HOW AND WHY LOVERS CHEAT

And What You Can Do About It

HOW AND WHY LOVERS CHEAT

And What You Can Do About It

Gigi Moers

A division of Shapolsky Publishers, Inc.

S.P.I. BOOKS

A division of Shapolsky Publishers, Inc.

For any additional information, contact:
S.P.I. BOOKS / Shapolsky Publishers, Inc.
136 West 22nd Street
New York, NY 10011
(212) 633-2022
Fax (212) 633-2123

10   9   8   7   6   5   4   3   2   1

ISBN 0-944007-18-X

PRINTED IN CANADA

This book is dedicated to my three kids—Jesse, Gidget and Bambi. They are the reason I get up each day. I thank God for blessing me with them.

Acknowledgments

I want to thank my kids for putting up with a mom too tired to get up with them in the morning because she wrote all night, for the endless cups of tea I gave them, but most of all for their loving and supporting me.

I want, also, to thank my best friend, Marge Hess, who spent hundreds of hours talking with me, advising me and allowing me to read her yet another revised paragraph.

I want to thank my agent, Bill Birnes, for believing in me and this book, as well as my publisher, Ian Shapolsky, for having the courage to be the one who said Yes.

Last, I want to thank all the lovers who have shared a part of their lives with me—and with you.

Gigi Moers
Hanover Park, IL
1991

Contents

WARNING BELLS

I once again picked up Annie's letter and read the following narrative: "I slumped deeper into my chair. I wished inwardly I could just fade into the woodwork. I watched as my husband crossed the courtroom and took the stand. Listening to his testimony, I felt as though I was watching everything I ever held dear ebb away.

"I tortured myself with questions that day. Those same questions eat at me even now as I write to you. Why hadn't I acted on my gut feelings months ago when I had an inkling Chris was having an affair? Why didn't I check out the clues I had come across? Why didn't I try to discover the truth instead of hiding my head in the sand? Maybe, just maybe, I could have done something. At best I could have suggested we get counseling. But at the very least, if I would have known the truth, I could have protected my own interests and assets. I could have prepared myself both mentally and emotionally for this eventuality. But most of all I could have shielded my children from this mess. I will always ask myself WHY?"

As I continued to read Annie's letter describing her day in court and her feelings of regret, my attention was transfixed on the words in the very last paragraph in which she said, "Had I only allowed the all revealing light of truthful reality to shine on me, I would not now be reaping what I thought was the dark protection of blissful ignorance."

Boy, had she said a mouthful. I wish Annie could have had this book when her intuition was telling her something was wrong, terribly wrong in her marriage. But she didn't. It is too late to help Annie but it is not too late to help you.

If by becoming your own do-it-yourself detective you can discover the truth in your marriage and thereby arrest an affair, Annie's good advice and experience will not have been given in vain. If by becoming a "Bond" you are able to stop an affair before it spreads like a cancer and consumes your life and your family, then all the Annies of this world have given you a gift. If by becoming a sleuth you are able to maneuver yourself into a position in which you can protect your children and your assets, if the truth affords you just one moment of peace, then all those who have gone before you have done so with an unsuspecting purpose. Your obtaining the truth is my hope—no, my goal.

It was because of and for people like Annie that I created Spouse's Infidelity Service, a service that teaches mates how to become their own marital investigators. But it is to reach people the world over that I have written this book.

In the years since I began Spouse's Infidelity Service, I have had the opportunity to work with thousands of clients in our offices and through correspondence. Working with so many clients that span every social, economic, geographical, religious and age group, I have discovered common denominators and patterns that are universal in all affairs. It is, therefore, my intention to give you the benefit of the collective knowledge and insights I have amassed, to arm you to do battle with ignorance. But before embarking on your investigation, you will need to make a decision that, in fact, an investigation is warranted. So, therefore, you must start at the beginning. A good place to start, if I do say so myself. You will presently become acquainted with the warning signs of an affair. If a warning bell is sounding, then it is my counsel and advice that you proceed to became a do-it-yourself detective.

It was through my research at Spouse's Infidelity Service that I was able to identify and classify the warning signs of an affair. I have divided these signs into seven categories which I call "warning bells."

I have chosen the term "warning bells" not in an effort to

overdramatize the clues of an affair, but rather to make literally clear to you that these are infidelity's warning manifestations and they should sound off as loudly to you as if they were audible.

The understanding and awareness of these warning bells are the foundation of your forthcoming instruction. It is on this foundation you will build your case. So it is essential that you fully comprehend the warning bells of an affair.

You will discover that a warning bell is based on a change. These changes take place in your spouses's behavior, the dynamics of your relationship and/or the normalcy of your collective routine.

Beyond defining each warning bell, I have included a case history of a client. These client histories are a conglomeration of many actual cases. The names are fictitious however. That kind of sounds like the opening to an episode of *Dragnet*, "the names have been changed to protect the innocent." Nevertheless, it is important that you understand that I have never betrayed a confidence with a client and I will not do so now.

So let us begin our journey into infidelity investigation. What are some of the "warning bells"?

1. Change in Personal Habits

A personal habit would include, but is not limited to, personal hygiene, use of cologne, grooming, clothing and anything pertinent to one's appearance.

In examining the importance of personal habit changes we need to take an anthropologist-type look at the dynamics of our relationships. How one physically looks, smells and is adorned, are the stimulators which attract the opposite sex. Unless, of course, the object of his or her affections is blind, can't smell or doesn't care. If this is in fact the case, I say put this book down, enjoy a good laugh at his incredible bad taste and throw the bum out because you can obviously do better. However, as this is usually not the situation, you should recognize that all animals including human beings are attracted to both sight and smell.

In fact, it is almost exclusively the male of the species that is brightly colored to attract the female. If you doubt this for a second, I recommend you go to your local zoo. It is there you will find, among other examples, the male peacock spreading his vibrant plumage endeavoring to attract the plain brown female.

You may argue that our economy would grind to a halt without women's cosmetic and hair coloring companies' revenues. While I would agree that the human population has shifted to the females adorning themselves, I believe the attractor/attractee principle remains intact. The only significant difference is the human female lets the males think they are doing the choosing.

You may argue further that our human interactions have been refined beyond those of the lowly animals. I agree. We have refined our primal mating rituals beyond Neanderthal man and animals. However, let me submit the following observations. We females continue to play hard to get, but are fully prepared to scratch the eyes out of our rivals. Our males still puff out their chests and promenade about inspecting and soliciting the available females. Further, our males continue to protect their marked territories against all comers.

These are but a few observations of what is the continuation of our perennial mating rituals. Yes, we are refined, but we remain basically unchanged.

So if your peacock is attempting to attract another mate, he will, and usually does clean up his act. His present "act" is one of marital complacency (i.e., showering when necessary rather than as a routine).

Let's be a fly on the wall and consider the circumstances and conversation that began the case of Susan M.:

Susan listened with silent amusement as her forty-two-year-old, balding husband Tom gave her a lengthy dissertation on the attributes of an eight-hundred-dollar hair piece. When he had finished enumerating the dozens of reasons a hair piece would change forever not only his life, but her life as well, Susan felt compelled to speak.

"Are you crazy! That's more money than we paid for our first car!" Susan shouted, but then added in a calmer tone, "Tom, if you want a hair piece to look better for me, I've told you I love you with or without hair. The amount of hair on your head could never affect my feelings for you. But if you want a hair piece for yourself, to make you feel better, I will try to understand."

Undaunted, Tom continued his previous dissertation, "It's not just that I happen to to care about my appearance, I also happen to care how I look to others. What good does it do me to workout three times a week if my bald head makes me look ten years older?"

"Who are you trying to impress? Certainly not me, cause I have already told you I couldn't care less, and by your own admission you're not getting a hair piece for yourself. So what you're saying is that we should take eight hundred dollars out of the savings account so the people at the bank think you look thirty-two."

Tom M. did get his toupee but he discovered it was uncomfortable and it made him perspire profusely. Therefore, he only wore it when he went out with his friends.

As it turned out Susan M. caught her wigged-out husband one evening with another woman who appeared to be about twenty-two. So as to point out the difference in the "happy couple's" ages, Susan de-rugged Tom to the horror of his young thing.

I am not suggesting that every man purchasing a hair piece does so as a prelude to adultery. Adultery certainly can be committed without hair. Yet, in the case of Tom M., the rug was motivated not by his wife's feelings or Tom's feelings, it was in this case Tom, the peacock, adding to his plumage.

2. Change in Hours

A change in his hours would include any change, and the operative word here is any, in his daily comings and goings.

We homo sapiens are creatures of habit, especially within the confines of marriage. We create and live within a routine, so much so that our daily lives take on an air of comfortable predictability. This comfortableness in a marital sense conjures up, for some, scenes of the "old ball and chain." Yet it is this "ball and chain" comfortableness that so many single people are seeking.

Our timetables are affected by many factors within the

scope of our obligations. For example, if our work hours are from nine to five, we will rise at an hour that will afford us enough time to shower, dress, have breakfast and drive to work. Adding the responsibility of children to just our morning agendas, we then need to increase that allotted time to include dragging the kids out of bed, washing their "good" jeans and so forth.

Delving even further into our predictable scheduled lives, we may find that we eat the same foods, drive the same way to work, and say the same things week after week. While all the sameness may be said by some to be dull and mundane, it does give us a sense of both order and security.

As married people, we have a certain accountability, to each other and to our families, to allow them to know our whereabouts. Beyond this being a common courtesy, the rationale is that we could save our loved ones undue worry, and in the event of an emergency, they could get ahold of us.

Further, endeavoring to function within our yuppie society, we strive to make the optimum use of our time. Beyond our daily work and family schedules, we usually have our recreational activities slotted in, such as card night, girls' night out, boys' night out, club night and so forth.

If all this preceding behavior is that to which most married people subscribe, we could surmise that most married people have an accountability to their spouse. Further, we could say that almost without exception we are creatures of habit either by disposition or by circumstance.

Dissecting further the reasoning of married people's daily schedules, it may be safe to theorize that accountability, routine and making the optimum use of our time all contribute to our predictability.

Having said all that, you need to be aware that when accountability and/or the daily habits of your spouse alter suspiciously, you should be alerted. The motivating catalyst could be the presence of an affair.

Consider the plight of Beth L.:

Beth awakened to the sound of her husband Pete's truck pulling out of the driveway. Sleepily she rolled over and glanced at their digital alarm clock. The actual time did not register to her sleep-blurred mind. Instead, panicked, she jumped out of bed, believing she had overslept. Hurriedly she pulled on her robe, as she did so she looked at the clock again. Five-thirty!?! "Five-thirty!", she said out loud. Slowly it occurred to her, she hadn't overslept. But since she was up, she decided to stay up, so she shuffled off to the kitchen and put a cup of tea in the microwave. She lit a cigarette, and watched the cup turn on the carousel.

The morning was not when Beth was at her best. Her family knew her vocabulary was limited to ten phrases including "Get it from Daddy's wallet" and "when pigs fly." But this morning, as Beth sat at the kitchen table smoking her cigarette and sipping her tea, she forced her fuzzy brain to function. Normally, Pete never left the house before seven o'clock or without saying good-bye. Yet for the past few weeks, he had left several times very early and surprisingly abruptly, without a word. These occurrences hadn't gone by without her taking notice of them, rather they had been absorbed into her busy day and she simply forgot to ask Pete about them.

"Maybe he's putting in some overtime," she said to herself. "I'll give him a call at work and check before I jump to any conclusions."

Dialing, she lit her fourth cigarette and listened as the phone rang. Finally a burly voice answered, "Hello, the Printing Press."

"Is Pete there?" she asked.

"No, lady, this is security. Nobody comes in before eight," the voice answered.

"Are you sure—" she began, but was cut off in mid-question.

"Listen, lady, I said I'm security. Shouldn't I know whether somebody is here or not!"

Beth hung up loudly, partly because there wasn't anything more to say and partly because she hated being called "lady." She then called her friend Marge and asked her to come over as soon as the kids had left for school. Over tea they discussed all the possibilities to explain Pete's early morning disappearances. They decided that swift and decisive action was warranted. So they arranged that Marge, who lived a block over, would park her car every night two doors down from Beth and leave her car keys under the floormat.

Beth began sleeping as lightly as she did when the kids were babies. Her nerves were strung as tight as strings of a violin. She woke each time Pete moved in their queen-sized bed.

Monday, Tuesday, Wednesday mornings all passed uneventfully as Beth feigned sleep and watched Pete through half-closed eyes. Then early Thursday Beth watched as Pete cautiously rose from the bed. He dressed quietly and left the house. The second the door shut behind him, Beth was in her robe and out the back door. She rounded the side of the house just as Pete was getting into his red truck. She stepped carefully back and ran through the two neighbors' yards to get to Marge's car. She watched Pete pull out of their driveway from her vantage point in Mr. Graziano's hedge. It occurred to her then how ridiculous she must have looked crouched there in her frilly robe and fuzzy slippers. She inwardly prayed that Mr. Graziano was a late sleeper. She didn't have to wait there long, however—at that moment Pete passed by. She ran to Marge's car, trying to stay low. She jumped in the car and sped after him. She lost him for the next couple of blocks, but since there were only two ways out of their subdivision she decided to head toward Higgins Road. Beth's eyes searched up and down the streets trying to spot Pete's truck. She spotted him two blocks before the traffic light, but he caught the light and she did not—so she lost him again. After an hour of fruitless searching, she gave up and went home.

Beth continued this shadow routine every time Pete left the house early. Many a time she started to ask him what he was up to, but the opportunity had always been there for him to stop his behavior or to talk to her. Since he had not elected to do either she decided this was her only course of appropriate action. Beth followed Pete many a morning, but he always somehow eluded her. Then one morning she saw a red truck pulling into an apartment complex. She sped towards it. She pulled in just as Pete was putting a key in the lock of the outer door of one of the buildings. Because she couldn't think of anything else to do, she began honking her horn. Pete turned. His expression was one of disbelief and confusion. He stood looking at her for what seemed like an eternity. Finally he came toward her. He suggested they

How and Why Lovers Cheat

go home and talk. Beth was torn between her own disbelief and a nagging compulsion to run him over.

They went home and talked. Pete confessed to the affair. Beth and Pete are separated now though they still love each other. Only time and Beth will tell whether or not their marriage is over.

3. Change in Sex Life

A change would include more sex, less sex, unexplained sexual requests or positions and changes in desire and satisfaction.

Infidelity is having sex with a partner other than your spouse. That act is what this book is all about. If it were simply a matter of one's spouse or lover confiding in or doing lunch with someone of the opposite sex, there wouldn't be a problem.

What we are legitimately discussing within the parameters of this book, is SEX, an act we philosophically or spiritually believe should be limited to one's spouse or at least one's significant other.

That limitation encompasses so much of what is the fiber of our natures, our upbringing, our sociological indoctrination and our religious beliefs. It is not a boundary most people enter into lightly. However, it is a boundary we self-impose seriously. So seriously, in fact, that the betrayal of monogamy has ended marriages, motivated murders and ended sanity.

Some have asked, why bother swimming against the tide? Why not just give it up and move with the times? Why? Because it is so much like the character Tevya in *Fiddler on the Roof*, there must be a place where we cannot bend. To do so is to lose one's balance. If this were not true, why are we suffering from the "new" morality? We bent to the sexual revolution. We have the pill to prevent pregnancy yet we have millions of teenagers having babies. We have penicillin to cure venereal diseases, yet it will not cure the sterility the disease can sometimes leave behind. And now we face the worst, AIDS. This disease can not as of yet be cured with a pill or a shot. Its wide-reaching implications are not yet known.

Because we are dealing with changes in *your* sex life, I believe it would be unnecessary and intellectually insulting to further explain why there would be a change in your sex life.

4. Change in Personality

A change in personality would include any difference in one's persona.

It is important to understand what a personality is. Personality, defined according to *The American Heritage Dictionary*, is the embodiment of the collective character: behavioral, temperamental, emotional and mental traits of an individual that makes his experience of life unique. Sounds pretty heavy to me. Simply put, personality is what makes us each unique.

John may put fake dog doodoo on the stove, that's his personality. And Ben may sit alone by the hour and contemplate the nuclear question, that's his personality.

The personality of a person engaging in adultery changes for many reasons. *One* reason is guilt. Whether or not one justifies his behavior as being causal is unimportant, the guilt is usually there. He may rationalize that his wife is frigid, or is a nag, or is overweight. So, therefore, *she* is the reason he is straying. But regardless of the rationale, most people feel some degree of guilt when deceiving another person, especially if that person is someone he loves or has loved.

An analogy I find well suited is that of shooting a deer. Like a deer within the sights of a high-powered rifle, the uninformed spouse is living on the edge without even knowing it. If you shout to let the deer know you are there, you give it a chance to change its destiny. If you give the deer a high-powered rifle with a telescopic sight and thereby give him a 50/50 chance to defend and protect himself, maybe even blow your horns off, then I believe your accountability is minutely lessened.

Personality changes run the gamut from happy to sad and from turned-on to confused. The personality will change based on the feelings of the person committing the adultery and the situation in its entirety.

It is, therefore, extremely important in an infidelity investigation forum to be in tune with your spouse's personality. This is good advice for a healthy marriage, but it is imperative to your investigation. If you don't know him, you will not be able to spot changes in him.

While discussing Vicki B.'s case with her in my office, she related these changes in her husband: "It's really weird," Vicki began, "Mike is acting so strange. It almost scares me."

"How so?" I questioned. "Give me some examples."

"Well, I woke up the other night and Mike's head was propped up on one elbow and he was wide awake and staring at me as though he was angry with me. Then a couple of days ago we were discussing our plans for our anniversary party, and he went into a tirade. He began shouting that we didn't have the money to do anything. Another time I was singing and rocking the baby to sleep, when I looked up, he was watching me and tears began rolling down his cheeks."

"Has he ever behaved this way before?" I asked.

"No. Mike is the most even-tempered person I know. I don't think it could be drugs because he is allergic to almost everything pharmaceutical. No, it's something else. I know. One minute he is his normal self and the next, he is sad or mad," Vicki explained.

"Is it possible there could be stress at work he is not telling you about?" I asked.

"Well, I guess it could be possible, but not probable. See, we own our own small construction company and it is doing better than ever before. I do the books, so I would know if there were any outstanding debts we couldn't take care of. No, I really don't think it has any thing to do with the company or money worries," Vicki answered.

"It seems to me that you have already made up your mind to the cause of Mike's personality changes," I suggested.

"I'm not sure exactly. It's just that I know a person doesn't go from happily planning an anniversary party to screaming at the top of his lungs about nothing. And then there's the way he holds the baby sometimes. I get the impression that he is holding her so tight like he is afraid he's going to lose her. It sounds crazy, but it's the truth," Vicki said, almost as if she were talking to herself.

"There are so many possibilities why a personality could

change," I challenged, pressing my fingertips together and leaning back in my chair. "It is important to examine all those possibilities in order to come to the truth. After you have eliminated the improbable, whatever is left must be the truth."

"O.K., I buy that. I talked to our doctor; Mike isn't sick. As matter of fact, he is as healthy as a horse. I cautiously questioned his friends, he is not in a fight with any of them and he is acting like his normal self with them. I talked to his mom and there isn't a problem with her or the rest of the family. And I know everything is great with our company and our money. So what does that leave? What is left? You tell me!" Vicki screeched, becoming more excited and more upset with every statement.

I answered her quietly, endeavoring to calm her, "No, Vicki, what I think is not what is important here. What is important, is what you think. So you need to tell me." I sat back in my big leather chair and closed my eyes, giving her plenty of time to think it through. I pressed my fingertips together, but otherwise I sat motionless. I am not sure if my behavior while talking with clients is a manifestation of my own persona, or whether I have read too many "Sherlock Holmes" stories. Either way, I try to relax clients through my voice and body language and allow them to draw their own conclusions.

"All right, I'll tell you what I think. I think the big sonovabitch is having an affair. I also think he is so racked with guilt that he either takes it out on us, or he feels so bad about it that he gets sad and scared he may lose us. Is that what you wanted me to say?" she said between sobs.

As I handed Vicki a tissue, our eyes met and I think she finally understood that her admitting her worst fears was what we had accomplished. She had just voiced to me what she probably wouldn't tell her best friend and it was hard. But now we could go on from here to discover the whole truth.

Vicki's understanding of her husband's personality played a vital part in her becoming aware of changes in him. It was on the basis of those changes that Vicki began her investigation. She was able to put together a personality change with an occurrence of an act of infidelity, thereby allowing her to catch Mike cheating on her. Vicki and Mike are still together and receiving marital counseling.

5. A Change in Money Matters

A change in money matters would include a change in who handles the money from one spouse to the other, or if one spouse becomes secretive about how the family money is being spent.

It is a well known fact, or at least a good generalization, that all affairs will cost between a little and a lot of money. The reasoning behind this cost is the setting of the mood and the abode in which the encounter will take place. Abode in this context can range between a motel and an apartment, depending on affluency.

Looking back over our own dating days, we know that a date usually consisted of a meal and an activity, such as a movie. It also may have been preceded by flowers and candy. And it may have ended with drinks and a motel.

While as "kids" it may have been circumstantially necessary to neck or make love in the back seat of a car, very few adults will do so. Adults know, for instance, that policemen cruise forest preserves and parks looking for lovers. We are also aware that there are public indecency laws. Further, most adults can no longer straddle a steering wheel, throw one leg under the gear shift while balancing themselves on their elbows which are lodged in the glove compartment. These contortions are now known to us as acrobatics.

We adults, in general, expect a date or sexual encounter to be romantic and exciting. The sex act is no longer new to us, so the trappings are important even with a new partner. Also, for many of us lighting is extremely important.

We can, I think, safely agree that most adults' standards of a "date" are higher than those of teenagers. We can further assume that most dates will cost money. For a cheating mate, money will come out of the family budget. (Let me note here that a lover not living with you will be more difficult to track, but it can be done.) If the family happens to be in the lower-middle class bracket economically, the monies will be easily missed. This is true whether a family is living within their means or not. A matter of twenty dollars could mean the difference between eating macaroni or hot dogs.

Within the middle to upper-middle class bracket, cash taken from the family budget isn't as easily or as quickly missed. It is, however, missed. Most of these families are carrying large debts, such as car and mortgage payments. These families may, indeed, have greater incomes, but they usually also have greater obligations. Where twenty dollars may just be considered mad money, a hundred dollars is serious money. Further, middle class usually date middle class, so a date is going to be more expensive. This is because the expectations are higher and in keeping with what is expected from one's peers. In other words, money will be spent on the same level it is available.

If I am coming off as snobbish, I don't mean to. Believe me, if you could see my bank book, you'd know I have no reason to even contemplate becoming a snob. Rather, I am endeavoring to dissect "money matters" with you and, in doing so, to understand the difference in changes that occur, broken down by economic classes.

The upper class and the very affluent are the most difficult of all of economic classes in which to spot money matter changes for many reasons. Those reasons include: company credit cards, expense accounts, an excess of money, and the lifestyle that affords them the ability to blow hundreds of dollars without any family accountability. At the same time, however, this class also is the easiest to monetarily backtrack as most expenditures are usually made with credit cards rather than with cash.

This was true in Sondra's case. Sondra P. is a wealthy woman in her forties. We will pick up her investigation as she attempts to find out how her husband Phillip has been spending both his evenings and their money:

Sondra waved to Phillip from the porch as he maneuvered down their long, curving driveway in his silver Mercedes. She watched until he was out of sight.

Then she rushed inside to his office. Reaching into her bra, Sondra pulled out a small golden key that she had had made last night. Sondra felt a sense of real accomplishment, thinking of the feat she was able to pull off.

Her mind wandered back through the events of last night.

She had gone to a restaurant alone. After finishing her meal, she paid the check and walked out to her car. She didn't avail herself of the valet parking purposely.

Sondra waited a good ten minutes in the parking lot and then walked into the restaurant appearing to be very agitated. The maitre d', to whom she was known, inquired as to her trouble. She informed him that she couldn't locate her car keys. The restaurant personnel searched the booth she had sat in and the cloak room without success, so Sondra decided that an emergency locksmith should be called. After the locksmith arrived, pulled out and replaced the ignition and door lock, she miraculously located her keys at the bottom of her purse.

The locksmith rolled his eyes as she suggested he make duplicates of all of her keys, so this type of thing wouldn't happen again. But as it was money in his pocket, he said nothing and made the duplicates. One of those keys was the well-guarded key to Phillip's desk. Sondra managed to get ahold of the key earlier that night. Since she knew Phillip would miss it in the morning, she had devised this plan to get a duplicate and replace it right away. Her plan had worked like a charm and she would be ready to search Phillip's desk the moment he left the house.

That moment had come, she thought, as she fished the key from its bosom hiding place. She turned the key in the lock. Sondra began to search the desk looking for credit card receipts, matchbooks, anything to give her a clue to where or on whom their money was being spent. Sondra found incriminating receipts that gave her the first clues for her investigation.

Sondra and Phillip have since divorced due to Phillip's adultery. But thanks to the small golden key, Sondra was able to lay her hands on the "second" set of books to Phillip's business. The one the government didn't see. Her possession of a copy of those books proved very valuable in an equitable divorce settlement for Sondra.

6. Strange Telephone Calls

A strange telephone call is either an incoming or outgoing call that you believe is strange or mysterious.

The call's strangeness is relative to what is normal in your home. Of course if you have always received prank or obscene calls, the continuation of those type of calls would not alarm you. Remember if you will, that all the warning bells are based on a change. If a change occurs as it pertains to the incoming or outgoing calls in your home, this is a warning bell.

A call's mysteriousness is subjective. It will be just your opinion a call is draped in mystery. So, therefore, an assertion that a call has fallen into this category is for you alone to decide.

In an effort to help you with this decision, I have classified the three types of strange telephone calls. Further, I have provided you with the probable rationale behind these calls.

Class One Calls

(A) Half a ring.

(B) One to several rings and then a hang-up.

(C) A sequel ringing such as one ring, hang-up, then two more rings.

Class one calls are usually prearranged signals between your spouse and their "other." These calls are telling your spouse something specific. The meaning could range anywhere from "I need you," to "I love you," and from "Call me back," to "Meet me." Whatever the meaning, if the call was a signal, your spouse understands it.

Your spouse's behavior and reaction after such a call will determine whether or not it was a signal. For example, if your spouse suddenly needs to buy a pack of cigarettes after a stange call, you can bet it was a signal, especially if he doesn't smoke.

Class one calls could also have an entirely different meaning. The call may be a form of intimidation. This intimidation could either be directed at your spouse or at you. If it is directed at your spouse, the meaning could range between "I want to talk to you now, whether you want to or not," or "You had better tell her (him) before I do." IF the call is directed at you, it has one of two meanings. The first meaning is that the "other" is jealous of you and she (he) is trying to purposely disturb you. Her (his) jealousy is perfectly normal if you are mindful that she (he) not only knows about you, but you are with the one she (he) wants to be with. The second meaning is that the "other" is preparing to let you know about her (him), but she (he) changes her (his) mind at the last minute and decides to hang up. She (he) may do this many times, always changing her (his) mind just as you answer. If she (he) speaks to you, she (he) may not get the result she (he) is seeking, and that is why she (he) hesitates. The reaction and the result she (he) is hoping for is to get your spouse. However, this may back-fire on her (him) depending on your reaction and your spouse's true feelings for her (him).

Class Two Calls

Class two calls are like class one calls except that the calls are placed frequently and are usually a form of distinct intimidation. Class two calls also include obscene or bogus calls, such as constant wrong numbers and survey calls. The calls are placed not to speak to you or your spouse, but to disturb and intimidate either one or the both of you. The fatal attraction concept is not a new one. My case files include dozens of examples of "fatal attractions." It goes back to the old saying "Be careful what you wish for, you might get it."

Class Three Calls

Class three calls include all the outgoing calls that your spouse makes from your home that you deem strange or mysterious. If your spouse begins to whisper on the phone or hangs up quickly when you walk in the room, you can safely assume there is a reason behind this behavior. Common sense tells you that if your spouse is talking from the garage while shut in the car, he doesn't want you to overhear the conversation.

One such example of a "fatal attraction" is the case of Alexandria L.:

Alexandria eased into the tub of hot, bubbly water. She closed her eyes and began to let herself drift away. Jerry was out in the garage and the kids were in bed. Alexandria relaxed and allowed the heat of the water to wash away the day's concerns and aggravations. She let her imagination wander through the pages of the novel she had begun to write. The blank page she had stared at for three days seemed unimportant now. She closed her eyes and watched as if she were a quiet bystander as her characters' lives unfolded before her. From somewhere far away she heard bells. They kept ringing, insistently intruding on her. Suddenly she realized that the bells were real and not in her story. She yelled to Jerry to get the phone, then realized she was wasting her time. There simply was no way Jerry could hear her in the garage, especially if he had his power tools going.

"Just like the old cliché," she said to herself, "the second you get in the tub, the phone rings." Alexandria climbed out of the tub and threw on her robe. The robe stuck to her skin and she dripped as she ran to catch the phone.

"Hello, hello," she said, not even trying to disguise the sharpness in her voice. No one answered. "Hello, are you there?" she asked, and still there was silence. "Damn, I nearly kill myself to answer this stupid phone and they hang up. Great!"

Alexandria dripped back to the bathroom and took off her damp robe. Just as she put her foot into the lukewarm water, the phone rang again. This time she didn't bother to put her robe on. She draped it across the front of her and half-slipped, half-ran to the phone. "Hello!" she gasped. No one answered, but she could hear breathing on the other end. "Come on, I know you are there, answer me," she snapped angrily. Still there was no reply. "All right, it's your quarter!" she yelled, hanging up.

She left the phone off the hook and went once again back to her bath. But by this time she was angry and the water didn't look as inviting. She dried off and put on her pajamas. She got into bed with her pad of paper and pen and tried to envision the development of her heroine before she had been interrupted. Inspired, her pen now seemed to fly across the page.

"Hey, who left the phone off the hook?" Jerry yelled from the kitchen.

"I did. Be quiet or you'll wake up the kids," Alexandria yelled back without considering that her voice carried too.

Then the phone rang. Jerry must have hung it up, she thought. She listened as he answered. She heard him slam the receiver down. "Who was it?" she asked as he walked into the bedroom.

"I don't know, must be some kids playing games. I took it off the hook." Jerry quickly changed the subject and asked, "I thought you were taking a bath?"

"I was and my block just disappeared. Then the phone rang and I nearly killed myself trying to answer it and no one was there. As soon as I got back into the tub, the phone rang again, so I ran to get it and whoever was on the other end didn't say a word," Alexandria explained, pausing over the page.

Jerry threw himself onto the bed and put his hand on top of Alexandria's head. He always did that when he needed to be close or if he was going to get frisky.

"Are you going to write all night?" he whispered.

"Well I had intended to," she answered.

"You just go ahead, don't mind me," he said as he slipped his hand under her pajama top.

Alexandria let the pad of paper drop as she turned toward him.

After they had made love and Jerry had fallen asleep with his hand draped over her head, Alexandria got up and quietly put on her robe and slipped out of their bedroom. She went into the kitchen and made a pot of coffee. Walking into the family room that doubled as her writing studio, she turned on her computer and put in her word processing software. As it was loading, she went back into the kitchen for a cup of coffee. While pouring a cup, she decided to put the phone back on the hook. No sooner had she replaced the receiver in the cradle then the phone rang. She picked it up quickly, not wanting it to wake Jerry up. Again no one answered her entreaties.

In the weeks to come, the phone would ring constantly and she would constantly be met by silence on the other end. Jerry claimed that it must be kids, yet when he answered the calls he slammed the phone down after seeming to be listening for a few moments.

The calls took on an evening pattern. They would begin about six and persist throughout the night. After several weeks of this, Alexandria realized that these kids, if indeed it was kids, were not going to stop on their own accord, so she called the police. After hearing her story, Detective Waston agreed that she should sign a complaint and allow the police to put a tracer on her phone line.

Alexandria kept a careful log of the prank calls. She noted the date and time of every call. She didn't tell Jerry about the trace, partly because he seemed so angry about the calls, and partly because she had the feeling he knew who was making the calls. She couldn't help being suspicious. Every single time he had answered one of those calls, he had listened first and then slammed the phone down as though he was reacting to what was being said.

Several days after the trace had been put on her phone, Detective Waston came over to compare the traced calls with her log. And to Alexandria's astonishment they found that every call she had logged as a prank call had been traced locally to one single number. That number turned out to belong to a woman.

"Are you sure you want to press charges?" the seasoned detective asked. "Maybe you should talk it over with your husband."

"No, I agreed when you put the trace on my phone that I would press charges if you could locate the caller, and that's what I intend to do." Alexandria tried to make her voice sound nonchalant and to calm the turbulence she felt gathering within her. But somehow she couldn't bring herself to meet Detective Waston's black, piercing eyes.

Alexandria followed the detective to the station and signed the complaint. He patted her hand as she was preparing to leave. He looked at her as though he sympathized and understood. Yet it was an understanding that she couldn't or wouldn't allow herself to contemplate.

The next afternoon Alexandria received a call from Detective Waston asking her to come to the station with her husband. She called Jerry at work and asked him to meet her at the police station. She didn't explain or give him a chance to question her.

At three forty-five she was seated outside Detective Waston's office, he came out of his office just as Jerry walked up. Detective Waston led them into a conference room and shut the door. He sat down and lit a cigarette before he spoke. "She claims she knows your husband, Alexandria," he said, never once taking his eyes from her face and then added, "I thought we better discuss this before we proceed any further."

"Who knows me?" Jerry questioned.

Alexandria looked at the detective for help, so he explained the detection and arrest of the prank caller. Jerry had gone white as he listened. He looked at Alexandria and then at the detective. Then it all came out just like a Perry Mason episode. He had, he confessed, a very brief affair with this woman and he had ended it. But she would not let it end. She followed him, called him and sent notes to him at work. It almost scared him, he said. She was, in his opinion, a real nut. He didn't know what to do, so he had decided to do nothing and hoped she would stop on her own.

After hearing Jerry's story, Detective Waston suggested that they go home. He told them that he would let their caller know that he had a signed complaint against her and her fate would lay in her own hands. And, that if she ever called or contacted them again, he would guarantee her that she would be prosecuted to the fullest extent of the law.

The woman did stop. Alexandria and Jerry divorced. And Alexandria is dating Detective Waston.

7. Intuition

Intuition is an immediate and instinctive perception of the truth. It is the ability to directly understand without reasoning. It is also, I believe, our sixth sense.

Of course, the degree and the intensity of one's intuition varies greatly from person to person and from one sex to the other. Though men are intuitive, it is women that seem to possess a superior capacity for intuition. The justification and explanation is that women are predominately the emotional half of the species. So, therefore, they are, by design or by disposition, more in tune with not only their own feelings, but of the feelings of those around them. They pick up on unseen vibrations and draw uncannily accurate conclusions.

Intuition, per se, doesn't fall within the parameters of the parapsychological, but it is definitely mysterious. Although we are usually skeptical of those things we can't easily explain, most people agree that the ability to be intuitive does exist.

I remember distinctly the first time I came into contact with my mother's strange power I now know to be intuition. I was up in my room with the door shut. My little sister, who we called "the informer," was not home. My brother and I were looking at some magazines we had found in the garage, when my mother called from downstairs. "Stop that right now! Or would you like me to come up there and take them away from you." We threw the magazines in the trash but from that time on I kept one eye on her. How she knew Dad was playing cards and not bowling, how she knew we had stopped for candy on the way home from school, how she knew what we all were doing when she couldn't see us, lead me to believe she was a witch with magical powers, until I grew up and had a husband and children of my own. Now they look at me funny and wide-eyed when I KNOW. I've got it too. And it's called intuition.

Let's look back at some of the case histories of the women in this chapter because though they may not have known it at the time, they have got it, too.

In the case of Susan M., Susan FELT that Tom's motivation to purchase a hair piece went beyond vanity. She pursued her investigation based on both a change in a personal habit and on that FEELING. Why didn't Susan accept the fact that Tom wanted a rug to look better and leave it at that? The reasoning is twofold: one, of course, is the change had occurred in Tom's personal habits, and two was Susan's feeling, her hunch if you will, and that was an entirely different warning bell going off. It was intuition. It was her perception that this change meant more, much more.

"When looking over the case of Beth L., you will see that Beth proceeded into her investigation with an instinctive knowledge of the end result. If she did not unconsciously already know the truth, why did she not question Pete? Beth's investigation was undaunted from the time she had ruled out Pete wasn't working overtime. Although she continued to seek hard evidence, I believe that she knew the truth on a level that defies the physical.

The case of Vicki B. is the best example of an intuitive

How and Why Lovers Cheat

feeling working together with another warning bell. The personality change warning bell was indeed sounding, but intuition played a greater role in Vicki's understanding of this change. If you look back at our conversation, you will see that Vicki explored and eliminated all of the probable answers. Her intuition alone had guided her to focus on the real cause of her husband's personality change.

Now you may argue that intuition does not exist, that these are merely examples of coincidence or of feelings radiating directly from a change. Though you are certainly entitled to your opinion, let me state that in all the years I have worked in this field, I have never known of one case in which the wife's intuition was wrong. Not one! Further, the wife's instinct has borne out over insurmountable appearances to the contrary. If I were a gambling woman, I'd put my money on a woman's intuition over physical evidence everytime. Also, let me state for the record, that the men I have worked with, have had, with few exceptions, an uncanny accuracy rate. So therefore, intuition is the loudest bell of all. If you feel it, you are more than probably right.

THE TALENTS OF A DETECTIVE

You are now prepared to detect and discern the warning bells of an affair. Armed with this awareness and knowledge, we can now proceed to turn you into a Cherlock Helmes, or at least a good Clouseau.

In this chapter we will dissect those attributes which are necessary to BE a detective. I am not endeavoring to launch you on a new vocation. Yet it is imperative you have a good understanding of the characteristics and talents one needs to become an investigator. Further, you now must absorb this information and undergo a metamorphosis that will allow you to emerge as a "Bond." While this may sound ominous and beyond your reach, it truly is not. You would not have even picked up this book unless you have the need to discover the truth. Where there is a will, there is a way. This is the way and you have the will. Believe me, somewhere inside your breast beats the heart of Cherlock Helmes.

Let's begin at the beginning. First you need to think the way a detective thinks.

1. The Mind of a Detective

A detective is a puzzle solver. She views a "case," as fragmented pieces of a once whole truth. She endeavors to logically and methodically, put the pieces back together.

A detective observes. She does not simply see. To see is to make an optical note. To observe is to take note of what one sees. Observation is to systematically watch and attentively examine.

A detective deduces. After she observes, she makes a deduction. A deduction is the act of drawing a reasonable conclusion through the intellectual process of elimination. After eliminating the improbable, whatever is left must be the truth.

A detective never takes anything at face value. Everything from a facial movement to an upturned collar has both a meaning and a motivation. One may wear tight jeans because she likes the way she looks in them and the way they attract the attention she enjoys. The wearing of the tight jeans is both for her good self image and for her need to attact others. So, therefore, there is both a meaning and a motivation.

A detective explores all avenues. She can not disregard any possible answer based on a preconceived supposition. Instead she approaches every "case" and every "clue" with a totally open mind. Further, she allows for the exploration of all possibilities by refusing to predetermine the solution. It is one thing to see and then deduct and quite another to deduct and then see. While it is fine to have a suspicion of something's outcome, it is quite different to let your preconceived outcome cause a false suspicion. Detection and deduction are difficult enough without your throwing in monkey wrenches and sending yourself off on wild goose chases.

Now let me set up a scene and you apply the mind of a detective. Through the application of thinking like a detective, try to determine who, what, why and when.

One cloudy summer afternoon while watching for my mailman from my second-story apartment window, I saw a 1986 silver Chrysler LeBaron drive very slowly up the street. The car turned down the side street, and I didn't think anymore about it until a few moments later it drove by again. I opened my window and watched as the female driver parallel-parked at the end of the block and got out of her car.

She was thirtyish and blonde. She was casually dressed in a sweatshirt, jeans and tennis shoes. She was also wearing dark sunglasses. She crossed the street and pulled out a pack of cigarettes. She dropped her lighter twice before she finally got her cigarette lit. Then she began to slowly walk down the block. She reached in her purse and pulled out a pair of gloves and put them on.

As she walked, she glanced nervously at the windows in the building directly across from me. She then walked past the building to a new, blue Ford pick-up truck. Reaching into her jeans pocket, she pulled out two separate keys. She inserted one of the keys into the door lock, turned it and climbed into the driver's seat. Again she nervously glanced up at the windows, but now she wore a defiant grin on her face.

I watched as she started the truck and pulled very quickly on to the street. She sped up to the end of the block and turned left. I ran to my side window and threw it open. I watched as she turned the corner and eased the truck to one side of the street. Leaving the engine running, she jumped out and, to my amazement, she scrambled on to the hood. She wrote "SNEAKY AS A SNAKE" on the windshield with white shoe polish. Then she ran around to the rear of the truck and wrote "COPS STINK, TOW ME IF YOU DARE" on the tailgate. Having left her messages, she climbed back into the truck. She paused momentarily until the street was clear in both directions, she then angled the truck lengthwise across the street. It blocked the entire road. Then she hopped out of the truck and ran down the alley. Dashing once again to my front window, I saw her get into her car. She then sped down the street in front of my building; I could see she was both laughing and crying.

WHO ARE THE PEOPLE INVOLVED IN THE SCENE I WATCHED FROM MY WINDOW?

Observations: (a) she looked attentively at a particular building; (b) she wore dark sunglasses on a cloudy day; (c) she had a key to the truck; (d) she was wearing gloves.

Deductions: (a) the woman knew someone inside the building; (b) she attempted to disguise herself because the other person knew her; (c) she has, at one time, had access to the other person's keys (i.e., the copy); (d) she was concerned about the other person's reaction, so she wore gloves in case the police dust the truck for fingerprints.

WHAT IS THE OWNER OF THE TRUCK'S AND THE WOMAN'S PROBABLE RELATIONSHIP TO EACH OTHER?

Observations: (a) the woman dropped her lighter twice; (b) she glanced a number of times at the windows of an apartment; (c) she wrote her messages in white shoe polish; (d) the messages themselves.

Deductions: (a) the woman was nervous; (b) she was worried; (c) she wrote her messages with an easily removable substance, so, therefore, she wished to leave the message without actually damaging the truck; (d) the front message was directed at the owner, while the back message was meant to incense the police and, thereby, cause the truck to be towed; it is obvious there had been a break between the two and the woman saw herself as the injured party.

WHY DID THE WOMAN LEAVE THE CAR IN THE STREET?

Observations: (a) all of the previous observations; (b) the woman laughed and cried as she was leaving the scene.

Deductions: (a) the woman purposely caused the owner aggravation through her actions; (b) the woman obviously felt this was a fitting act to retaliate for the wrong she felt was done to her, yet she found revenge bittersweet.

WHEN DID THIS HAPPEN?

Observations: (a) it was a cloudy summer afternoon.

How is it that you know who, what, why and when?
You know because you have observed. You have made deductions from your observations. You have looked for both the meaning and the motivation in her dress and actions. You have listened. You have explored all of the possible explanations for her actions. Then, after eliminating the improbable, you have deduced the basic identities of the parties involved and arrived at an understanding of her actions. What you have done, my friend, is successfully applied to this scenario the mind of a detective.

By the way the story is true. The truck was towed and ticketed. My client now regrets her actions and understands that vengeance is best left in God's hands. But she also feels that her cheating husband paying $97.00 for towing charges and tickets somehow doesn't begin to make amends for the costs she paid in the form of a broken heart when she caught him in the act of infidelity. Personally her action appeals to both my sense of humor and my sense of fair play.

2. The Tenacious Attitude of a Detective

A detective's demeanor is one of persistence and determination. She zeros in on her objective and relentlessly pursues it to its conclusion.

A detective's attitude is confident. She brings an air of daring to her search for the truth.

A detective's manner is purposeful and targeted. Her bold resolve is one of her greatest assets.

So a detective's attitude is one of tenacity which is a conglomeration of persistence, determination, relentlessness, confidence and bold daring.

This is the attitude that you must adopt to be successful in your investigation. It is with a tenacious attitude that a detective swaggers up to a waitress to question her about her steady customer. A timid mouse will neither have the nerve to do so nor the bearing to extract the information she is seeking. This attitude is not difficult to adopt. You simply need to believe in yourself and in the expectation of your success. The attitude we bring to any given situation almost invariably predisposes its outcome.

The student who assumes he will fail the test may just blank out entirely when the paper is placed in front of him. What he is actually doing is living up to his own expectations. My friend, live up to yours. Be tenacious and set your expectations high. If you do not do so, you will doom your investigation to failure from the outset.

Let me set a scene so that you may have a better understanding of the attitude a detective brings to a case:

Problem: Mary wanted to discover if her husband was cheating on her while on his recent business trip.

Objective: To obtain a copy of the hotel receipt.

Attainment of the objective:
(1) Mary called the hotel's registration desk with a plan.

(Purposeful)

(2) Mary asked for a copy of the bill after she had explained the original had been misplaced; she was told to get a copy from her husband's office.

(Determined)

(3) Mary explained that the bill never reached the office and without it her husband can not be reimbursed for his expenses.

(Persistent)

(4) The hotel agreed to send a copy to the office; Mary insisted they send the copy of the bill to her home address; she explained that this is the proper procedure for the submission of employee expenses.

(Relentless)

(5) The hotel agreed to send the bill to Mary immediately; then Mary asked for particulars on the bill as long as they had it out; she requested the amount of the total on the bill and the number of guests that had stayed in the room; further, she asked that the telephone charges incurred from the room be included.

(Bold)

This scene includes all of the variables of a detective's tenacious attitude. Mary had a plan to obtain her objective and she carried it off without the slightest doubt that she would be successful.

Yes, this story is true. The names have been changed to protect the innocent. Mary confronted her husband with this bill, but only after obtaining other supporting evidence of his infidelity. They are now receiving marital counseling.

3. The Courage of a Detective

A detective must possess courage. It is her courage that fuels her investigation.

It is not enough to have the mind of a detective and, thereby, be able to formulate a plan. It is not enough to also have an attitude oozing with tenacity, and thereby, be determined and daring. No, it is not enough because without the courage to carry out the plan, the determination to do so is useless.

Consider the case of Skye. You should be alert to where her tenacity leaves off and her courage begins:

"What do you mean the account has been closed? I have had this savings account in your bank for twenty years," Skye yelled.

Skye stared at the teller, unbelieving. She was told that all of the accounts she had held jointly with her husband had been transferred into new accounts. She couldn't understand how he could do this to her. Everything was gone. The savings accounts, the checking account and the IRAs. He had transferred the money into new accounts in his name alone. So, therefore, she didn't have access to any of them.

Skye realized that she was standing there like an idiot with her mouth hanging open. It suddenly occurred to her that she must appear normal and get to the safety deposit box. She mumbled something to the teller about PMS and becoming forgetful and turned on her heels. She made herself *walk* to the vault where the safety deposit boxes were. Her one thought now was to clean it out before Barry got to it too.

Filling out the form for admittance with a shaking hand, she prayed that he had overlooked the box. She walked quietly behind the matronly attendant to their box. Holding her breath as she watched the key turn in the lock. She nodded politely as the attendant chatted happily away about her new grandchild. Then with her box in her hand, she rushed into one of the small rooms. Skye slowly lifted the lid. She felt as though she had entered the *Twilight Zone*. The box was empty. Nothing was left.

Skye did not remember driving home or dropping on to the living-room couch. All she could remember were the tears. She felt as though she were drowning in them. It was not enough she had caught her husband having an affair with his secretary and his moving out of their house into hers, now he had taken all of their money, the jewelry, the stocks, bonds, everything.

Skye lay on the couch curled in the fetal position. She stared unseeing as the day gave way to night. Then as if emerging from a bad dream, a plan began to take shape in her mind. She decided to get even, not mad.

Very early the next morning Skye drove to her husband's office. She put her key in his door hoping the locks had not been changed. The key turned. Skye opened the door and went straight to his desk. She opened the bottom drawer and pulled out a small wooden box. Skye lifted the lid and pulled out three passbooks, a checking book and a set of keys. She hadn't lived with this man for twenty-two years for nothing. She knew his habits as if they were her own. It stood to reason, she thought, that if he had kept his keys and account books there before, he would stay true to form and she was right. She hurried from the office after returning the box to its place and locking the door behind her.

Now she knew she was in a race against time. If Barry discovered his loss before she could get to the bank, she was sunk. She waited outside for the bank to open. She was the first in line at the drive-up window. Wishing the teller a good morning, she placed the checks inside the tray.

"Excuse me, your husband just opened these accounts, why is he pulling out most of his money now?" the teller asked.

"I don't know. I think it has something to do with the stockmarket. I really don't understand money matters. He handles all of that," Skye answered nonchalantly.

The teller shrugged and said something to the effect that she would have to check signatures. She asked Skye to come into the bank because she couldn't give this amount of money out through the drive-up window.

Inside, Skye watched as the teller checked the signature on the checks against the bank file. Satisfied with the match, the teller counted out the money. Skye smiled to herself knowingly, after almost twenty-five years of marriage she was able to sign her husband's name better than he could.

How and Why Lovers Cheat

"You realize that now your husband has a remaining balance of one dollar in each of his accounts," the teller remarked as Skye turned to walk away.

"Oh, yes, I realize it. Maybe he will get lucky in the stock market," Skye retorted as she headed for the vault.

Skye once again filled out the form to her safety deposit box. She watched as the attendant checked her signature and picked up the masterkeys to the boxes

Asking about the attendant's grandchild, Skye purposely dropped her keys. She bent and picked the keys up, except now she was holding out her husband's box key not hers. They walked to the back of the vault chatting. The attendant asked Skye for her number. Looking down she read off her husband's number from his key. The attendant inserted both the master and Barry's key into the locks and withdrew the box. She handed Skye the box and walked out with her. After locking the small room door, Skye lifted the lid and there were all their papers and her jewelry. She took out everything and dumped it into her purse. She gave the box back to the attendant and walked out of the bank. Pulling out of the bank's parking lot, Skye passed her husband's car. His face was bright red. Quickly she rolled down her window and yelled, "You have just entered the TWILIGHT ZONE."

Skye's story is a terrific example of courage. It took courage to go to her husband's office. It took courage to go to the bank and withdraw the money. It took courage to switch the safety deposit box keys. But I think the most courageous thing Skye did was getting off the couch and pulling herself together to protect her assets. Skye and Barry are divorced now. I understand that his secretary left him for a better "job."

4. The Creativity of a Detective

A detective is creative. She must be an innovative storyteller and an imaginative actress.

A very intelligent person once said, "If life hands you lemons, make lemonade." This is creativity. This is what you must possess in order to be an investigator.

The ability to be creative is the incandescence of a detective. This is the attribute which illuminates the darkness of the unsolved problem. It is with this talent you will be able to resourcefully handle anything that comes your way during your investigation.

My all time favorite example of creativity is something I like to call "Muffin." As a matter of fact, I have incorporated it into the list of needed tools for a detective. We will be discussing that list in great detail in the next chapter.

"Muffin" came in very handy while Marge was on her case.

Marge knew her investigation was in its final hour. If she blew it now she would have to start back at square one. With this uppermost in her mind she drove cautiously around the corner of the block looking for her husband's ten-year-old beater. Finding it parked in the same general area in which she had discovered it last week, she released a sad but satisfied sigh.

Marge eased her borrowed car next to the curb and parked it. She checked the placement of her brunette wig in the rearview mirror before grabbing her large purse and getting out of the car.

She walked confidently past her husband's car to a small ranch which was badly in need of a good paint job. She knew through her investigation both the layout of the house and its yard. Quietly she approached the side yard and ventured up to the kitchen window. She peered inside the darkened room. From this vantage point she could see the front room was dimly lit. She moved slowly to the back of the house, looking into each window as she went, trying to discern the whereabouts of the occupants.

In this manner she made her way around to the other side of the house, cautiously she looked into the sidewindow of the front room. She could barely make out the two figures on the couch. But as her eyes became accustomed to the darkness she recognized her husband's familiar outline.

She moved away from the window shaking, with aversion at the sight of them. She felt sick to her stomach and began to question her need to catch him red-handed. But she only faltered for a moment as she remembered the months of begging him to tell her why he was so cold and unfeeling.

She decided that this was the only way. After all of these

months of thinking that she was nuts and overly suspicious, she was going to have proof of his infidelity. The proof she needed would have to be irrefutable, so that neither he nor, more importantly, she could doubt its validity.

Marge walked back to the corner of the house and crouched in the bushes. She readied her camera with its low-light sensitive film. At first her mind raced as seconds seemed like hours, but as time went by her mind gradually became numb, very much like a hunting Australian aborigine. Like those hunters, she was awake, but now she did not think, instead only her senses and instincts were alive. It is said that the aborigines can sit motionless for hours in a kind of wake-sleep as they wait for their prey to emerge from its burrow.

Suddenly she sensed someone approaching even before she heard him. She decided to remain where she was. A man dressed as though he were out jogging, glanced at her and asked, "What in the heck are you doing there, lady?"

Marge looked up. She knew he could not see her hands as it was a dark and moonless night. So she quietly dropped her camera and stood up with a leash in her hand and said, "I was looking for Muffin. She seems to have gotten out of the yard. Have you seen a little black terrier? She has a pink rhinestone collar on."

"No, I haven't, but I'll keep a lookout for her," the man answered as he began to jog down the street.

Just to make things look good, Marge got up from the bushes and moved away from the house calling, "Muffin, Muffin, darling, where are you?" Looking back over her shoulder, she watched as the figure of the man was swallowed up into the darkness. She then returned to her vigil.

It was about a half hour after her run-in with the jogger that her husband emerged from the house. He stood entwined in his mistress's arms, kissing on the stoop under the porch light. Quietly Marge stood up and took several pictures of the lovers' embrace and then she walked sadly back to her car.

Without the ploy of Muffin's leash and a plausible story, the investigation could have been irrevocably damaged. A leash changes a person from a would-be burglar into a harmless, worried dog owner. This, my friend, is creativity.

Marge and her husband are divorced now. He is living in

that small ranch which is still badly in need of paint. Marge can take some solace in statistics that show that most men do not stay with their mistresses long—nor women with their lovers. These people are usually simply transitional individuals in their lives.

5. A Detective Is Well Prepared

A detective must be well prepared for any eventuality. It is only through careful and well-thought-out preparation and organization that a detective is successful.

The essential preparation of a detective includes both the intangible and the tangible. Some of the intangibles we have already discussed.

A detective needs to prepare her mind so that she can devise a sound and appropriate plan. A tenacious attitude must be adopted so that she possesses the determination to carry out the strategy of the plan. She must fortify herself with courage, and creativity must radiate from the very fiber of her being.

Yet with this preparation of mind, attitude, courage and creativity, she has only just begun. She must also outline and assemble all of the tangible details she will need in her investigation. Those tangibles may include disguises, a camera, a good cover story and so forth. The preparation and organization of these details is imperative as the entire success or failure of any investigation can hinge upon them.

Let's sit on Jacqueline Clouseau's shoulder as she endeavors to catch her husband in the very throes of his rendezvous. You should be mindful of her lack of preparation and how this affects her performance as a detective.

Jacqueline sat seemingly content at the dining room table working a crossword puzzle. She barely glanced in Devon's direction as he breezed past her. He kissed the air a good six inches from her cheek and said good-bye.

"Big meeting at the lodge tonight, dear?" she asked, nonchalantly not looking up from the puzzle.

"Hey, you know they can't get along without me," he answered as he walked out the door.

The moment the lock snapped shut, Jacqueline's demeanor

changed from a disinterested mouse to a fierce lioness. "I just bet," she yelled throwing the crossword book at the door.

Then Jacqueline sprang so violently from her chair that she almost upset it. She bolted to the kitchen and yanked the phone from its cradle. She dialed Patty's number. Without even saying hello, she informed her that Devon had lcft. She begged Patty to hurry over and hung up.

Jacqueline ran to her bedroom and grabbed a huge shoulder bag from the closet. She dumped its contents onto the dresser and then shoved in a camera and a gray wig. Hearing Patty's car turn into the drive, she snatched up her keys and ran to the door. She opened the door just as Patty had begun to knock. Jacqueline's outward force and Patty's simultaneous inward force resulted in the women colliding in mid-air. There was a loud thud as their foreheads came together.

"Thanks a lot," Patty moaned and then added, "Will you calm down, we already know where they are going."

As though she hadn't heard her. Jacqueline grabbed Patty's arm and rushed to her car. She completely ignored the pain of the already forming lump on her forehead. She practically pushed Patty into her car. Jumping in herself, she ground the motor and before Patty could say a word, she threw the car into reverse and hit the gas. There was a sickening sound as her car slammed into Patty's front bumper.

"I don't believe this," Patty yelled. "You are going to kill us before you ever get a chance to kill Devon."

"Just forget it, I'll pay for the damage," Jacqueline answered as she pulled her car forward to disengage the bumpers. Then swinging wide she backed onto the lawn to avoid Patty's car and get onto the street.

Once on the street, she accelerated to such a speed that Patty immediately put on her seat belt. Looking out her window, Patty watched objects slip by obscurely. They hadn't gone a mile before the red blinking lights of a squad car lit up their interior.

They both sat silently as they watched the young policeman saunter up to Jacqueline's window. "What the heck do you think you're doing?" he asked.

"Listen, if you are going to give me a ticket just start

writing. I'm in a hurry," Jacqueline answered curtly.

Thinking quickly, Patty interjected, "Um, she didn't mean that, Sir. See, we are on our way to the hospital. My friend's grandfather is dying."

"Well I'm sorry to hear that, but I'm going to have to give her a ticket. She was going thirty miles over the limit," he said, adding, "your license, please?"

Jacqueline reached for her wallet and only then discovered she had forgotten to bring it with her. Looking up into the policeman's eyes, she sighed and began to cry. "I forgot my wallet. I was so upset when they called about Grandpa," she whimpered.

Patty took up the ruse and patted Jacqueline's hand and asked, "Can't you see the woman is beside herself with grief?"

Guiltily the policeman mumbled a few words of warning and condolences. Then he gave them a pass.

The cop no sooner got back into his car than Jacqueline's tears turned off and she laughed, "Those acting lessons sure paid off."

"Yeah but slow down, or next time we won't be so lucky," Patty retorted.

Driving at a relatively normal pace, they once again made their way toward the "Pheasant Run." Jacqueline had discovered Devon's hide-away spot last week quite accidently as she was shopping.

They drove in silence. Suddenly the motor began to sputter. Jacqueline looked down at the gas gauge just as the car rolled to a stop. Patty did not say a word while they trekked nine blocks to a gas station. The quiet was almost deafening as Patty handed over her last three dollars to Jacqueline to use for both the gas in the can and in her tank when they returned to the station.

"That gas gauge has been giving me trouble," Jacqueline said, once they were on their way again. But Patty remained silent. She just looked out the window and shook her head.

"Oh my gosh, there he is," Jacqueline screamed and threw a U-turn in the middle of the street.

"Are you sure?" Patty asked, setting aside her anger and again snapping her seat belt in place.

"Don't you think I know my own husband's car?"

Jacqueline answered breathlessly as she chased the car down a side street.

They watched as the car pulled into the driveway of a strange house. Jacqueline pulled out her camera. She snapped a lovely picture of the elderly couple that emerged from the car.

Later, as they arrived at the "Pheasant Run" Jacqueline stammered, "Anyone can make a mistake, Patty."

"Just forget it and put on your wig. Let's get this over with," Patty answered.

Jacqueline tried desperately to get all of her red strands into the wig without much success. Finally she said, "Well this will just have to do." Patty went back to being quiet.

They entered the lounge and spotted Devon and his ladyfriend in a dark back booth. Choosing a table out of his view, they ordered two drinks. Jacqueline bolted her's down and ordered a shot to bolster her courage. They decided to ask for the check so they could clear out fast as soon as Jacqueline got her picture.

Patty reached into her purse to pay the check and looked at Jacqueline dejected. They had forgotten they were out of cash. They had to banter for some minutes before they were able to convince the waitress to hold Patty's watch until they could return with the money.

After the waitress had left, Patty said between clenched teeth, "After you kill Devon, I'm going to kill you."

Jacqueline didn't answer. Instead she decided that this was the time to get the picture. Getting up quickly, she walked over to Devon's table and took a rapid succession of pictures. Turning on her heels she ran back to Patty and yanked her to a standing a position. Together they sped to the door while Jacqueline's wig flew off.

Jacqueline Clouseau's story is a classic example of everything not to do while on a case. The funny thing is though, that unlike television, this is probably a more accurate account of an actual investigation.

If you are able to bumble your way to the truth, it's worth it.

This is a true story. Jacqueline and Devon are now separated. Jacqueline's confrontation later would have been so much more effective had she remembered to load her camera. I also understand that Jacqueline and Patty are not on speaking terms to this day.

6. A Detective Is Patient

A detective's patience is one of her most important attributes. This type of patience should be immeasurable and continue unceasingly.

An excellent comparison can be drawn between a working investigator and an animal behaviorist in the midst of a study in the field. The behaviorist may sit for hours on end (literally) and never spot the animal she is seeking. A detective may sit and watch an apartment complex for hours and come up empty-handed. An animal behaviorist will return again and again to keep her watch, and so will a detective. Once spotting her subject, a behaviorist will track it, observe it and try to understand not only the what, but the *why's* of her subject's behavior. A detective once spotting her subject may need to follow him, keep him under surveillance and try to deduce his next move.

Let's continue the analogy and look at the work of the world-famous animal behaviorist Jane Goodall.

In 1960, famed anthropologist Louis Leakey was searching for a person to study wild chimpanzees. He wanted someone without an academic bias. He also wanted someone who possessed uncommon patience and dedication. So he chose Jane. She went on to make scientific history.

At twenty-six, Jane traveled four thousand miles from her home to the Gombe game reserve in the African country of Tanzania. Her mother acted as her companion and a few natives made up her staff.

No sooner had the tents been pitched and the provisions been stored, than Jane set out. Unarmed, untrained and alone, she ventured into the jungle of the reserve in search of the wild chimpanzees.

For months she couldn't even find any chimpanzees or if she found them, they would flee at the very sight of her. Yet she continued day after day to return to the jungle to begin her search anew.

Finally she discovered a peak from which she could see the entire valley. Sitting there daily, she began to piece together the movements of the chimpanzees. For many months she watched them and became accustomed to their nomadic habits. As she was watching them, they were watching her. Slowly they accepted her presence. It was through her painstaking patience over several months that she was able to gain their trust. Through this trust, they would allow her near them and, thereby, allow her to conduct her study.

Jane Goodall's study has spanned over a quarter of a century. Our knowledge of the wild chimpanzees' behavior and habits can be attributed to her.

Ms. Goodall's example is an object lesson to us all. It speaks of painstaking fortitude and endurance. It speaks of exceptional patience and dedication. Further, it was those attributes that became so much more important than academic training. If you possess just a fraction of her patience, I'm sure you will also be successful.

It will be your ability to combine and unite the attributes of analytical reasoning, a tenacious attitude, courage, creativity, excellent preparation skills and patience that will allow you to BE a detective.

Now that you are an investigator, we will discuss the tangible tools you need to do your job.

CHAPTER THREE

TOOLS OF
THE TRADE

The tools of the trade are the basic tangible equipment you will need in order to conduct your investigation. If you cannot find some piece of equipment mentioned in this book, write to me at S.I.S., P.O. Box 370, Schaumburg, IL 60103, and I will help you if I can. Your particular investigation may run a course that may not necessitate the usage of every tool mentioned in this chapter. However, I suggest that you outfit yourself completely, so that you can embark on your quest fully prepared. Like a white water rafter, you can not begin your journey with only one oar and no lifejacket. You can not know for sure where the course of your investigation will lead you. You can not anticipate there will be no rushing rapids or waterfalls. So, therefore, you must acquire all of the basic equipment that you MAY need so that you will not end up on the rocks or, more importantly, up a creek without a paddle.

Right about now you are asking yourself, "How much is all this going to cost me?" I know this because this is the same question I would be asking myself. So let me address your probable concern, your costs can be kept very low. One of the best ways of keeping costs down is by borrowing or renting any piece of equipment you do not absolutely have to buy. I will keep you apprised of costs as we cover each piece of equipment.

I have divided into three categories the areas in which you

will need investigative equipment. These categories include your home, your car and your tool bag. Beyond addressing the cost of equipment, I will briefly clarify the reasoning which makes each tool essential. Further, I will instruct you in the operation of each piece of equipment if such instruction is warranted. I suggest that you obtain each tool as we cover it. If you do so you will complete this chapter by emerging as a totally outfitted detective.

(Note: I have put an asterisk by those tools which I believe you are not compelled to acquire immediately. However, I suggest you create a plan for the tool's procurement so that you are prepared when you need it.)

Your Home

1. Telephone . . . . . . Cost: $0

The telephone is one of your most valuable tools. It is through its use that you will be able to amass the bulk of your information. I have, therefore, set aside an entire chapter exclusively dealing with its utilization, so I will not endeavor to detail here and now all of the ways in which you can use this tool. It is enough to state now that the telephone has been purposely and properly placed at the top of your equipment list, as it is imperative to your investigation. Also, as I am sure you have noticed, I have put its cost factor at zero. I believe that most homes already have a telephone. In this day and age the phone has become a necessity rather than an luxury.

2. Telephone Recording Device . . . . . .
Cost: $30 (for TRD only)

The telephone recording device is one of the least known and the most revolutionary little gadgets ever invented. Aside from being very inexpensive, it is also extremely easy to obtain.

The telephone recording device has a built in VOX mode which simply means it is voice activated. (Now, so I do not have to type the words telephone recording device several times, I have shortened its name to TRD.) When the TRD is plugged into both a tape recorder and any telephone line jack in your home, it will record ALL calls made to and from your home. It does not matter on which phone in your home the calls originate from or are answered. Absolutely any call coming into your home and, thereby, through your line will be recorded. The way it works is when the phone is taken from its cradle, the TRD activates the tape recorder into which it is plugged and all activity on the call is then recorded. Once the call has come to an end, the TRD stops the recorder. The tape recorder is always on and in the record position. It is the TRD that starts and stops the tape recorder. Further, it is completely noiseless so it is not in any way detectable to those persons on the telephone. I should caution you at this point to make yourself aware and acquainted with any and all eavesdropping laws. So consider yourself cautioned! Please consult both your own state statutes that can usually be found in your local library and the legalities chapter contained in this book to assist you. Further, you should know that the TRD was designed to be the poor man's answering machine. (Read between the lines). The TRD is, indeed, just a terrific, little, easily hidden, inexpensive answering machine.

There are just three interconnected components that make up a working TRD system. First, as I mentioned before, you need a TRD. Second, you need a tape recorder which has a receptacle marked REM. REM stands for remote jack. The remote jack receptacle allows the tape recorder to be AUTOMATICALLY turned on and off by the TRD. Last you need a telephone line jack. A telephone line jack is just a technical term for the jack in your wall that you normally plug your phone into.

Now in order to set up the TRD system on your phone line, follow these step-by-step instructions or refer to the manufacturers' package directions.

INSTRUCTIONS

Step 1. Plug the TRD into a tape recorder. You will be using both the microphone and the REM receptacles.
Step 2. Plug the TRD into the telephone line jack.
Step 3. Turn the recorder to the ON position.
Step 4. Place both the TRD and the tape recorder in the RECORD position.

If you are limited by the available jacks in your home, or if you need to be able to use the phone to which the TRD system is set up, simply include a multi-jack adapter to the setup. Then plug the adapter into the telephone line jack. It allows two jacks to be plugged into one wall jack. Then by plugging in both the phone jack and the TRD system into the multi-jack, everything will work simultaneously. (Note: If you foresee your use of the TRD system as a lengthy one, I suggest you purchase a tape recorder that works off electricity rather than depending on batteries.)

3. Wireless Monitor . . . . . . Cost: $59 to $?

The wireless monitor was basically designed to allow a mother to hear the cries of her baby when she is busy in another room. The apparatus includes both a transmitter and a receiver. A transmitter transmits radio waves through space. A receiver picks up those radio waves. The transmitter is placed in the baby's room while the receiver is with the mother. So mom can hear what is going on without actually being present.

Some of the wireless monitor units are as small as 2"x 3"x 4", which, of course, means they can be easily hidden. No wiring is needed between the units so its uses are limitless. Further, there are some models that run on batteries so they can be used in areas without electricity.

Last, there are some models that have reception ranges up to 300 feet. So one could be outside of the house and hear what is going on inside. Now doesn't this little gem suggest all sorts of possibilities to your detective's mind and imagination? I know it makes my blood pump faster.

I had one client who "accidentally" left a small, battery-powered, wireless transmitter with a 300-foot-range duct-taped to the underside of her husband's front car seat. She followed him to his recently discovered base of operations which turned out to be a lover's lane. My client just happened to have the receiver with her in her car. She also "discovered" a tape recorder in her car which was on and running. Subsequently she was able to tape the "baby cries" coming from her husband's car. I understand the recording brought tears to his eyes after he lost his shirt in divorce court.

The possibilities are only as limited as your imagination and creativity.

Your Car

1. Car . . . . . . Cost: $6,000-$?

To an investigator, an automobile is important. Its primary function, of course, is to allow the detective the transportation and the freedom to run down leads. In the pursuit of these leads and clues, the absence of an available vehicle can be overcome. You could borrow or rent a car. There are many areas that have rental outfits which rent very old and very used cars for extremely reasonable fees. These cars are ideal as long as you have some assurance that the engine won't fall out if you accelerate past thirty miles an hour. Public transportation is also another excellent way to get around. But if all else fails, you could walk.

That said, you need to know that there is a secondary function of an automobile, while on a case, that does not lend itself to substitution. A car is crucial in the area of tailing and vehicular surveillance. It is in this capacity that the absence of a vehicle will only run you up a brick wall. Could you see yourself telling the bus driver to "Follow that car!" Believe me, it doesn't work. I tried it. I was kicked off the bus in, I might add, not a very nice neighborhood. But that's another story.

But before giving up on vehicular investigation, make sure you have explored all of your possibilities. There is more than one way to skin a cat or a spouse. You could either ask a friend to drive you, or you could hire a taxi for a one-price/one-night fee. Most taxi drivers would rather have a guaranteed night's income than have to hustle their tails off all evening long. While Checker Cabs are great for the city, they usually look out of place in the suburbs. In the event that you live in the suburbs, you could call a limousine service. Many of these companies have regular passenger cars in their fleet. And most of these companies allow you to hire them by the hour or by the night.

The type of vehicle you utilize is just as consequential as your ability to get your hands on the vehicle itself. The ideal "detective" car would be a very boring, four-door sedan, probably dark blue with absolutely nothing about it that would make it notable. I always think it is unbelievably hysterical when I see the television and movie private investigators driving around in red Porsches. Then to make matters worse, their cars also usually have T-tops or are convertibles. Now tell me seriously, would you notice a white convertible Mercedes behind you or not? Your fundamental objective while on a case, and specifically while tailing, is not to be noticed. You do not want him to catch you trying to catch him.

So, therefore, if at all possible choose a vehicle that will blend into the crowd. Believe it or not, it is not important that your car be equipped with automatic changing license plates or a smoke screen button. When it comes to a detective's car, the more undetectable the better.

I realize that you will be breaking all of the guidelines I have just set on the utilization of an unnoticeable car if you have to use your own vehicle. Your spouse has driven this car, washed it and probably put some of the dents in it. Therefore, we can surmise that he might recognize it. However, after dark, the family car probably wouldn't be noticed by him unless you were right next to him. Between the obscurity of the darkness and blinding headlights, the atmosphere is not conducive for clear identification. Further, it would be foolish for you to go through the unwarranted expense of renting a car when you can make use of your own. So more often than not, you will probably be using your own car. Just because I instruct you in correct procedure, I do not necessarily expect you to be able to follow it to the letter. It is because I am aware that you might be forced to both follow your husband and do so in your car, I have included a chapter dealing with the art of tailing and surveillance. That chapter should enable you to keep from getting caught. So do not become discouraged concerning the possibility of using your own car. Remember, just because you know your own car does not mean you can pick it out of a crowd. If this were not true, you would not see people walking aimlessly through big mall parking lots searching desperately for their cars while walking past them several times.

2. CB . . . . . . Cost: $45-$?

A CB is a citizen band radio. It allows communication between vehicles. Its primary use to a detective would come into play when more than one car is involved in vehicular surveillance and tailing. So let's say you are in car number one and you are following your husband. Your friend in car number two, would be keeping abreast of your course on a parallel street. Car number two would stay in position to pick up the tail in the event your husband turned, or if you felt he had become suspicious that he was being tailed. Then car number two would pick up the tail. But the way the two cars would stay in touch with each other is through their CB's.

Even if you do not believe you will be involved in a two-person vehicular surveillance, a CB might prove to be very useful. A CB turned out to be a godsend for a client of mine who was tailing her husband alone on the highway. She became ensnarled in traffic and lost him. So she got on her CB and asked her "good buddies" to help her locate him. Subsequently she had every trucker in a ten-mile radius looking for his car. It was through their help that she was not only able to continue her pursuit of him, but eventually caught up to him just as he met his mistress. Let's hear it for the eighteen-wheelers!

I would recommend that you invest in a portable CB as your installing the stationary type, with a ten foot antenna, may cause your husband to become suspicious. The portable CB plugs into your cigarette lighter and usually comes with a magnetic antenna. Utilizing the portable CB affords you the ability to easily hide it in the trunk when you do not need it. Further, given the popularity of the citizen band radios, the cost difference between the stationary and the portable types is relatively insignificant.

3. Screwdriver . . . . . . Cost: $2-$3

It is a good idea to have a complete tool kit in your car. But for our purposes, you need to have at least a screwdriver. Now you may be asking yourself, "What am I going to do with a screwdriver?" Well, I'll tell you; you need a screwdriver to punch a hole in your spouse's tail-light. The reasoning is that a car with a broken tail light is much easier to follow. At night it appears as a beckoning beacon. However, punching a hole through a tail light is actually easier said than done. Ideally you would want to have just a medium size hole in the red plastic cover. But for some reason, the automobile manufacturer has made these covers somwewhat difficult to break. You may encounter some problems while trying to penetrate the cover with the screwdriver. You can try hitting the screwdriver with a hammer. If all else fails, simply turn the screwdriver around and smash the cover in. Do not be frightened about doing this, remember that his car is legally marital property. So you can break the windows if you want, it is your property too.

4. Thermos and a Cooler . . . . . . Cost: $15

While my inclusion of a thermos and a cooler may appear as an insult to your intelligence, it really is not. A fully prepared detective will need to have a thermos full of hot coffee and a cooler for sandwiches and the like. If you are on a stake-out dying of thrist, falling asleep and ravished with hunger, you can not concentrate on anything. Further, you can be sure that just as soon as you leave and run to McDonald's for a Big Mac and a cup of coffee, your spouse will slip out of his office for his rendezvous. It is hard, long work being an investigator. So you will need liquids and sustenance. Why do you think the cops are always at the doughnut shop? It is because they don't know what you now know. Bring your own.

5. Sunglasses . . . . . . Cost: $5

Sunglasses are terrific for keeping the sun out of your eyes. They can also double as part of a disguise. Further, I know I look good in a nice pair of shades and I am sure you do too.

6. Maps . . . . . . Cost: $5-$12

You should have a few good maps of your area in your car. You may also want to invest in a street map book. Rand McNally puts out several different kinds which can be invaluable while you are on the job. It is one thing to lose him while on the job and quite another thing to lose yourself.

7. Paper and Pen . . . . . . Cost: $2

It is very important to have paper and a pen with you at all times. Many a a time you will need to keep notes as you proceed. You may also need to note license plates, addresses and so forth. Only a Clouseau would have to jot down an address on her hand using an eyebrow pencil.

Your Tool Bag

1. Binoculars . . . . . . Cost: $30-$?

I use my binoculars quite frequently, especially during the football season. Looking through a pair of binoculars at a game makes one appear as though she is studiously following the action on the field, which is, of course, exactly what I am doing. It was only through this meticulous study that I was able to spot a cute, little mole on the stomach of Jim McMahon, the former Chicago Bears' quarterback.

You, on the other hand, will probably contain your use of binoculars to distinguishing identities of people across the street. So you need a decent pair of binoculars. The 7x35 type should suffice nicely. The 7 in the binoculars' rating refers to its power, and the 35 refers to its millimeter rating. You could invest in a more powerful type, such as a 10x50 or a 20x60, but you will be doubling your monetary outlay for them. For that matter, you could purchase infrared binoculars that would allow you to see in the dark. I have included a chapter on advanced tools of the trade for those of you who want to get fancy. But it really isn't important for you to put yourself through more expense than is absolutely necessary, unless of course you want to. The same binoculars I used for Jim's tummy will work for you.

I suggest that you canvas friends and relatives before you go out and purchase any piece of equipment. Many sport fans, former servicemen, policepersons and hunters will have a pair of binoculars laying around the house that you could borrow.

2. Camera Equipment . . . . . . Cost: $26-$350

I recommend that you purchase or borrow a 35mm camera. You can also usually rent this type of camera from your local photography store. I have several reasons for suggesting a 35mm camera rather than the 110 or the 126 types. But the bottom line is versatility. Before we explore the versatility of a 35mm camera, let's focus in on why you need a picture at all. The most important reason is so you can confront your spouse or lover with undisputable evidence of his infidelity. He may be able to lie his way out of a hotel receipt or lipstick on his collar. But an 8x10 glossy of him entwined in another woman's arms is irrefutable. Someone once said a picture is worth a thousand words and she was so right. It probably was a betrayed spouse who originally said it. Regardless, a picture is tangible evidence of his indiscretion. So not only will you know and he will know you know, but a picture is admissible in a court of law, if you choose to use it there. This then is the secondary reason why you will want a crystal clear photograph.

The 35mm camera itself is relatively easy to use. But if you are all thumbs when it comes to anything other than a Polaroid, I can suggest two options. The first option is to use a 35mm with as many automatic features as possible. There are 35mms with auto focus, rewind and flash. If you still do not feel as though you can take a decent picture, you may want to use my second suggestion and do what a client of mine did. She placed a notice in a college newspaper for an amateur photographer. She was able to find an excellent photographer for budget prices. As I mentioned before, the 35mm camera's versatility makes it the detective's choice. I will breakdown some of the advantages of this camera:

1. Flash: The flash runs off the camera's batteries, so as long as your batteries hold out, so does your flash capability.
2. Film: Not only can you get 36 pictures per roll, but there are several different types of film. For instance, you can purchase film that allows you to take a picture in very low light and without a flash. A popping flash would give away your position while on a stake-out. Do not be afraid to ask questions at your local photography store. The store personnel are usually very knowledgeable and helpful.

3. Telephoto lens: The telephoto lens will allow you to clearly focus in on an object at long distances. If I had been using a 35mm with a 300mm telephoto lens instead of binoculars, I would have been able to get a picture of Jim's cute little mole. Because you do not want to blow your cover, you will want to photograph your "action" without him ever knowing you were close enough.

These are just a few features which make the 35mm camera a detective's best friend.

3. Wigs and Toupees . . . . . . Cost $2-$?

We will be fully discussing disguises in an upcoming chapter, but a wig is definitely on your equipment list. You will want to scour garage sales and discount stores for a wig with a different hair color than your own. Remember, just like in the case of your car, your spouse's subconscious antenna will quiver whenever a person with his spouses's hair color is around. It is his guilt and his desire not to get caught which keeps him aware of those near him. So if you are blonde you will want to don a brunette wig. This simple and subtle change may mean the difference between slipping by him unnoticed or not.

4. Walkie-Talkie . . . . . . Cost: $35-$99

A pair of good walkie-talkies are vital to an on-foot tail and surveillance that encompasses more than one person. Like the CB, it allows you to stay in contact with your cohort. Also, remember that using your creativity means that any tool can be adapted for any purpose. One client "accidentally" left one of her walkie-talkies taped to the underside of her husband's desk. Her use of this piece of equipment enabled her to discover that her husband gave more than dictation to his secretary. Sneaky huh, over and out.

5. Tape Recorder . . . . . . Cost: $35-$?

Your tape recorder is a critical tool in its own right. You will need it to document interviews, addresses, license plates and so forth. If you simply rely on your notes, you may forget to add an important piece of information. Also, there will be many times when you will be too busy doing other things to make legible notes, like driving.

Further, as you have probably surmised by now, you will need more than one tape recorder. It is used in conjunction with so many other pieces of equipment. I suggest you purchase the regular size recorder with a REM receptacle that runs on both batteries and electricity. Also, you should have a compact, hand held recorder that can be easily used and hidden.

6. Leash . . . . . . Cost: $5

Remember the case of Marge in Chapter Two, in which she was able to plausibly explain her presence when she was discovered in the bushes? A simple leash may get you out of a difficult or potentially embarrassing situation. Further, one client suggested it could also be used to drag home a stray dog of a husband. But I guess everything has more than one application.

7. Flashlight . . . . . . Cost: $5

Once again, I do not mean to insult your intelligence. But rather, I am endeavoring to give you a complete listing of your investigative equipment needs. So get yourself a good flashlight and generous supply of batteries. In this way you can be "ever ready" to catch him.

Now that you are an outfitted detective, we will go on in Chapter Four to explore and establish the goal you are seeking to achieve. Like the captain of a ship, you need a map to guide you, and a predetermined port of call—without which you will flounder and sink.

ESTABLISHING A GOAL

Your ability to establish a goal focuses and centers your efforts. It also solidifies and structures your investigation. So therefore, a goal directs you and places your feet on an intended path with a planned destination. To pursue an investigation without first contemplating and making a decision on your goal is to set yourself adrift. It is a tremendous waste of time and energy.

At the end of Chapter Three, I closed with an analogy. The analogy compared a detective without a goal to a ship's captain floundering at sea without benefit of a map and wandering aimlessly without a predetermined port of call. If this conjures up a ridiculous visual picture of an idiot lost at sea, then I have more than made my point. You must make a decision concerning your intended goal. The goal then becomes your destination, your port of call, if you will. Further, the plan to achieve that goal becomes the map that will guide you.

We will discuss in this chapter decision making, both short and long term goal-setting, following through and achieving your objectives. However, there is one area we can not deliberate on and that is whether or not you are making the right choices. There is, and should be, only one person who can make your decisions. Only one person who could possibly determine the "rightness" of your decision. That one person is you. The decision and the goal you set now could affect the rest of your life. At the very least, it may alter your thinking and many of your personal relationships.

So therefore, I call this type of decision a life decision. You have made so many, maybe without even realizing the gravity of your decision until much later. It is a life decision to marry or to have a child, or, for that matter, to separate or divorce. These decisions affect you your whole life. You can not make these types of decisions quickly and without weighing their outcome. Rather, you must agonize over your decision and endeavor to analyze and explore your feelings. A life decision comes from deliberation and from introspection. Introspection is self-observation; simply put, it is the examination of your heart and mind. Then you choose a path that you feel is right for you. These choices are personal. While it will be helpful to you to gather input from those closest to you, the ultimate responsibility of choice is on your shoulders alone. This is how it should be. You should never allow anyone to manipulate or pressure your decisions or goals because it is your life. Further, only you will reap all of the benefits and all of the disadvantages from your decision. Therefore, only you will be able to discern whether your decisions are the correct ones.

It is important for you to be aware that the goals you set now are the framework on which you will conduct your investigation. A client once asked me whether or not she was stuck with this goal once she made it. Although you are never stuck with any goal you set and it is not written in granite, you would have to make several adjustments to your investigation if you change your goal later. However, it is our prerogative to change our minds, and you certainly always have that latitude. But if you change your mind midstream, (notice how I am staying within the nautical theme of this chapter), you will have to backtrack on the original course you had set. Let me give you an example. Let's say Tammy decided her short-term goal was to discover whether or not her husband was cheating on her, and her long-term goal was to go to counseling in that unhappy event. But while in the midst of her investigation, she decided she would rather see her husband tied to stakes naked on an ant hill with honey poured all over his paunchy body, than to stay married to him. She would have to readjust her investigation and her long-term goal. While we may all agree Tammy's husband's behavior justifies such painful and slow punishment, it is illegal in some states to do this. (Check your local state statutes.) So she will probably just have to settle for divorcing him, which could be just as slow and painful a torture for him.

Before we get into decision making and goal setting, I believe you need to begin the process of delving into your feelings. In order to help you do so, I have compiled the following list of possibly hard questions that you may not have previously wanted to explore. However, it is very important that you confront yourself and your innermost thoughts now. While it is a challenge that your best friend may not be heartless enough to ask you to face, I implore you to meet yourself head on. It will be through this mental encounter with your heart and mind that you will be able to sort through what it is you really want to accomplish by conducting this investigation.

List of Questions

1. Do you really want to know whether or not he is having an affair?
2. Can you prepare yourself mentally for the rigors of conducting your own investigation?
3. Do you believe the affair will just naturally end if you leave things alone and feign ignorance?

Now, in the event that he **is** having an affair . . .

4. Will you confront him?
5. Can you live with the fact that he had an affair?
6. Do you think marital counseling would help?
7. Would you want to see a counselor?
8. Would he see a counselor?
9. Would you want to stay married to him?
10. Do you believe he would have another affair?
11. Do you want to separate?
12. How would a separation help you?
13. Do you want a divorce?
14. Under what grounds would you want to divorce?
15. What would the divorce solve for you?

Believe me my friend, no one likes to look this closely in the mirror, especially when she is in pain. It is like trying to clinically examine your own wounds. But, yes there is always a but, in order to open the dam on your feelings, you must first pry open the lock that holds them fast. And now you can go on to making some decisions about youself and your life.

As we all know, making up our own minds is one of the most difficult things we can do. The reason is, we discover as children that there are definite repercussions and circumstances to every decision we make. Further, we all have probably lived long enough to have made a wrong or bad decision and had to live with it. So, unlike the small child who says, "What the heck. I'll stick this key in this eletrical socket! What could happen to me?" we proceed carefully. We know what could happen; at best our hair will end up looking like Bozo the Clown. At worst, we will mentally become Bozo the Clown.

So, like it or not, we are not children. Mommy can not come and kiss this boo boo away. And though I wish He would, God will not give you a sign; I know we have all tried that one. Instead, you must fathom your own heart and come up with what is right for you. But before you begin to make any decisions, I would suggest you throw off the pair of handcuffs we all wear. The handcuffs I am referring to are those that have been made with the material of "what other people think is right for you" and forged in the fire of "popular thought." Until such time as another person can live your life for you, those handcuffs are useless and shackle you from being you.

Decision Making

Exploration. Explore your heart and mind. Look honestly into yourself.
Definition. Define the problem, both verbally and in writing. In doing so you can mentally and tangibly see it.
Saturation. Saturate yourself with information and input from sources such as friends, clergy, articles and books.
Incubation. Most major problems produce a period in which all attempts at a solution will be futile. The problem is being

worked out on the subconscious level. So set it aside and allow it to simmer in your mind.

Illumination. After the problem has simmered, an illumination process will occur. This process is a rapid insight or a series of insights. It is like the cartoon character with a light bulb over his head who says, "BY GEORGE, I think I've got it!"

Verification. In this final step, test your decision out on yourself critically. Check your thought process to be sure this is what you want to do. If you discover your light bulb was not a wattage you could really live with, go back to the incubation step.

Goal Setting

After you have come to a life decision you can comfortably live with, you need to set up your goals. A goal is the destination, or port of call, you are working towards. Further, you will need to outline both your short- and long-term goals. For example, let's say you were very hungry but the cabinets are all but empty. Your short-term goal would be to open a can of soup and satisfy your immediate hunger. Your long-term goal would be to go to the store so you wouldn't have to ever again resort to eating split pea soup that was so old that the peas had solidified into one green mass.

In order to set your goals, you simply need to understand your decision so that you can map out where you want to end up.

Short-term goals. A short-term goal is a goal that can be attained immediately or within a reasonable amount of time. Hence the name "short."

Long-term goals. A long-term goal is a goal that usually either takes a longer amount of time or can only be attained after the short-term goal has been realized. For example, you want to lose weight. Your short-term goal is to lose ten pounds right away so you can fit into your jeans. Your long-term goal is to get down to 125 pounds, which is all together thirty pounds less than what you now weigh.

Following Through and Achieving Your Goals

Anyone who has ever been on a diet can testify to the difficulty of following through and achieving a goal. I know, I have lost hundreds of pounds over the years. But, the inability to follow through on one goal does not doom you to failure on another one. Although my closet is filled with clothes from size seven to eleven, I can complete the writing of a book. I am sure you can find many examples in your own life to edify the truth of my statement. The bottom line, as in progression to a goal, is hard work and a real need to attain the goal. In other words, if my doctor said, "Either you lose twenty pounds or you will be dead in a month!" I would look great! If he really cared about me, he would threaten me!

I am going to give you two case studies of two different women with the same short-term goals, but with very different long-term goals. So that you can see how an investigation must be structured to fit in with the goals that have been set up. You will see that Pam's type of investigation does not require her to document details as her goal is to discover the truth (short), but to stay married (long), if at all possible. Vicki, on the other hand, wants to discover the truth (short), but she has already decided to both divorce him and do so on the grounds of adultery (long).

(*Note*: Some states have completely done away with adultery as cited grounds for a divorce. You should check your local state statutes. Regardless of whether you are planning to divorce him or not, in the event he is cheating, you will want to document both the affair and your investigation. You would be surprised how a well-documented case could put you in the captain's seat. And afford you the ability to protect yourself, your assets and your children.)

PAM'S STORY

It was gloomy morning late in May. The rain fell in a gray mist rather than in actual droplets. Pam looked out her second-story bedroom window. She felt like the weather, it epitomized the dismal depths of her very soul. Pressing her face against the window pane, she finally let the tears begin to fall, as she stared down at the empty driveway. Daniel still wasn't home. All night she had laid awake, jumping at every noise and rushing to the window. She had spent so many nights alone waiting for him, sleeping fitfully but always alert to every noise, just as she had when the kids were babies. Somehow this morning she KNEW, as she let the sobs consume her. She KNEW she had been waiting faithfully while all the time they had been living some terrible lie.

For several weeks now Pam had a sense of foreboding. Since she was a child she could just feel things that were going to happen. Though she didn't believe in the supernatural or premonitions, she knew she possessed a sixth sense that made her more aware of those around her. Daniel had emanated a feeling that she had picked up on.

Daniel was a Chicago newspaper reporter—which had always made his comings and goings irregular. Very often his job would keep him out of the house well into the night so that he could meet his deadlines. But his behavior in the recent weeks, together with his being gone more than he was home, had set off Pam's warning bells. Daniel had become secretive and jumpy and not at all like his normal self. There were so many things, that Pam couldn't even articulate them to her best friend, Kaye. How can you tell someone, she thought so many times, that you KNOW because he hadn't gotten upset when she had worn her low-cut peasant blouse? Who would understand that was not part of your "couple," that this blouse always drove him crazy? So much so that if she wore it in defiance to his unreasonable jealousy, he would stare all night at her barely noticeable cleavage. Even Kaye would think she was nuts if she explained it was things like her blouse that let her know that Daniel was having an affair.

Suddenly, as though the sun shone directly through the gathering mist, she knew what she was going to do. She was going to find out who this other woman was and she was going to stop this cancer that was growing in her marriage. With this resolve planted firmly in her mind, she snatched up her clothes and went to shower and to face the kids at the breakfast table with the best attitude she could muster.

When Daniel came home, she made him breakfast and spoke pleasantly to him about his article. She listened quietly as he apologized for not calling home. She went about her routine in the house as he drew a hot bath for himself. But once he had settled into the tub, Pam went into action. She gathered up his discarded clothes from the bedroom floor and his briefcase from the hall table. She carried everything down to the basement. Meticulously she went through every pocket in his clothing. Then she emptied his entire wallet and briefcase and looked at every scrap of paper. At the end of her search she discovered two matchbooks from the same restaurant, a recent credit card receipt from a hotel downtown and several scraps of paper with phone numbers on them. She returned everything to its proper place but jotted down the names, addresses and all other suspicious information on some notebook paper. This is where she would begin.

Pam's investigation was tireless and relentless. She felt as though she was fighting a snarling enemy that was attempting to rip her marriage and family apart. Somehow she found the strength everyday to face Daniel with an unknowing smile and an air of unassuming pleasantry. But the nights when he would take her in his arms were the worse. It was then that it took all of Pam's reserve to will the tears from her eyes so that he never guessed that they were now wide open to his infidelity.

Within five weeks Pam was able to discover the identity of Daniel's mistress. But she was not satisfied to stop there. She delved into the woman's life and past, looking for some ammunition with which to fight her. The mistress was a co-worker of Daniel's, and Pam was determined that she would get this woman away from her man at all costs. Then Pam found an indiscretion. The woman had lied about her education on her résumé to the newspaper. This is what she would use. She armed herself with this evidence and quietly arranged to meet the mistress under the guise of being an informant with a hot story.

Pam sat at the restaurant that she knew this woman and her husband had frequented and waited nervously for the mistress to enter. Pam had asked her to wear a red rose in her lapel so she could recognize her. As the mistress entered the restaurant, Pam waved her over to the table. The ensuing conversation was trite, but as sophisticated as Pam could make it. In it, Pam revealed her true identity, her investigation and finished with her discovery of the woman's lies concerning her education. Then Pam gave her an ultimatum: The mistress could either have her career, or fight Pam for her husband. Pam insisted she give her an immediate answer. The mistress chose her career. Pam then asked her to arrange for another job and break things off with Daniel quietly and quickly. After receiving from the mistress all that she had wanted, Pam left the restaurant exhausted.

But she knew her fight as not over, it had scarely just begun. Now she must talk with Daniel.

She had arranged for the kids to spend the weekend with her parents, so when Daniel came home he found her alone waiting at the kitchen table. After he had seated himself in his usual place, Pam dumped the shoebox she was holding on the table in front of him. She showed him all of the evidence she had spent weeks compiling on his affair. She told him about the hours of work and tears she had endured. She told him about her meeting and her ultimatum to his mistress, and the answer she had received. Lastly, she told him that she still loved him, and she was willing to fight for him and their marriage if he felt the same way. Then she waited for him to digest all that she had said and done.

They talked all evening long. They didn't bother to turn the lights on as the darkness began to surround them. The darkness somehow made the talk and the tears bearble. Breaking in on them like an uninvited guest, something exploded. They ran together to the door and rushed outside. It wasn't until that moment as they watched the sky, holding tightly onto one another's hand, that they realized that it was the Fourth of July. They laughed and sat together on the porch, watching the lights fill the sky. Somehow they knew that this was not the end. That like the fireworks that lit up the night, they could once again light up the love they knew was still alive in their hearts.

VICKI'S STORY

Vicki sat in her four-year-old mini-van which she detested. It represented, to her, classic housewife drudgery. Though it was practical for hauling football teams, groceries and shuttling herself and her friends between hot garage sales, it depressed her. She preferred to think she was the red convertible type. In her soul she was red convertible, but her life was mini-van. It was something she had accepted years ago. Yet, sometimes she would long not to have to drive such a crystal clear symbol of her life.

Vicki sat in her van outside her own house for what seemed like hours. She remembered running out to her van, but she couldn't figure out how long she had been sitting there or for that matter why. Then she looked down at the long gold earring she was holding in her hand. Still she couldn't get her thoughts together. Her only impressions thus far had been that she hated her van. But then her mind switched gears and propelled her back eleven years to when she first met Bill. They had met and fallen in love at college where they were both majoring in law. They spent hours debating precedents and making love. They had planned to graduate law school together, marry and, one day, open their own law firm. But Vicki had gotten pregnant in her senior year, and they had to alter their plans. Vicki dropped out of school and they got married right away. By the time the baby came, Vicki was supporting the family and putting Bill through law school. She took a job at a day care center so she could take the baby to work with her, and at nights she earned extra money typing term papers. Yet through it all, they were happy and she was so proud of Bill. He had promised that as soon as he graduated and landed a job, he would take up the slack so Vicki could go back to school for her law degree. But that day never came. The weeks slipped into months and the months into years without Vicki ever seeing the inside of any other classroom than those of her kids.

Bill went on to become a senior parter in a very prestigious law firm. Somehow he entirely forgot the promises he made to that brilliant young law student that had become his wife. Bill believed it was high time that she gave up her pipe dreams of a law career and become satisfied with being his wife and the mother of his children. He had done a wonderful job of arguing his point of view, and as the years slipped by, Vicki contented herself with being an extension of Bill. As her life unfolded in her mind like a Danielle Steele novel, Vicki once again became aware of the object she held in her hand. Looking down at it as though it had just been placed there, she tried to force herself to remember where she had found it and why she was still holding it so tightly that it was cutting into the skin of her palm.

Suddenly, the mist she had been floating in began to melt away and she remembered she had found the earring in her own bed. She had come home exhausted last night after being away for three days in Springfield burying her grandmother. The entire ordeal had been like some horrible dream as she arranged her grandmother's funeral. Her own mother had tried to haggle costs with the funeral director. At one point, she clearly remembered her mother telling the director that if that was the best price he could give them, she would just leave Grandma on ice in his basement. Vicki stepped in then and guided the director to another office, where she made the arrangements herself. But her mother continued her badgering and bleating throughout the entire weekend, and she had all but freaked out when she discovered at the reading of the will that Grandma had left all of her meager belongings to a close friend. The only thing Vicki had wanted was her grandmother's law degree. It meant so much to her that she awkwardly asked her grandmother's friend for it. Vicki's grandmother had not only become an attorney when it was thought that women were best, barefoot and pregnant, but her grandmother had gone on to get her doctorate in law at the age of fifty-two. It was with her dead grandmother's law degree wrapped safely in her luggage that Vicki had parted with her sisters and mother in Springfield. She then drove all night so she could see her children before they left for school in the morning. But instead of extracting herself from a bad dream, she had been plunged into a nightmare.

Vicki had arrived home at approximately two o'clock in the morning. She dragged herself wearily inside. As soon as she had shut the front door, she heard a commotion coming from upstairs. She climbed the stairs and whispered loudly that she was home, assuming she had alarmed Bill because he had not expected her home until the morning. Just as she stepped onto the second story landing, she ran head on into Lori, her sister's roommate. She had asked Lori to take care of the kids while she was away. Tiredly, Vicki mumbled a few words to Lori about the funeral and told her that she would talk to her in the morning. She had known Lori all of her life, and felt confident leaving the kids with her while her sisters, her mother and she left to say good-bye to her grandmother for the last time.

Vicki fell asleep almost as soon as her head hit the pillow. Several times during the night she had woken with a strange feeling that she couldn't sort through. She assumed it was grief for her grandmother and complete exhaustion. But it was something more. Something that she couldn't quite put her finger on. Since she was too tired to even try to think, she willed herself to sleep. When she woke again it was morning; the house was completely silent. She reached for Bill, but he was not there. She turned over and looked at the clock; it was ten-thirty in the morning. She groaned as she realized that she had missed seeing the kids before they went to school. She wished Bill would have awakened her, she wanted so much to talk with them and hug them, to assure herself that everything was all right.

But everything was not all right and never would be the same again. She couldn't shake this awful feeling, and it wasn't just her grandmother's death. It was something more. She tried to get a handle on it, but realized in her muddled state of mind, it was useless to even try to think. Yet the feeling hounded her to the point of being maddening. So, Vicki decided the only thing that would clear her head was work. She got up and began to strip the four-day-old bedclothes from her bed. She pulled off the blankets and then the top sheet. It was then that she saw the earring. One gold earring. She wasn't sure at first sight whose it was, but she knew it wasn't hers. Lori! It was Lori's! She had seen her wear these earrings several times, they were her favorite pair. Now everything made sense and the feeling that had come so strong all through the night. Lori had been upstairs last night and there was no reason for her to be there. The guest bedroom was downstairs. That haunting look in Lori's eyes last night was not concern for Vicki's grief, it was guilt. Lori

How and Why Lovers Cheat

had been in her bed with her husband.

Vicki grabbed the guilty sheets and blankets and ran to the garage. She threw them all in the trash. Then still holding tight onto the earring, she ran outside and jumped into her van. But she realized she didn't have the keys nor was she dressed. So she decided to sit in her van and try to think of what to do. It was then that the thought process began about how much she hated her van and the events of her life with Bill. As the mist faded, Vicki looked down at her now bleeding hand that was still clutching the earring. She knew she must go back inside the house, so she stepped down from the van and walked, shaking, back to her door. She was coming home again, after enduring yet another death. This one was the death of her marriage. But there would be no gathering of family and friends. No elegy, no clergy, no ceremony to help ease the pain. No, this death was different, with no rites of passage. Vicki wandered through the house and finally came to her daughters' room. She went in and sat in the same rocking chair that she had sat in to rock them to sleep when they were babies. She sat and tried to rock and console herself, as she had done for them so many years before. But the consolation never came. Then, as though emerging from a distant place, Vicki stood up and she knew what she was going to do. She was going to confirm and document Bill's affair with Lori and then she was going to divorce him. There was no counseling, no discussion, no excuses that would help. This was the line that she had drawn years before. She had endured her father's philander-ings as a child and watched her mother cry once too often to ever allow an affair in her own marriage. She went and retrieved the bedclothes from the trash and put them back on the bed. It was justice that Bill would sleep on the sheets that she had further soiled in the trash, just as she had slept on sheets that he had soiled with his unforgivable trash.

Vicki was lucky. She knew the law. She knew what type of case she had to prepare. She knew she had to keep a detailed log including dates, times and places of her entire investigation. She knew she had to substantiate all of her accusations with creditable witnesses. So she built her case slowly and meticulously. She enlisted her sister's help. While *her sister* watched Lori, *she* watched Bill. They each had access to their respective person's belongings, home and telephone. They listened to the "couple's" conversations and observed their meetings. They gathered receipts, took pictures and compiled evidence. At the end of several weeks, Vicki had a complete iron-clad dossier on Bill's affair. She had ironically prepared her first court case, and she knew she had done an excellent job. She hired a well-known and respected divorce attorney and had her file for the divorce. She decided there was one more thing she had to do before she confronted Bill and presented him with his summons. After she had done it, she was ready.

The next day she dropped her kids off at her mother's apartment for the weekend. She packed all of Bill's clothes into boxes and put them in the van. Then she sat down at the kitchen table and waited for Bill to come home. As soon as Bill came into the house, he began to ask a question, but she waved him to his usual place at the table instead of answering him. After he had seated himself, she opened her briefcase and handed him the summons. She told him that there was no need for conversation and that his clothes were packed and waiting for him in the van. He cleared his throat and tried to speak, but he could not find any words. Minutes slipped away as they sat together in the gathering darkness and the deafening silence. Suddenly they heard explosions. They ran together to the front door and threw it open. Looking into the night sky, they saw fireworks lighting up the neighborhood. Only then did they realize it was the Fourth of July. Vicki looked at Bill, speaking quietly she asked him to leave. He nodded and trudged towards the van that was parked in the driveway. Vicki shut the door of the house and followed him down the drive. As he pulled out of the driveway, Vicki got into a sporty red convertible.

"Whose is that?" he asked.

"It's mine!" she answered and then added, "Today truly is INDEPENDENCE DAY!"

Then they both pulled out on to the street and went their separate ways.

Two different women, two different stories, but they have so much in common. Each woman made a decision that she felt was right for her. Each set both short- and long-term goals. Lastly, each structured and conducted her investigation based on those goals. This is what you must do. It does not matter whether you are a PAM or a VICKI. What does matter is that you follow their example and make your own decisions and establish your goals.

I will end this chapter by noting to you that there is no clear formula to prove adultery in a court of law. It doesn't add up like one hotel receipt plus two lipstick smeared collars equals adultery grounds. However, the legal rule of thumb is "What a reasonable person in similar circumstances might assume." The burden of proof will be on you, as in all cases when a person has been accused. He is, in a court of law, assumed innocent until you prove his guilt. What you think in the privacy of your home is your own business.

Further, it is a good idea to document your investigation thoroughly, regardless of your long term goal. It could turn out that you change your mind in the same way Tammy did. It is better to have the facts, just in case you later decide you would rather see him staked naked on an ant hill, than to stay married to him.

STRUCTURE OF AN INVESTIGATION

You are, at this point of your instruction, an outfitted detective who is planted firmly in the captain's seat of your ship with both a map and a port of call. But before you can weigh anchor and design your investigation, your journey if you will, you must acquaint yourself with your vessel. Your ship is a "structured investigation." Your assimilation and absolute understanding of how an investigation is structured is critical to your ability to carry one out; if a captain does not know his ship, his tenure at the helm is completely questionable. Can you see the same idiot who was lost at sea being asked by one of his sailors where the anchor was located? Of course, since he was dumb enough to set sail without a map or a known port of call, we can only assume his mental deficiency would be complete and he would retort, "I think it's by the pointy end."

Your job as captain is not to THINK, rather it is to KNOW. There is so much riding on your doing your job well. The end result of this investigation could affect the rest of your life, your children's lives and your financial well being. Are these not good enough reasons for you to understand the vessel you intend to command? I know your answer is yes, so therefore, I will acquaint you with the components of your ship which I call the SS-SOAI. (The SS I threw in because it sounds so nautical, and the SOAI stands for "structure of an investigation.")

The structure of an investigation can be broken down into three distinct sections. They are: section one, "the starting point"; section two, "the body of an investigation"; section three, "the goal." In this chapter I will define a "starting point." However, it will be in Chapter Six that I will endeavor to help you find your particular starting point to afford you the ability to actually begin your investigation. The body of your investigation is the nuts and bolts of your ship. It is the fabric from which you will weave yourself to the truth. Lastly, the goal is, of course, a derivative of the decision making process we have just concluded in Chapter Four. Therefore, we will just touch on section three as we have already extensively explored this area.

Section One:
The Starting Point

The starting point of any investigation is the first or most important clue that was discovered. The clues I am referring to are the warning bells that went off. They not only stirred your suspicions, but they also began this entire process. It is with that ringing bell that you will start your investigation. It does not matter whether the clue was something tangible such as a hotel receipt, or something as intangible as a strange feeling in the pit of your stomach. What does matter is that YOU have determined it to be a warning bell. Trust your own instincts, only you can decide if, in fact, you have an important clue.

All the great detectives throughout history have possessed one vital common denominator. Each have had an immense amount of faith in his or her own instincts. So what might be passed over by a lesser investigator as unimportant or trivial will ring the bell of a great one. Further, she will act upon her intuition and follow up the clue. If we looked back through the annals of crime detection, we would see many examples of monumental investigations that stemmed from what initially appeared to be a seemingly superficial and paltry clue. But it is not a clue's immediately apparent significance that puts the wheels of justice in motion, rather it is the detective who pursues the clue because she instinctively knows it is important. This type of detective would trust her own instincts far beyond any predisposed supposition that a piece of evidence was meaningless and valueless. Something as simple as broken twig has begun many a manhunt.

The uncovering of a clue incites in a detective a questioning process. Then instinct carries the questions forward until suspicions begin to emerge. This is an intellectual chain reaction. It is as though something sounds within her. Something isn't what it seems. She may not even be able to express the totality of what she believes is the clue's relevance, yet she starts to act upon it. Solely because her instincts tell her that the telephone call just didn't sound right or her husband's palatable story simply can't be swallowed. Instinct is an innate propensity, urged from within. The detection of clues flows from without, while intuition flows from within. So it is the blending of these two forces that strikes the chord of harmony that makes a detective great.

Let me reiterate again that the starting point is both the warning bell that went off and the first stitch in the blanket you are endeavoring to crochet.

Let's look at the unique case of Carrie M.:

Carrie shut her apartment door and called out to Glen. But she did not receive a reply. Kicking off her white nursing shoes she called out again.

"That's strange," she said to herself, and proceeded to search through the entire apartment for him. This did not take long since they had a very small one-bedroom walk-up. They could barely afford this place because money was so tight. Carrie was a nurse working at the local hospital which didn't pay well. To make money matters worse, Glen had been laid off from the steel mill just after they had become married. Though this was not the little white honeymoon cottage Carrie had always dreamed of, she had made it into a home.

Carrie went through the apartment to satisfy herself that Glen wasn't asleep in the bedroom and just didn't hear her. Finding the apartment empty, she walked back to the front door. She turned the four various locks she had insisted Glen install shortly after they had moved in. Then she put a new alarm around the doorknob and switched it on. Carrie had become very security minded as a child. Her family had come home from vacation one summer when she was ten and found their house ransacked. Carrie could never shake the feeling of having been invaded for as long as they lived there.

It was almost midnight by the time Carrie stripped off her nursing uniform and threw it into the hamper. She sat in the living room curled in a ball on the couch, with her anger growing as she watched the minutes tick by. She didn't mind so much that Glen had gone out; it was his behaving so inconsiderately that got to her. If he had left a note, she would be in bed now, reading herself to sleep. Books were like old friends to Carrie. She reread them until she could almost recite them word for word. But she refused to go to bed because she wanted Glen to see the dark circles she imagined were forming, even now, under her tired eyes. She always had a flair for the dramatic. So as to give the picture of the maligned wife the final touch, she draped her grandmother's wool shawl around her shoulders. She was going to clutch it to her chest and shiver every once in a while, but she decided that was overdoing it. Instead, she practiced sighing deeply, so she could have it perfected when Glen finally got home. Looking back at the clock on the mantle, she saw the hands strike two. Carrie got up from her place on the couch exasperated and decided to try to go to sleep. She would sigh at Glen in the morning when she wasn't so exhausted. It had been a long day at the hospital. She worked in the pediatrics ward, and the only way she could push the sick children from her mind was to read one of her old friends.

She had just begun Chapter Two of Dickens's *Great Expectations*, when she heard Glen's keys turning in the locks. She jumped out of bed and ran to the door to disconnect her new alarm from the knob. But she got there too late. Suddenly the house was filled with the loud vicious barking of what seemed like a very large dog and the shouts of a woman's voice saying over and over again, "Down Killer, down! We will get your rabies shots in the morning!" By the time she was able to shut the alarm off, Glen was halfway down the stairs. She had neglected to tell him about the taped alarm because he already thought she was taking this "security business" too far.

"Glen, it's all right!" she yelled. "It's just a tape!" she added, gesturing to the recorder in her hand. But then she got a good look at his pale face as he climbed back up the stairs and burst into a fit of laughter. As he walked past her doubled over body into the apartment, she turned the tape back on for a second.

"Thanks a lot," he muttered.

"Serves you right. Where have you been?" she retorted, closing the door and once again turning the locks.

"I was at Tom's place. He got up a card game on the spur

of the moment and I lost track of th- th- th . . ." he began to explain but was interrupted by a series of sneezes.

All Carrie's anger vanished when she came closer to him and saw that his eyes were red and watery. He couldn't seem to stop sneezing and his breathing sounded wheezy and irregular.

"Oh my God, what's the matter? Come and lie down on the couch and let me have a look at you," she commanded in her nurse's voice, pulling him along to the sofa.

She checked him over, and even though he claimed it probably was all the smoke at the card game, she undressed him and put him to bed. She brought him an antihistamine and some hot tea. Then she got into bed beside him. Carrie mothered him as though he were a child, and Glen, quite frankly, ate it up. After a while she turned off the light and mused, "We will talk about the card game in the morning, young man."

Yes, ma'am!" he whispered back, and they both laughed.

In the morning Glen still didn't look well, so Carrie insisted he make an appointment with her father, who was a doctor. His eyes had cleared up, but his breathing still sounded wheezy.

Glen's symptoms were gone by the next day and the incident was entirely forgotten until it happened again about a week later. Glen had come home very late and sneezed his head off all night long. Carrie was torn between her worry over Glen's health and her anger about his late hours. She decided to rule out the health question first so she called her dad.

"Dad, I am sorry to interrupt you at the office, but I'm worried about Glen," she said.

"What's the problem, Babe?" her father asked.

"You tell me, you're the doctor. What do you think it is?" she asked, trying to keep the edge off her voice.

"Babe, how would I know without seeing him?" he asked gently.

"But he said, I mean I thought he said, that he had seen you," she began and then stopped, confused.

"I don't know what is going on, but Glen has not come to see me. Is he sick, or is it something else you're not telling me about? Your voice sounds funny. Listen, meet me for lunch and tell me all about it," he said, disguising the concern in his voice as much as possible. He didn't like Glen, but for his daughter's sake he would have welcomed a Martian in the family if she loved him.

They met later that day and Carrie poured out her troubles to him, just as she always had done. She saw him as a cross betwen Marcus Welby and Bill Cosby. Their relationship had always been very close. At the end of their lunch she felt so much better. They had agreed that he would come over to Carrie's place the next time Glen had a sneezing fit.

Neither Carrie nor her dad had to wait long. The next week Glen came home again sneezing. She went into the bedroom and called her father. Then on a hunch she called Tom. As nonchalantly as possible she questioned him about the card games. But he didn't know what she was talking about. Further, he told her he hadn't seen Glen in months. Carrie did not tell Glen about either of the calls she had made. Instead she watched television while Glen continued to wheeze and sneeze. When the buzzer sounded, she went and unlocked the door for her father. Quietly she explained to Glen that she had asked her dad to come over and look at him.

Glen begrudgingly followed Carrie's dad into the bedroom and allowed him to examine him. Her father gave Glen an antihistamine and went into the kitchen to talk to Carrie.

"Well, he seems to be having an allergic reaction," he said after a while and then added, "I think he is allergic to cats."

"Dad, how can you say that? You haven't even tested him yet. I mean I know you are a great doctor, but you don't have x-ray eyes."

"Don't I?" he answered, handing her clumps of cat hairs he had picked off of Glen's pants.

"But we don't have a cat," Carrie murmured. It was then that things started to fall into place in her mind. She looked at her father, squared her shoulders, and thanked him for coming as she walked him to the door.

After he had left, she sat down wearily on the couch. She knew what she had to do. The cat hairs were where she would begin. She was determined to find out who Glen had been catting around with.

Section Two:
The Body of an Investigation

The body of an investigation is the actual detection of the facts. It consists of many elements. The elements include pattern discernment, uncovering clues, note taking, disguises, tailing, surveillance and so forth. In a few words, it is everything you will do from here on. It is conducting your investigation. Though we will cover each element in depth in the coming chapters, it is vital that you fathom both how to approach and how to effectuate a successful investigation:

Your approach should be focused. You should clearly visualize your goal. Then you need to move toward your goal with single-minded determination. To allow yourself to become side-tracked or hung-up on insignificant data is detrimental to attaining your objective.

Your approach needs to be systematic. Taken one step at a time, just about any aim can be realized. So therefore, deal with one clue at a time. A professional investigator may be able to juggle fourteen different unrelated leads to successful conclusions, but I think you would be asking too much of yourself to follow suit. In the first place, this is not your vocation, rather this is a task you have taken upon yourself under duress and out of necessity. More importantly, the professional investigator is almost never personally involved in the case. You most certainly are, so your state of mind is always under attack by your emotions. To prod that struggle any further is unwarranted and unnecessary. Do not put more on yourself than you should have to bear. Take one step at a time. To aspire to pursue several clues simultaneously is to make your efforts fragmented. A methodical and orderly progression is what you are seeking. If you attempt a juggling act, you may end up as if you were in an *I Love Lucy* episode. It is like trying to answer the phone, untie the kids from each other and pick up broken glass from the floor at the same time. What ends up happening is you will hang up on your mother-in-law, get hopelessly tangled up with the kids and step on the broken glass. And who would want to hop bleeding to the phone, tied to three children, so a mother-in-law could have the opportunity to nag you loudly? Certainly not me, and I'm sure not you.

Your approach should be one of intensity fraught with fervor. Of course, I do not expect you to be able to jump up and down enthusiastically while you are endeavoring to discover whether or not your spouse is having an affair. But if you undertake your investigation half heartedly, you will muddle it badly. If your approach is lackadaisical, then you will realize the same results. There is an old saying "You get out of something what you put into it." This is also true for detection work.

The organized effectuation of an investigation is really quite simple. It is the chaining together of clues and leads. It is, in fact, as though you were crocheting a blanket. The first step to crochet a blanket is picking up the yarn and making the first stitch. The first stitch in your investigation is the starting point, that we have already discussed. Further, we know it is going to be a blanket because that is what we decided upon earlier. That decision can be likened to your setting your goal. In either case, you know what you are aspiring to achieve. So with your first stitch completed and your goal in mind, the only thing left is hard work.

Let's continue with this analogy. I know you are probably getting sick to death of my analogies. But I just love them. Since I am the author, you are stuck having to endure them. Try to imagine how my kids feel; you can stop and put me down, but they are trapped like so many mice in a cage. When I say, "Let me give you an analogy," the most they can do is groan, and they had better do that respectfully. I digress. When one crochets a blanket, she would begin by making a chain stitch that extends to the desired length. When a detective has a clue, she will follow it and chain the information she gathers from it. She would continue to do so until she exhausted the clue or it afforded her another lead. After coming to the end of the first row of the blanket, you must turn it and stitch in the opposite direction, incorporating the second row into the first. The detective does the same thing when she discovers another lead. She follows it, chains it and incorporates it into the information she has already gathered. So in order to both complete the crocheting of a blanket or to obtain your goal, you need to weave it together one stitch at a time.

Let's go back and pick up the case of Carrie M. When we left her, she had become very suspicious and she was determined to discover who Glen was pawing.

Carrie decided to take the cat hairs to a veterinarian to see if he could tell her what kind of cat they came from. She gave him a plausible story concerning her pedigree Russian blue

How and Why Lovers Cheat

that was in heat and had a unfortunate encounter with an unknown partner. He checked the hairs under a microscope and then against some of his patients. After about fifteen minutes, he gave her his best educated guess that the cat hairs had come from a grey and white Persian.

Carrie then checked as discreetly as possible all of Glen's friends and acquaintances to see if they owned such a cat. But she came up empty. She decided she had taken the hairs themselves as far as she could. So she verged off on a different path.

She began to log the days Glen would come home late and those times when he began to sneeze. She was looking for a pattern. In the meantime, she kept up an appearance of complete ignorance in front of Glen. It took a couple of weeks for a pattern to become apparent. Glen's rendezvous day was Wednesday. So she took the next Wednesday off from work.

Carrie switched cars with one of her friends and positioned herself a street over from their apartment building. From her vantage point she could see the parking lot of their building. She sat in the car sipping coffee listening to *Pride and Prejudice* on tape. She had checked out several books on tape from the library to give herself something to do while she held vigil over her apartment. Snacking on Ding Dongs, she made notes on all of the events of her investigation.

At a quarter past seven, Glen emerged from their building and got into his car. He pulled out on to the street and headed east on Irving Park Road. Carrie had practiced tailing moving vehicles since the onset of her investigation. She would pick a car out at random and try to follow it to its destination. She became quite good at it. Although one time she did find herself explaining her story to a policeman when she blew a stop sign. He didn't buy her story and she paid a twenty dollar fine. But she knew the practice had more than paid for itself, as she weaved through traffic behind Glen.

Glen continued due east on Irving Park Road for several miles and then turned north on Barrington Road. Finally he swung into the Full House restaurant's lot and parked his car. Carrie passed the restaurant and then doubled back, looking for a good place from which to watch his car. By the time she made an inconspicuous U-turn and arrived back at the restaurant, Glen was going inside. She parked her car down a side street and watched Glen's car through her binoculars. She knew she had been lucky. Glen had not made many turns, nor had he gone on the highway. In either case, her ability to follow him would have been made more difficult.

Carrie sat and waited. After about an hour, she realized that she had drunk one cup of coffee too many. The urgency she felt made the next fifteen minutes almost unbearable. Just as she had begun to eye some nearby bushes, Glen emerged from the restaurant. He was with a tall, raven haired man. Carrie scanned the entrance of the restaurant for any females that might appear as being with them. But none surfaced. She felt like an idiot. Here she had taken the day off from work when they needed the money so badly, only to discover Glen had had dinner with a MALE friend. But as soon as the doubt came, it also vanished. Though it was true that Glen was just having dinner with a friend, it still neither explained his late hours nor his cat hair allergy. So Carrie decided to continue to tail him.

After saying a few words to his friend, Glen got into his own car and pulled out onto Barrington Road. He headed towards the highway. Now Carrie knew she was in for it. This would be tricky. She would have to stay far enough away so as not to be noticed, yet close enough not to lose him. Enough, of course, is the operative word. She thanked her lucky stars that she had had the foresight to break one of Glen's rear lights the day before. It made this tailing a little easier. Carrie managed to stay with him the entire way as he drove down the highway and exited at Harlem Avenue. He went north on Harlem for a few miles and then turned off on a side street. But just as Carrie turned, a man ran across the street causing her to screech on her breaks. In the meantime, Glen continued on. Subsequently Carrie lost sight of him. She pulled over. She felt like crying and would have if another car going past her hadn't arrested her attention. It was Glen's friend from the restaurant. She eased out of her spot and followed him to an old brick bungalow. He parked and went inside. Carrie passed the house and began to search for Glen's car. She didn't have far to go. It was up the street and Glen wasn't in it.

Carrie's mind was full of questions. What was Glen doing? Was he playing cards? If everything was so innocent, why didn't he tell her what was going on? Was he involved in drugs? Did they have girls in this house? It was maddening. But Carrie decided to wait it out and see what happened. By now her urgency problem could not be put off any longer. Come what may she had to find a facility. She left and was back within ten minutes. Glen's car was still there. So she decided to cruise by the house once again. It appeared to be completely dark. She felt it wasn't worth it to try to look in the windows. Instead she jotted down both the address of the house and the license plate number of Glen's friend's car. Then she went up the street and parked. She sat there all evening long. Around one o'clock in the morning, Glen came out of the house alone and got into his car. He pulled out and so did she. Carrie followed him for a few miles before she realized he was heading for their apartment. She knew she had to beat him there, so she passed him and sped all the way home. She was barely able to strip off her clothes and jump into bed before she heard his keys in the locks. She pretended to be asleep and began to plot her next course of action.

The following week was a busy one for Carrie. She had Glen's friend's plate number run through the Department of Motor Vehicles. In this way she was able to get both his name and address and establish that the house both he and Glen went into belonged to this man. She also discovered he was listed, so she called him. She pretended it was a survey call and was able to discern that he was a laid off steel worker, who was not married. By the following Wednesday, she was able to amass a sizable amount of information on Richard, Glen's friend. But she still did not know what was going on. Then she got an inspiration.

Section Three: The Goal

Although we have gone into this area very thoroughly, it is important that you retain a few points vividly. First, you must always keep your goal in mind and be focused on it. You are endeavoring to discern the truth. Do not get hung up on trivialities. Second, your goal can always be changed if you change your feelings about it. Just like the blanket we were crocheting can be adapted into a sweater, many sweaters in fact. Last, the attainment of your goal does not end this progression, rather it begins another phase. When you discover the truth, you will have just embarked on the more difficult process of dealing with it. You need to realize this now, so that you may begin to prepare yourself for this eventuality. Put this advice on the back burner of your mind and let it simmer. So when the time comes for dealing with it and healing, you will have already gained some strength for it.

Let's go back one last time to the case of Carrie M. and see if she was able to bag her prowling tomcat. When we last left Carrie, she had just had an inspiration. Carrie decided not to follow Glen around this Wednesday. She was pretty sure that his eventual destination was Richard's house. So instead, she laid in enough supplies to afford her to comfortably stake out her prey. She was in disguise and had a special piece of equipment lying on the back seat of her car.

She drove to Richard's place and parked up the street. She watched as again both Glen and Richard parked and went inside. It was nine o'clock. She had decided to give them plenty of time to get involved in whatever it was they were doing. So she turned on a tape of *The Hunchback of Notre-Dame* and settled in. At ten-thirty she slowly passed the house. Although it appeared to be dark and empty she knew they were still in there. Parking once again in her now familiar spot, she turned off the engine. Carrie then got out of the car, adjusted her wig, and opened the door to the back seat. She reached in and pulled out a cold pizza. Shutting the door and attempting to catch her breath, she walked down the street. She didn't hesitate for a moment. This was the showdown. She was going to find out what was going on in there. She climbed the stairs of Richard's bungalow and rang the bell.

"Who is it?" an unfamiliar male voice asked.

Disguising her voice as best she could, Carrie answered, "Pizza delivery!"

"Pizza, I didn't order a pizza," the voice retorted.

"Listen, if you don't take it, I will have to pay for it out of my own pocket," Carrie whined.

Then she heard a short conversation between two men. One of those male voices she clearly recognized as belonging to Glen.

"All right, we'll take it," the other man said as he opened the door.

He was the man she had come to know as Richard. He opened the door in his bathrobe. He stood there dumbfounded as Carrie stared past him at her half-naked husband on the couch.

Richard was not merely Glen's friend; he was, in fact, Glen's lover. Carrie heard and saw more than she ever wanted to. She threw the pizza at them and dashed down the stairs. Just as she reached the sidewalk, she tripped over a gray-and-white Persian cat which was in the midst of ascending the steps.

Carrie and Glen are now divorced. Glen moved in with Richard. Carrie is now dating a doctor who is an avid cat hater.

You now know your ship and you are ready to set sail.

CHAPTER SIX

THE
STARTING POINT

This, my friend, is where it all begins. Every word, every sentence and every paragraph that came before this chapter was just preparatory material. It is now that you will begin your investigation. You are ready. You can hear, recognize and taste a warning bell from twenty paces away. You now possess the analytical mind of a detective. You have the right attitude, courage, creativity, preparation skills and the patience of a saint. You have amassed all of the tools of the trade, and your fingers are itching to use your binoculars. You have made your decisions and set your goals so you know where you are going. Lastly, you understand how an investigation must be structured, so you are prepared to carry one out. You have been metamorphosized into a outfitted, educated detective. And you are ready to begin your quest to discover the truth.

In Chapter Five we explored the definition of a starting point. Further you became familiar with both its significance and its precise placement within the framework of an investigation. "Your mission now, if you choose to accept it, is to find YOUR particular starting point. These instructions will self-destruct in five seconds. . . ." It is too bad we couldn't have some *Mission Impossible* theme music here.

Remember that your starting point is the original warning bell that went off and aroused your suspicions. It is from there that you will embark on your mission.

What is it that began your questioning process mentally? After you have discerned which of the warning bells are going off, you are on your way to launching your first offensive. Actually you are choosing to wage war. This war is against your own ignorance of the truthful circumstances within your marriage. There are as many Pams reading this book who are determined to "fight for their man" as there are Vickis who are just as determined to fight their way out of a marriage that they feel is not acceptable or does not conform to what they want in their lives. Many aspects of an investigation make it an act of war. Besides the truth and marriage factors, there are financial questions and, most importantly, the children's lives to be considered and protected. Those spouses or lovers who choose to hide their heads in the sand, rather than know the truth or do battle with the enemy, will always get it in the end. I mean that literally. They get it in the "end" because that is the part of their anatomy that they left vulnerable. The person who stands erect and faces adversity head on may not win, but she will have, at the very least attempted a position of defense. To allow life to happen to you rather than you to happen to it, affords you only the cloak of the personification of the poor, poor victim. End of speech!

In the following pages I will be dealing with the warning bells one at a time. I will explore each warning bell briefly and then move on to suggest an initial course of action. By initiating the first offensive, we will taking your starting point and begin the chaining process I discussed in the previous chapter. Moving in this fashion, we will be able to not only pinpoint the modus operandi (method of operation) of your alleged infidel, but we will also begin to combat the maneuvers he is engaging in.

There are two points that I must make before we go any further. The first of these is: In order to recognize any warning bell, we must remember that the word change is synonymous with it. Second, working with every warning bell you will notice that I will recommend that you log behavior to establish a pattern. Your first question, therefore, will be: How do I go about keeping a log so that I can ascertain forming pattern? Good question. The answer is, read the next chapter. In it we will cover logs and pattern discernment. What we are doing in this arena is discovering the enemy's vulnerable areas in which he as left himself open to infiltration. Further, we are creating and blueprinting an initial assault into the adversary's territory.

Change in Personal Habits

A change in personal habits includes any deviation of what you, the spouse, or lover, has come to know as the norm. These alterations include, but are not limited to, the use of cologne, grooming, clothing or anything pertinent to one's appearance.

Remember the discussion on cleaning up one's act to better attract the opposite sex. The words "state of wedded bliss" are usually synonymous with the state of complacency. Marriage is in itself a routine we all fall into. Very few rise a half an hour before our husbands to apply warpaint so he won't have to see what we actually look like. Very few us sleep in our makeup so in case he gets up in the middle of the night to go to the bathroom and happens to glance our way, we are gorgeous. Even if we did glue on false eyelashes before going to sleep, this doesn't guarantee he will not look elsewhere for sexual exercise. A certain evangelist's wife that we all know proved this fails. If you noticed, I said sexual exercise because, in fact, I believe that sex without love is no more fulfilling than lifting weights or jogging. Also being a product of the late Sixties, I think the best things in life are free and *el natural* is the only way to go. But that's me. In any event, if there is a change there may also be a problem. Remember the old adage, "where there is smoke, there is fire."

Now let's say this warning bell is sounding. Let's further suppose that he has purchased a whole slew of new clothes. Because this bell is subjective, meaning it could be just your opinion that something suspicious is happening, you will need to do two things. The first of these are to log when he is leaving the house looking especially good. Further, you may want to log when he purchases these terrific threads. One will usually buy a new outfit in preparation of an event such as a "date." A log is meant to be a means to establish a pattern, so do not log insignificant data on it. The second item on your agenda is to test your theory, that a pattern has been ascertained. To test your theory, you may want to check that he wasn't in desperate need of new clothes, or you might check your receipts to discover the last time he purchased new clothes. Theory testing is where you will be assuring yourself that this is in fact an actual warning bell and not a figment of your imagination. You must question yourself here and now so that you can dispel any doubts you have and allow yourself to proceed confidently. You are playing devil's advocate. It is no sin to be wrong. While I challenge you to press on and go for it in all things, I do not suggest you do so blind to the facts. If there is a problem, then there is. But if there is not one, don't make one. You are the only person who can make these decisions. I say go for it but do so cautiously and intelligently. So test your theories.

When you have established a bona fide pattern, this will be the time to do some surveillance and possible tailing work. Unless, of course, another lead affords you with the ability to forego this leg work. You know by now that I am not one to engage in exercise for exercise' sake, but this is not why I would suggest you always opt to conduct your investigation with as little amount of vehicular surveillance as possible. The reason I recommend that you try other methods in which to engage the enemy and locate the truth is, tailing is an art in its own right that takes a considerable amount of practice. Further, if you are out there physically following him around, you are leaving yourself open to being caught trying to catch him. In a military exercise, a good general will always opt to move under the cover of night or in a covert manner. It affords her both the element of surprise, and she does not run the risk of ambush. Be a good general. Explore all your options. If another lead presents itself, pursue it before you hop in your tank and chase him across an open field in "broad" daylight. However, if tailing him is the only means to your end, Chapter Twelve will help you do it as skillfully as possible.

To recap:

Hear the bell.
Log the changes and find a pattern.
Test your theories.
Chain another lead to the first clue.
Tail him on those days that the change is occurring if no other leads present themselves.

Change in Hours

A change in hours includes any fluctuation in his daily routine.

In order for an affair to be taking place, your spouse must be physically with the "other" person. Elementary, my dear

Watson. Yes, as elementary as this statement is, it is fundamental to this warning bell. So keep it in mind. The fact is, one can not commit adultery telepathically. So he must go to where "she" is. When he does go to her, he is not where he would normally be. So these "goings" can be discerned.

We all live within and on schedules even if we are not aware of them. So, therefore, to add an activity to our normal schedules takes some planning. Further, to add an activity covertly is strategically complicated to say the least. It is not as easy as you now believe. The where and the when must be deployed with the utmost care by him. To understand the enemy's difficulties is to understand how to combat them. He must arrange a "meeting" with her in a manner that does not arouse your suspicions. So he must give you a plausible story concerning his whereabouts and the necessity to be there. Further, he has the extra burden of plotting this tactic with the utmost concern. He must carry out this deployment and launch his campaign with an optimum degree of attention to all of the details. The last thing he wants is to be caught. He wants to have his cake and eat it too. If this were not true, he would simply ask you for a divorce and go after this person zealously. No, he wants all the creature comforts of home and family, and he wants to play too. The comprehension of the adversary's objectives allows you the capability to both see the intricacies of his maneuvers and to understand the reasoning behind them.

Put yourself in your spouse's shoes mentally and try to imagine the dilemma he is facing. How would you go about grabbing a few hours of unencumbered freedom? In order to spur your mind into action, I will give you a few examples of the approaches some of my clients' spouses have chosen. One client found that her husband left a couple of hours early in the morning to meet his mistress. Another client's gallivanting husband took long lunches with his co-worker. Another husband joined a bowling league with his lady. While another wandering husband feigned business trips to allow himself several uninterrupted days of playtime. Walking in his combat boots grants you the capacity to see things from his lowly perspective so you know when to check the foxholes for him. It is said that a good soldier does not walk erect, rather he crawls on his belly. This method of movement keeps him from getting his head shot off. So if your soldier is crawling through the underbrush on his belly, your best vantage point is in a tree. The way to place yourself in the right tree is to discover when he will be venturing forth. The sniper in the tree may not be able to shoot the enemy's head off, but she will probably have his tail end clearly in her sights. I mean this metaphorically. I always think how incredibly stupid it is to actually shoot a cheating spouse. If you kill him, you have ended *your* life too. Further, you will miss out on all those years of making him feel guilty. Seriously, this investigation, this military exercise is about the ascertainment of the truth and not about a body count. Twenty years from the time you discover the truth, you will want to be able to live with yourself. Will his prone and bleeding tail end be worth the price YOU will pay? I think not. So, proceed, but do so intelligently. If it turns out he is having an affair, the worst thing you could do to him or his mistress is give them to each other, and welcome her to your misery.

So dissect your spouse's schedule. When is it that he is not with you or at home? What is he doing? What is he supposed to be doing? Is he working, bowling or what? This is what you will need to find out. Most people work for a living. This means that there are between eight to twelve hours every weekday he is gone. Further, in order to get to work there must be some driving time allotted. Then there are weekly activities. If you chart these hours, you will be able to visually see when it is that he is gone and not within easy access of your scrutiny. So these are the hours which you will be investigating. If he is engrossed in an affair, it will be happening sometime within the perimeters of those hours.

Your next step, if this bell is ringing, is to log his daily comings and goings. If he is having an affair, there must be a time in which he is doing so. If there is a time, then it can be discerned. It can be found by logging his hours. There is, however, one inherent problem within this logging formula. If he does not break his normal routine yet you still believe he is having an affair, then he has incorporated the affair into one of his existing activities. If this is the case, then you will have to move on and locate another clue to help you determine the *when* of the affair. It may be a change in his personal habits prior to leaving on a normal activity that alerts you to his timetable modus operandi. Sooner or later he will slip up. There are no perfect crimes and no perfect criminals. Eventually he will do something stupid. When he does, you will catch it.

After you have logged his hours and found a suspicious block of time, the charging bugle will have been blown. You will be on your way to encountering him on the battle field. But before you rev the engine on your tank and proceed after him in hot pursuit, be sure you have chained enough information together, tested your theories to warrant your moving out of cover and onto the front lines.

To recap:

Hear the bell.
Chart his hours away from home.
Log the changes and find a pattern.
Test your theories.
Chain another lead to the first clue.
Tail him on those days that the change is occurring if no other leads present themselves.

Change in Your Sex Life

A change in your sex life would include any variation in what you, the spouse or lover knows to be the norm.

Your questioning your own sexual intimacy is exceptionally difficult for many reasons. The first of these is: Very few people flag those days of their sexual contact and keep a running critique of individual performances. Further, it is the very intellectualization of your spouse's intimate contact with you that throws open the doors to the real source of pain here. By this I mean, to examine one's own sex life in this context, one cannot help but confront the pain that he might be in contact with another person, thereby giving the pain a catalyst to pour forth. But like it or not, in order to discuss changes with the analytical mind of a detective, your emotions must stay in check. I know this is so easy for me to say and so much harder for you to do. What the hell, have a good cry. I cry with you. But go on, for your sake, go on. I wish I had a Mobile Army Surgical Hospital to tend to you as you move through this emotional bombardment. But unfortunately, you must act as your own medic and heal yourself. All I can do is wish you God's speed.

The final point I feel I should address now is, this discussion may have some of its own inherent or built-in taboos which makes any open thought process a hardship. In any event, this change must be explored. Though we are treading in deep waters emotionally and personally, I know we can overcome the obstacles. To clearly perceive the mine fields in any undertaking is to allow yourself the ability to side step them.

This area is extremely subjective because it is equally emotional and personal. Therefore you will need to take a Swedish-type position of ambiguous neutrality in order to view this matter without bias. By affixing yourself to neither the right nor the left, you can make a centered and coherent appraisal of the facts. A good general rarely gets down in the trenches to evaluate a battle. Rather she remains positioned atop a nearby hill to afford her an overview of the entire field. Of course quite insentientially, from this perch she also makes an inaccessible and difficult target. I seriously do understand and agree with the basic premise that the general's safety ensures the surviving soldiers with a leader. But I can't help but wonder how many fewer battles, and for that matter wars, would have been fought if the commanders, presidents, dictators and so forth were forced to make up the front lines. Would they have wanted to risk their legs for a line of longitude or latitude? I doubt very strongly we would have quite so long a black alphabetized marble statue if the first names were preceded by president, general or emperor. But that's another story.

In any case, you as the general will have to sit in detached judgement on both your own sexual frequency and your typical intimate contact and make a determination on whether or not a change has taken place. To be able to make a clear evolution that a fluctuation has, in fact, occurred, you will need to peer as though an unaffected bystander into those happenings behind your closed bedroom doors. This smacks samehow of voyeurism. But it is the only way that you can possibly make a concise assessment of your own sex life.

Both your sexual frequency and its ensuing intimate contact are open to question and debate. I feel like Dr. Ruth Westhiemer here. But it is necessary to delve into and dissect this sphere now. What we have unequivocally been talking about since page one is, in fact, SEX. Your concern that your spouse may be having intimate contact with another person. This is really one of the big questions here. While the infidelity in itself is the motivating catalyst of this investigation, there is so much more involved. There are unlimited ramifications to the act of adultery. I think we should explore exactly what it is that causes adultery to become a horrendous problem in a marriage.

The sex act in itself between committed people is an affirmation of their love for each other. It is also a part of a greater promise they once made to each other. That promise consists of "I give myself to you alone." And you had better give yourself to me alone. The marriage vows are the understood contract made between two people. We do not say, for instance, I promise to love you until you get fat or bald. We do not say I promise to be faithful as long as someone better doesn't catch my eye. We do not say until boredom do us part. No! We promise love and fidelity, among other things, until death do us part. Well, some say this is not real life. Okay, if this is not real life, then let's change the promises. Let's everyone be honest and say I promise you love and fidelity until I break my promises. When it is that I break my promises or think I am going to, I'll come to you and tell you what is going on with me so you can make changes in your life. Then in keeping with this twenty-first-century real life, you will be aware so you will not have to waste your time or energy running around with a pair of binoculars trying to find out on your own. But the fact is, this type of honesty is not real life. He lies. Why? I'll tell you why, because the real promises he wants kept are yours. Your promises of love, honor and fidelity. He is another entity in his own right. And that, my friend, is not only wrong but it is also incredibly unfair.

It was on those original promises that you contracted to enter into marriage or a relationship. This is the field on which you built your home and family. When he breaks those promises without even letting you know that he has done so, he has drawn first blood and turned the home field into the battlefield. Further, he has begun the war you must now fight, love-filled though it still may be.

It is by launching your offensive against your own ignorance of the truthful facts in your marriage that you begin to take back some control over your own life. In this day and age you may be actually saving your life. Our parents fought the unseen foes of pregnancy and venereal diseases that sprung from their infidelity wars. But we fight germ warfare for which there is no combatant. That foe is AIDS. AIDS is a sexually transmitted disease. AIDS at the time of this writing has no known cure. It is the bomb. But no concrete bomb shelter in the world can keep this first strike from killing. Some people talk of real life. Real life is broken promises, broken homes, divided families and the AIDS death sentence. That is truly real life. So if you ask me if you are justified to fight this war with every weapon in your power, I say YES!

When you hear this bell sounding through the awareness that your sex life has changed either in frequency or intimate contact, then you must log your sex life. My reference to intimate contact includes changes in the longevity of the sex act, his demonstration to you, his discovery of new positions or any alteration of what was normal for the two of you. For example, if he always held and cuddled with you afterwards but now he won't, that is a change.

Though we will be discussing logs extensively in the next chapter, let me once again caution you to keep only pertinent information on your log. His increased volume while snoring is his way of torturing you, your problem and totally unnecessary to note on a log. Your log is meant to help you ascertain a pattern within this change. By locating a pattern, you are on your way to discovering the reason behind it. One client asked me whether or not she should continue sleeping with her husband while she was conducting her investigation. My answer is do what you think is right for you. But if you don't sleep with him, your necessity for a sex log is void and does not apply. You can't log what you do not do.

After you have established a pattern, test your theory of it. I always refer to an untested pattern as a theory. The reason is, until you have tested your assertation, you do not know for sure whether you have muddled into it a series of "I thinks." So if you discover through your logs that he will not sleep with you on Fridays, buy a sexy nightgown and slink around. Test your theories. Because we are still talking about sex and the sexual creature is at best a fickle one, you may have to test your theory a few different ways before you can solidify it.

Then endeavor to chain this lead to another one in order to continue to gather information. But if no other lead or clues present themselves, tail him on the day the change is occurring.

The exploration of this warning bell is when you, as the general, break all the military rules and wallow in the trenches. Keep your head and rear end down! More important, keep a close rein on your heart and emotions. For it is now that the girls will be separated from the women and the boys will be separated from the men.

To recap:

Hear the bell.
Log the changes and find a pattern.
Test your theories.
Chain another lead to the first clue.
Tail him on those days that the change is occurring if no other leads present themselves.

Change in Personality

A change in his personality would include any fluctuation in his persona.

This change is one of the most subjective of all the warning bells. You can not rely on anything but your own opinion to make a determination that a change has, in fact, occurred. You must depend on your impressions of his persona. More often than not the changes that do occur in his personality will be so subtle and so gradual that they will be difficult, at best, to discern. But since even the most callous of individuals will be somewhat affected by a wrong doing, there will be some modification to note. The ability to note and predict your adversary's thought process will allow you to successfully outmaneuver him.

The personality can be defined in this way, "an embodiment of the collective character; behavioral, temperamental, emotional and mental traits of an individual that makes his experience of life unique." So, therefore, our personalities are not an uncomplicated appendage of ourselves that we can offhandedly presume we understand completely or direct. This little thing we call personality has been the subject of conversation, conjecture and a multitude of research by the medical community for centuries. They have endeavored to fathom our personality to better understand us and what it is that makes us tick. If the medical community could truly get a handle on how it works, then they would be able to better treat us when our personality goes haywire.

Sigmund Freud, the founding father of psychoanalysis, established a theory on the elements of the personality and how those elements work. His theory and data, will serve as your own CIA (Covert Intelligence Attack)—so that you can not only predetermine your spouse's behavior, but you will understand the energies that drive him forward. Freud believed that the personality is made up of three distinct parts of one whole. They are the id, the ego and the superego.

Freud theorized that the id is made up of inherited biological instincts and urges present in us from birth. He believed the id is self-serving, irrational, impulsive and totally unconscious. Further, he theorized that the id operates on the "pleasure principle," meaning that the pleasure seeking impulses of all kinds are freely expressed. Infants are sometimes described as "all id" since they desire immediate satisfaction to all their needs. Hilter's personality was probably all id. He beat up countries and people and then took his ball and went home.

Let's suppose your personality was only a manifestation of the id and you saw a drop dead gorgeous man that really tripped your trigger. Spurred on by your id, you would run up to him and immediately engage him in a sexual encounter. You would do so because, as Freud conjectures, the id demands immediate gratification of its wants and needs. Beyond this, he believed that the id is empowered and is energized by the libido. The libido is derived from the "life instincts" which include survival and underlying sexual desires. The id further contains the "death instinct" which is responsible for our aggression and destructive urges. So most id energies are directed toward a discharge of tensions associated with sex and aggression. Have you ever heard a better description of a dictator's personality. It is frightening to think that these men controlled weapons and armies. It is also interesting to note that not one female dictator comes to mind. (I know my male readers think by now that I am somewhat sexist, and they are probably right. I lean, I guess, toward the woman's point of view because I am a woman. So sue me!)

Now let's use the totality of Freud's id in the situation of coming upon a drop dead gorgeous studmuffin. If only the id were present in your personality, you would run up to him, rip off his clothes, throw him to the floor and make wild passionate love to him. You would not care that you were doing so in the middle of the local mall during a Christmas half-off sale. Your id would be only interested in an immediate sexual gratification performed with aggression, and done so without the slightest thought to the damage done to your life or to your reputation. This example embodies our id's immediacy, sexual desire, aggression and destructiveness. To make matters worse, you probably wouldn't be able to get a second "date" with this guy.

While being driven alone by the id might be fun to fantasize about, the fact is, if everyone was id only, there would be complete and utter chaos. We would probably be on World War 1001 by now. Luckily, as Freud postulates, the personality also contains an element that he calls the ego. The ego can be described as the executive. It draws its energy from the id. But the ego possesses the power to direct the personality. In direct contrast to the id, the ego is energized by the "reality principle" which involves delaying action until it is appropriate. The "reality principle" results in a second process thinking which is basically problem solving. So the ego is the system of thinking, planning and deciding. It is also the conscious control of the personality.

Applying the ego to our studmuffin groping, the scenario would go differently. The id says, "Yes, yes, yes and I mean now!" But the ego would say, "Hold on! I've got a plan. Let's ask him out, buy him a few drinks, drive him to a motel and then let's rip his clothes off!"

Now here comes the third and last element of Freud's conception of our personality, the superego. The superego acts as judge and censor to the thoughts and actions of the ego. One part of the superego is the conscience. The conscience represents all of the actions for which a person has been punished. If you act contrary to the standards of your conscience, you are punished internally by guilt feelings. The superego "ideal" represents all the behaviors one's parents approved or rewarded. So the superego is the internalized parent dispersing guilt on the naughty things we do.

By combining the superego with the id and the ego and bringing the totality of our persona to bear in our gorgeous babe story, things would probably go something like this:

ID: Wow, check out that studmuffin! I am going to go for it!

EGO: Hold it one second, Id! These things have to be done delicately.

SUPEREGO: Are you guys nuts? In the first place we are married, and in the second place adultery is a sin! Just look and keep walking. We are here to buy a sweater for our dear, old grandmother.

If you understand the components of the personality, you will then understand his internal conflict. The conflict is guilt. If you understand this conflict, you will be able to note the outward changes that are derivatives of the internal spanking he is giving himself. The degree of guilt he feels will act as a thermometer for the fluctuations in his outward actions. So, therefore, if he is feeling guilty, he may go from a demonstrative hubby who loves to spend time with you, to not being able to stand the sight of you. Who he really can't stand the sight of is himself. If he, out of the blue, gives you candy or flowers, he is probably trying to make amends for a crime he knows he has committed towards you and so forth. Guilt is a heavy burden to carry. Unfortunately, more often than not, it is not heavy enough to make him stop having the affair. But it usually makes him enjoy it less. POOR BABY!

Look for signs of guilt. Look for the changes in his personality. Has he gone from a talkative, happy-go-lucky guy to a closed book? If his personality makes any significant change, then there is a reason for it. Only you can determine the why behind the change and therein lies your burden.

After you have spotted a change in him, log those changes. This log, as always, will act as a tool to discern a pattern. Once you can map out that his personality has changed within a patterned dispersement, then test your theory. Your tested theory becomes your invasion stategy. The chaining tactic then can be launched and your campaign to attack his susceptible quadrants will be in full swing. Of course, if you can not chain on another lead, follow him on the day that the change is occurring.

To recap:

Hear the bell.
Log the changes and find a pattern.
Test your theories.
Chain another lead to the first clue.
Tail him on those days that the change is occurring if no other leads present themselves.

Money Matters

This change may include a shift between spouses in who handles the family finances or one spouse becoming secretive about how the family money is being spent.

The reasons behind this change have been enumerated in depth in Chapter One, so I will not reiterate them here. But if this change is occurring, it is an assault that you can bomb immediately. Further, it is a tangible change and, therefore, not subjective. It will not be just your opinion or your impression that a hundred dollars is missing from this month's family budget. So the ensuing chaining process is both apparent and can be done systematically.

Whenever a war is contemplated and decided upon, funds are appropriated for it. In order to engage the enemy, weapons must be purchased, soldiers must be paid, travel expenses must be allotted for and so forth. By the same token, if your spouse contemplates and decides upon a full scale sexual covert operation, he must appropriate the funds to fuel it. He must purchase new armor and be able to foot the substantial monetary liabilities of his quest. The funds will be derived and embezzled from the family budget. Therefore, if there are missing or misused funds, you are as justified as the committee that convened in the Contra scandal to investigate it.

For example, let's suppose one hundred dollars is missing from the checking account. By ascertaining the date and time of the withdrawal, you can establish and conclude that, in fact, the money was there and you were not the one who removed it. Several questions then present themselves. They are: Who, When and Where. This, then, would be your starting point. You will endeavor to trace the funds back to who commandeered them and then move forward to discover, if you can, when they were taken and where they went.

As soon as this bell begins to ring, you should immediately examine any and all monetary sources you have as a married couple. Your search should encompass the activity in the checking and savings accounts, on the credit cards, the stocks, the bonds, his business expense account and so forth. You must meticulously go through everything having to do with money. Further, you must do so without tipping off your spouse that you are investigating these entities. Your investigation must be done clandestinely, especially if he is in control of the finances. To obtain copies of bills, receipts, charge slips, account statements and so forth call the institutions and request them. A plausible story concerning a tax audit should do the trick and afford you quick results. Most institutions are very accommodating when it comes to mandates from the IRS. Usually they are happy to help and ecstatic that it is not them the IRS is checking up on. Be sure not to leave any stone unturned.

Once you possess all of these monetary leads, your work is cut out for you. Each lead must be traced down one at a time. For instance, if you have a credit card slip indicating that one dozen roses were purchased on a Monday night in a town ten miles from your home, you have a definite lead. Check it out. After you have taken it as far as you can, endeavor to chain it to another lead. You may be able to discern from your checking account statement that there was a cash withdrawal that same evening and in the same town. You then would be well on your way to establishing a pattern without ever picking up a pen or drawing up the first log.

There is an old song that says, "Money makes the world go around." Though we may believe that love keeps it spinning, it is, nonetheless, true that money does make the world sit up and take notice. Further, to have an affair he will have to spend money, and unless he does so on a strictly cash basis, that money can be traced. We have become a plastic society, without a credit card you are a non-person and without a checking account you simply do not exist. So where there are charges, withdrawals, and cancelled checks, there is paper documentation. Where there is documentation, there is concrete evidence.

In order to move through this change in a methodical and systematic manner, make a check list of all the money that flows both inward and outward of the family budget. Then acquire all the statements from each of these sources for the last three months. This will give you an overview of the activity both past and present. Graph your spouse's monetary output that can not legitimately be accounted for. This graph will create a visual picture of his patterned monetary activity. After completing this graph, compile on a separate piece of paper all of the leads you have gathered from it. Now you are embarking on the body of your investigation.

Just because you are keeping a monetary graph does not let you off the hook from keeping a log. A daily log will allow you to stay abreast of his continuing monetary activity and allows you to see where your money is going. So keep a financial log and note monetary fluctuations on it. You never can tell how handy this documentation may come in later if you pursue a divorce. Be sure you test your theory, checking that it was neither you nor one of the older children who made a seemingly suspicious purchase.

A war is neither won on one battlefield nor during one encounter; rather, its success is obtained in a relentless and systematic movement toward the attainment of its goals.

To recap:

Hear the bell.
Check all monetary flows.
Graph the activity.
Log the changes and find a pattern.
Test your theories.
Chain another lead to the first clue.
Tail him on those days that the change is occurring if no other leads present themselves.

Strange Telephone Calls

A strange telephone call is either an incoming or outgoing call that you believe is strange or mysterious.

This warning bell is not very subjective. An incoming mysterious call is somewhat conclusive with little room for error. The degree of subjectivity within a call encompasses those calls that are hang ups. Without any ensuing conversation, this type of call could have been either a wrong number or a childish prank. But a fishy survey call or a husky voice asking for your spouse is definitely the real McCoy.

So when you believe that this bell is ringing, the first offensive, or the starting point, is to begin to monitor your telephone calls. Read between the lines! Your second objective is to log all incoming calls that are of a suspicious nature. Third, you should check your telephone statements for the last three months. Although we no longer receive an itemized telephone bill listing of each call placed from our home, the bills still hold a wealth of information. They continue to list those calls that were long distance, billed from another number, and those charged to our calling card. By checking out each of these numbers, you may hit pay dirt.

Chapter Ten, which is "Telephone Goldmine," will help you extensively prospect for all sorts of little gems as they relate to your telephone. Since I have included this in an upcoming chapter, I will not go through each possible tunnel you might want to explore. Rather, it is enough to say that approximately 93 percent of all my clients have mined successfully by utilizing these methods. Many did not have to proceed any further than their own telephone to discover the truth. You may be in that lucky percentile.

After you have monitored your telephone and kept a telephone log, you will, at the very least, be on your way to gathering leads from which to work. Adopt a theory concerning the calls'relevance, then test that theory. Your next step is, as always, to begin to chain information, leads and clues together. Stitch your investigation together one step at a time. If it is then warranted, you may need to follow him on those days you have theorized to be suspicious. Let me caution you once again; audio eavesdropping is against most state statutes and inadmissible in a court of law. Your INTENT, however, in monitoring your own telephone in the privacy of your home with an instrument you have purchased, may be to discover whether your children are calling 900 numbers. If you should happen upon a conversation between your spouse and his mistress, do not, whatever you do, listen to this call. It is neither your INTENT to discover this information nor eavesdrop on their private, private conversation. While it is true that this area of the law, as it pertains to family members, is somewhat gray, you wouldn't want to break or even bend the law. So don't listen!

You can liken the pursuit of this warning bell to the calvary and Indian warfare in the days of old. The calvary would send out scouts into the Indian territory to locate the enemy's position and assess their numbers and strength. Further, the scout would try to get close enough to the Indian encampment to endeavor to discover their next move. Your scout is the monitoring of your telephone calls. She goes where no man suspects she will be. Further, she allows you to locate and assess your enemy. Beyond this, she provides you with the ability to get close enough to your wild savage to hear what move he is planning next. She runs swift. She runs quiet. She runs true.

How and Why Lovers Cheat

To recap:

Hear the bell.
Monitor your telephone calls.
Log the mysterious calls and find a pattern.
Test your theories.
Prospect in the goldmine.
Chain another lead to the first clue.
Tail him on those days that the change is occurring if no other leads present themselves.

Intuition

Intuition is an immediate and instinctive perception of the truth. It is the ability to directly understand without reasoning. It is our sixth sense.

The sounding of this warning bell is felt rather than heard. It is a vibration that reaches to your very soul. An analogy that I think is most apropos is one of a spider and her web. The spider spins its web. No one teaches her how, yet she does so with intricate attention to every detail. The spider instinctively drops a silken line and attaches it to an area that will be happened upon by its prey. The spider then begins to weave, moving from the center outward. Each thread is interconnected, one to the other. Many times, she will just sit in the middle of her web, waiting. It is from this centralized position, or actually any position, that she will feel the vibrations of anything that is entangled in her web. Although not as calculating as the spider, we all can feel the vibrations of those around us. Like the spider's web, we radiate an unseen milieu around us. Those persons closest to us emanate feelings and sensations that we pick up either consciously or unconsciously. Further, we have an understanding of those radiations without a direct reasoning of them. Somehow we know; we understand their meaning. This is intuition.

It does not matter that we can not completely intellectualize the how or why of this sixth sense. What does matter is that you can and may feel when something is wrong with your mate. It is then that intuition's warning bell is sounding in a pitch that only you can hear.

Our web is not an intended trap or a well placed ambush. It simply exists to keep us in tune with those we love and care for. Further, unlike the spider, we do not await a negative vibration to snare and devour our victim. It is, rather, a sensor to our loved ones' needs and desires. The fact that our web picks up negative as well as positive vibrations and feelings is neither our fault nor our intent. Nevertheless, if the negative force is present, that too will be assimilated. So, therefore, if he is having an affair, you may just feel it without any other outward evidence to substantiate the perception.

Is it kismet that we entrap ourselves when we commit a wrong? Like the tangled fly, we doom ourselves to our own fate. The more we struggle to free ourselves from intuition's web, the further ensnared we become. So his lies entrap him further and more tightly. The strange thing is, it is because you love him that your web was so sensitive to begin with. Strange that in the end, the war that he began he will lose, and in a way you will lose too. So, like every struggle that rips at the basic fiber of our being, there are no true winners; only war-weary soldiers asking WHY it ever began.

Regardless whether you are acting as a soldier in the trenches or as a general atop a nearby hill, you are enbroiled in a honorable war. There is honor in fighting to protect yourself and children. There is honor in launching a defensive to preserve your home and family. If this war is not honorable and justified, then we as a society have truly lost our greatest strength. The marriage and the family must be the foundation on which we build. Without it, our homes are indeed built on sand instead of rock.

How and Why Lovers Cheat

FIND A PATTERN

I am sure you have heard a policeperson, either in a news report or on a sitcom, refer to modus operandi. Modus operandi is defined as method of operation. The ability to establish a wrong doer's method of operation is crucial to nabbing him.

Let's take the case of an habitual rapist. More often than not, these people follow a distinct pattern. They choose the same type of victim. He grabs her in the same way and under the same circumstances. For example, let's suppose a newspaper reported the activities of "Rapist Sam." He had assaulted six women in the last two months. In every instance he accosted his victim in a darkened shopping center parking lot. Further, he always chose a victim who appeared to be over fifty and heavily burdened with packages. In addition, he was raping on the southwest side of the city.

By logging his method of operation, we could safely deduce that he would rape again on the southwest side of the city; his victim would be over fifty; and she would be attacked in a darkened parking lot. Now, by knowing and understanding his method of operation, the police have several avenues they could utilize in order to catch him. They may either stake out or set up decoys at several parking lots within the parameters of the rapist's previous offenses. However, these efforts still may not effectuate an arrest of the offender because an element of luck is necessary. There simply isn't a way the police could cover every lot in which the rapist might strike.

So the police may then go back over their logs of information. In doing so they may discover some facts that had been overlooked. They may be able to discern that the rapist is moving in a westerly pattern and is raping every other Tuesday. Believe it or not, human beings are extremely predictable creatures. You may have heard the old saying "a method to his madness." Even an unstable personality may behave in a manner that can be anticipated. Without boring you with the inner workings of an aberrant nutcase, we can safely assume that he will rape within an environment in which he feels safe. In other words, if an offender finds a certain set of circumstances works for him, he will probably stay within their confines.

I am reminded of a scene in the movie *The Longest Yard*. Burt Reynolds, who was portraying a quarterack, decides to try a risky play. The play involved the team covering every man except one burly linebacker on the opposing team by the name of Bogdanski. They allowed him to come straight up the field toward Burt. When he did so, Burt rocketed the football directly into his lower uniform area. This play turned out to be very effective. Although Bogdanski was in considerable pain and "slightly" dazed, he stayed in the game. So Burt decided to run the same play again. It worked once, so it could be supposed, it would work again. Once again, the team covered every man except Bogdanski and, once again, the football was smashed into his lower groin. Down he went. This time, however, Bogdanski went down and stayed down, permanently. What does this all mean? First, never play football with Burt Reynolds! Second, if we find something that works, chances are we will stay with it. We can, therefore, deduce that the rapist will "stay with it" too.

So if the police were, in fact, able to determine the day and westerly pattern of the rapes, they could dramatically narrow down their stake out campaign. They would then have one day and a smaller sphere on which to concentrate their efforts. Further, the more the police learn about the rapist, the better their chance to arrest him. As they piece together his method of operation, and log and chart his past movements, they can make educated speculations on his future actions.

In the arena of infidelity detection, you are the policeperson and your spouse is the wrong doer. But other than that, everything else remains the same. You must detect and plot your spouse's method of operation. This is the focus of this chapter.

How and Why Lovers Cheat

His MO is buried in the behavior that first aroused your suspicions. It is up to you to unearth it. You must once again take a good look at your sounding warning bell. You must pick it apart and log and chart his behavior as it pertains to this warning bell. As you do so, you will be able to find pattern which is his method of opertion.

Finding a pattern within a sounding warning bell is one of the most essential phases of your investigation. Once you have identified his MO, you will be able to draw an inescapable net around him. The ascertainment of his modus operandi provides you with the ability to observe his present maneuvers. Further, it allows you to predict his future behavior. When you can predetermine his ensuing escapades, you can place yourself in a position to catch him in the act.

In order to keep from going on wild goose chases, and thereby wasting a sizeable amount of time and energy, you must learn how to keep and maintain logs. Log keeping, in this context, is the documentation of a realm of behavior. A log gives you a definite device that will allow you to keep abreast of his ongoing behavior. Further, by doing some research, you may also be able to go backwards and attach past actions to it.

For example, let's suppose the telephone warning bell was ringing. You would create a log covering all of the incoming and outgoing strange telephone calls. Through this log, you should be able to note and establish a pattern within those calls. Further, you may find by matching this log to your itemized telephone bill, a recurring number that coincides with the plotted mysterious calls. So the log allows you to not only observe the present, but also research the past and predict the future.

The importance of log keeping can not be stressed strongly enough. Let's look at "The Case of the Stolen Heart"; log keeping figured prominently in the client's ability to discover the truth.

Helmes, the world reknown detective, lay prone and disenchanted in our apartment within the very heart of the city. While outside our window the metropolis' inhabitants were hurriedly bustling by, our inactivity hung in the air. Neither Helmes nor I had moved from our resting places the entire day. I had been thinking what a direct contrast we were to the passersby when Helmes stirred.

"From the point of view of the infidelity expert," said

Cherlock Helmes, "Chicago has become a singularly uninteresting city."

"I doubt that the decent citizens would join you in your lamentations," I retorted.

"Well, I must not be selfish," she answered, rising from the couch and poking about in the fireplace for the twelfth time that morning. "The community is the gainer and no one is the loser except one out-of-work specialist. The everyday cases are no challenge. I need the stimulation of the twisted byways and the mazelike intricacies wherein the application of my faculties are utilized to their fullest extent. What use is a great mind without data to apply it to. Even the personal columns are mundane and my correspondence is equally boring." She went once again to the couch. She glanced over the morning editions and then threw them on the floor with disgust.

"My dear Cherlock, it is to your own credit that this situation exists," I ventured, but I could see my words fell on deaf and despondent ears.

Helmes had done so much in her chosen field of investigation that any dry spell of cases always brought on this type of depression. She was happiest when she was applying all of her knowledge and expertise to a case. I had seen her go without food or rest for days on end while in hot pursuit of a clue. Yet here she lay in our quarters at 22 Bakerville Street as though her occupation had come to an end and her usefulness was no more.

Knowing her as I do, I let her alone. When she was in one of these moods, the only solution was work. I have shared this apartment with her for eight years and have the honor of calling her my friend. Although I know her better than anyone, I know that there are cubbyholes throughout this great detective that I could neither fathom nor hope to understand. The detection of clues and the righting of wrongs are the focal point of her life.

A knock at the door broke in upon my thoughts. I answered it and brought Helmes the telegram that had been deposited into my hands.

"You read it, Wastin," she said, waving away the telegram I held out to her.

I read it aloud:

"Dear Ms. Helmes,
I am at my wits' end. I beg an appointment with you

at 2:00 this afternoon. It is most urgent. Yours faithfully,
Mrs. Amanda Fitzwilliam-Demeter

Setting aside the telegram, I asked, "What can it mean, Helmes?"

"A case, Waston, a case!" Cherlock answered, jumping up from the couch and snatching the Who's Who journal from its place on the front room shelf. Turning the pages Helmes remarked, "We are moving in prestigious circles, Wastin." She read aloud from the journal, "Amanda Fitzwilliam, daughter of the founding father of the Fitzwilliam Chemical Corporation. Net worth 36 million. Born March 12, 1952. Graduated Yale 1976 with a Master's degree in Business Administration. Married John Demeter 1986."

"I remember reading in the papers of her father's death a few months ago," I said. "But there hasn't been anything in the news concerning Mrs. Fitzwilliam-Demeter herself. Why do you think she needs to see you?"

"I have no data, yet. It is a capital mistake to theorize before one has data. Insensibly, one begins to twist facts to suit theories, instead of theories to suit facts."

This was Helmes' last word on the matter. She disregarded my ensuing questions without an utterance. Instead, she sat in her chair behind her desk, smoking cigarette after cigarette.

At precisely 2:00 p.m. our doorbell sounded. I answered the door and ushered in a beautifully groomed but not overly attractive woman. Her hair was prematurely streaked gray and worn in a tight bun at the nape of her neck. Her green eyes were bloodshot as though she had been crying recently, but her composure was calm and direct.

"Ms. Helmes?" she asked, looking from Helmes to myself. "You can probably guess why I'm here."

"I am Cherlock Helmes. This is my intimate friend and associate, Dr. Waston, before whom you can speak as freely as before myself. Please take a seat, Mrs. Fitzwilliam-Demeter," Helmes said cheerily, motioning to the chair opposite her desk. "Aside from the fact you have had some trouble concerning your husband, have experienced a recent fall, and a disassociation with your late father, I know nothing of your troubles. Further, I never guess. I observe and detect.

The lady gave a violent start and stared in bewilderment at my companion.

"Ms. Helmes, you are a wizard! I have heard of your analytical powers but, I admit, never believed such powers actually existed," she remarked in awe.

"It is nothing I assure you, Madame," Helmes answered, delighting in the praise. "The fact that you have come to me suggests you are here to seek help in an infidelity case. Further, one can see that an impeccably dressed woman would never leave her home with a run in her stockings. The run perfectly corresponds to a small bruise. So, therefore, we must deduce that you have had a fall after leaving your home. Finally, the ring finger on your right hand is unadorned; there is, however, a visible pale circle which indicates that you normally wore a ring there. The entire country knows your father presented you with the heart shaped Pink Diamond on your eighteenth birthday, and you have worn it ever since that day. Its absence from your hand could only mean a break with your father."

"It is just as you have stated. I had a fall on the ice and am here about my husband. Further, it was constant disagreements over my choice of husband that caused the break between Father and myself. Father felt that I had married beneath me. He disapproved of my husband John and our marriage. As a result of one such disagreement, shortly before his death, I vowed never to speak to him until he accepted my husband. When I made that vow, I removed the ring he had given me. I never spoke to my father again," she said with a trembling voice. Helmes handed her a tissue and offered a few words of consolation. After a while she continued, "It seems Father may have been right about John after all."

"Madame, though I can see this is very painful for you, I can not help you unless you tell me exactly what the problem might be. Please begin at the beginning and try not to leave out any pertinent facts," Helmes said gently. She then leaned back in her chair, closed her eyes and, pressing her fingertips together, added, "Pray proceed, I am your attentive audience."

Taking a sip of the brandy I had placed on the table near her, our client began her strange narrative. "John and I were married two years ago. We met at one of Father's chemical plants. John was working on the line in the plant and saved me from what could have been certain death. A large cylinder of chemicals had been jarred from its protective casing and would have hit me had John not pushed me out of harm's way and caught it before it hit the floor. John had not been in Father's employ very long, so we really knew nothing about him or his background. Nevertheless John and I began to date. We eloped to Las Vegas six weeks later."

"May I ask which of you first proposed this elopement?" Helmes questioned.

"Well, it was John. But I was in complete agreement with him. I knew Father would never approve or give his blessing to our marriage. Father was vehement in his endeavors to dissolve our union. As a matter of fact, in the quarrel between us just before his death, Father swore he had conclusive evidence against John. He said that it would make me want to leave John forever. Of course, I would not even listen to such slander. Instead, I ended all further interaction with my Father until such time as he decided to accept us. I really do not wish to dwell on my private relations with Father. It was because he was seriously displeased with my choice of husband that we eloped. It was in an effort to raise Father's opinion of him that John decided to begin his own business. So I gave John a considerable amount of money from my trust fund to advance his business aspirations. He used these monies to establish his own company."

Breaking in on her narrative again Helmes asked, "What type of company did he begin?"

"I don't know. It might sound strange, but as John explained it to me, he didn't want me involved in any way. He desired to make it a success and prove himself to Father. To reinforce this resolve, John kept a strict accounting of all the monies I invested in his company. He did this so he could pay me back once it began to show a profit."

"I'm sorry to interrupt, but do you happen to have a copy of that accounting?" "Yes, I do," Mrs. Fitzwilliam-Demeter answered, withdrawing a long, blue envelope from her handbag and handing it to Helmes.

Helmes glanced over the ledger inside and remarked, "This is a handwritten list of amounts totaling over 1.5 million dollars! Didn't you have a formal contract drawn up between the two or you?"

"No," she retorted, "I just do not feel right about a contract between married people. John did suggest it once, but I knew he would be successful and I believed in him."

"Believed?" Helmes asked, "Have you had occasion to change your confidence in his trustworthiness?"

"That is why I am here, Ms. Helmes. Several recent events

have caused me to begin to doubt John. I thought if I put the case before you, you could dispel my suspicions."

"What exactly has happened to arouse your suspicions concerning your husband?"

"Well, after John started his company, he began to go away on business trips. For the first few weeks of our marriage he would be gone for just a day or two, but then his trips became as lengthy as a week at a time. Beyond this, I had no way to reach him. Although it is true John frequently telephoned me while he was out of town, it troubled me deeply that I had no way of contacting him. His explanation for not giving me a number to reach him was that he moves from place to place so much. My concern over John's constant business trips, and my inability to reach him, increased tenfold recently. I ran across some unsettling information a few weeks ago quite accidentally. I discovered John's business checkbook and there were checks for very large amounts written to a Mr. Joseph Drake. When I asked John about these checks, he became very upset. He said I didn't trust him. Then he told me that Mr. Drake was a business associate from whom he was purchasing tooling equipment. Very shortly after this incident, John gave me the number of his company so that I could reach him there. He said that he did not want any mistrust between us. I was more than satisfied with the situation; that is, until yesterday when I was unpacking John's suitcase from his latest business trip and found it contained someone else's clothes. Every article of clothing in his bag was not his own. John always wears business suits. When he is dressing casually, he wears custom made trousers and sweaters. These clothes consisted mostly of denim pants and flannel shirts."

Helmes leaned forward excitedly and asked, "Did you happen to notice the sizes on the clothes?"

"As a matter of fact I did. Every article of clothing was John's size. The pants, the shirts, everything was exactly his size."

Helmes smiled to herself. I, knowing her so well, could see she was on to a clue. She then inquired, "Were there any monogrammed items or correspondence in the bag?"

"I went through everything and the only thing I could find was a monogrammed handkerchief with the initials J.D., but that was it. I showed John the clothes and he looked frightened. He said the clothes must belong to his associate, Mr. Drake. Although that would account for the J.D. initials, it would not explain how Mr. Drake's clothes came to be in John's bag. John did offer a possible theory. He told me that Mr. Drake was with him during his last trip and they had requested that the maid pack for them. He remembered that the door was open between their adjoining rooms when she came to do so. He supposed, therefore, that she had grabbed the wrong suitcase in the midst of the packing. But, this time, I am not satisfied with John's explanations. I have a funny feeling in the pit of my stomach that something is terribly wrong. However, as John has always insisted on unwaivering and unquestioning trust between us, I just don't know what to do."

"I have a few questions, Mrs. Fitzwilliam-Demeter. To begin with, how soon after your marriage did your husband begin his business?"

"I believe it was less than one month after we had returned from our honeymoon."

"Did the advances of business capital also begin shortly after marriage?"

"Yes."

"Did you notice when the checks to Mr. Drake commenced?"

"Yes, John began buying equipment from Mr. Drake immediately after setting up his company."

I could tell Helmes was alive with energy, her eyes were shining and her fingers were trembling. Although it didn't seem to me anything was amiss with the Fitzwilliam-Demeter union, I would bow to Helmes' superior ability to make that judgement. I have had the honor of sharing many a case with Helmes over the years and have grown to respect her analytical powers. She never fails to recognize a clue. Further, when she discovers one, she becomes as excited as a bloodhound chasing a fox.

"I have two more questions, my good woman: how soon after your last argument with your father did he pass away and, finally, where is the Pink Diamond now?"

"Our last disagreement occurred just three weeks prior to Father's death. The coroner's report said he died of heart failure. In answer to your second question, my Pink Diamond is locked up in the safe at John's company," she retorted. She then asked, "What do you think Ms. Helmes? What does this all add up too?"

" My dear, I believe you have an undeniable problem here. The question is, how would you like to handle it?"

"I want you to look into it as discreetly as possible and I will do anything to help you do so," our client said with more spunk than I gave her credit for.

"All right, here is what I want you to do. First, make a log of those times your husband goes away on his business trips. Note the date, the day and the time he leaves and returns. Also, include in this log where he states he is going. Second, send me any information you have on Mr. Joseph Drake, your husband's company, and the number he gave you to enable you to reach him. Third, make a log of all the checks in your husband's business checkbook made out to Mr. Drake. Include in this log the dates and the amounts of those checks. Further, keep this log up-to-date, noting any further checks written to Mr. Drake. Also keep a log on any further occurrances of discrepancies in your husband's clothing or personal effects. Finally, send me a copy of the coroner's report concerning your father's death. I beg you, Mrs. Fitzwilliam-Demeter, say nothing to upset your husband or cause him to become suspicious. It is for both the success of our investigation and your own well being that I make this request."

"You suspect John of more than just infidelity don't you, Ms. Helmes?"

"I suspect everything, I know nothing for sure. Follow my instructions to the letter and keep me abreast of your progress. A telephone call will bring me to your aid immediately," Helmes said, rising and escorting our client to the door. "Please contact me when you have some concrete results with your logs. There is a pattern muddled in there somewhere."

As soon as Helmes had shut the door, she rushed into her room. I waited impatiently for her to emerge. When she did so she was dressed as a bag lady. The transformation was truly remarkable. Not only had Helmes donned a disheveled gray wig, tattered clothing and hole-riddled shoes, but her entire persona seemed to have faded into the character she was playing. The metamorphosis was so absolute that I found myself searching this vagabond's face in an effort to distinguish my colleague's features beneath the make-up and theatrically applied wrinkles. The stage had indeed lost a potentially great actress when Helmes turned her talents to detection work.

"Wastin, I am going out. Do not wait up. I suspect my excursion may be a lengthy one."

During the next few weeks Helmes said very little concerning the case. Judging from her various disguises and odd hours, I presumed the investigation was progressing well. She did, however, remark after reading through the information Mrs. Fitzwilliam-Demeter had sent by post that the case was becoming, "curiouser and curiouser."

I knew it was impossible to force a confidence with Helmes before she was ready to reveal in what direction her investigation was proceeding. So instead, I tried to busy myself with the writing of my latest novel, but my mind kept churning over our client's strange narrative. Although I endeavored to apply Helmes' methods and sort things out, I could make neither heads nor tails of it. Needless to say, I was greatly excited when, a few weeks later, Helmes informed me that Mrs. Fitzwilliam-Demeter was expected the following morning with some fresh developments. It was the twinkle in Helmes' eye that led me to believe that of the two women, Helmes, probably, had more to tell at this interview.

Exactly at 9:00 our client was seated in the chair opposite Helmes with a sheaf of papers in her lap.

"I see you have compiled the logs I requested," said Helmes. "Perhaps you will be kind enough to give us an overview of each of them."

"Well, to begin with, John's business trips have a distinct pattern to them. I have discovered by logging his comings and goings that he is on a definite schedule. It is amazing that the regularity of these trips was never before apparent to me."

"The regularity was not ostensibly evident because you saw with your eyes, but failed to observe and take note of what you were seeing. Please continue with the results of your hourly movement log."

"It seems that every ten days John leaves on a business trip and stays away for exactly ten days. I have been able to confirm the existence of this pattern with the help of my log. Further, in an effort to verify my findings, I went through John's business checkbook and noted those checks for airline tickets. It is uncanny, each trip falls within this ten day staggered pattern."

"You have done splendidly. Did you happen to note the airlines your husband traveled on?"

"Yes, I did. John used Airline Express for every business trip he took. Upon further checking, I was able to discover that, in every instance, his destination had been Boston."

"Capital! Your information concurs with mine thus far. Pray, continue."

"I know you received the information I sent you pertaining to Mr. Drake, my husband's business, and the number he gave me. I will give you the results of the second log you asked me to keep—those checks made out to Mr. Drake. Each of the dates of the checks coincided within the sphere of one of John's business trips. Each time John went out of town, he wrote a check to Mr. Drake. I have inquired with an old friend who is the president of the bank in which our funds are deposited. My friend was able to establish that each check was cashed and deposited into the account of Mr. Drake at the Boston Metro Bank. The checks totaled well over one million dollars, Ms. Helmes! It is impossible to believe that John spent the bulk of the monies I invested in his company for tooling equipment. I am at a loss as to what this means, but think that either John or I are being duped by this Mr. Drake," she exclaimed.

"Madame, please refrain from drawing conclusions until you are in possession of all the facts. What did you learn through your last log concerning your husband's clothes and personal effects?" Helmes asked, redirecting the conversation.

"Well, in this area I can report no new developments. Nothing whatsoever changed in John's attire or effects. I have checked his suitcase each time he returned from a trip in the past few weeks, but found nothing except clothes and such that I knew belonged to him."

"Can you think of anything else that you feel is important for us to know?" Helmes asked.

"Nothing. What does this all mean? Have you been able to discover anything through your investigation?"

"First, let me commend you. You have carried out your part of the investigation wonderfully well. However, your information only confirms my conclusions. I am sorry, but what I am about to tell you will pain you horribly. So I beg you to brace yourself," Helmes began as Mrs. Fitzwilliam-Demeter prepared herself as though for a physical blow.

Helmes continued, "Wastin can tell you I have been occupying my time recently dressed as a bag lady. Disguised as such, I was able to shadow your husband as he moved through the streets of the city. In addition, armed with the address of his company, I took up residence on the sidewalk opposite his business. Blending into the district, I was free to prowl about unnoticed. In this manner, I was able to discover that the warehouse comprising the whole of his company is completely vacant. There is, however, a front office containing a desk and a telephone. It is in this office that an elderly woman sits from nine to five every day. I struck up an acquaintance with this woman and was able to learn that her entire job consists of taking messages for her boss. She stated that she thought it was peculiar that no one ever called except his wife, but she wasn't about to jeopardize her cushy job by asking questions. I was able to further establish that, in fact, the lease, the telephone number and the business checking account all checked out to this address. So, therefore, I safely concluded that your husband's company is nothing more than a ruse to bilk you of funds and a means by which to hide his other activities, such as his out of town trips. You should know that your husband's police record and background have been traced. His history is that of a cunning and dangerous con artist. I am sure that his movements—from his employment with your father's company through the present moment—were, and are, all part of a premeditated scheme. I am convinced that it was not an accident that the cylinder barely missed injuring you on the day you met. Rather, it was his calculated tactic to meet you and endear himself to you. His pursuit of you, I have learned, was relentless. Further, he slowly and methodically detached your loyalties from your father so that he could have a free rein on your money."

At this point our client, her voice filled with desperation, interrupted, "Suddenly so much is clear to me. So many things I must have blinded myself to are ridiculously obvious. It is as though a light has been turned on. I simply can't fathom that anyone could so worship money that they would actually go to the length of being part of relationship for it. What an utter fool I've been. I shall never forgive myself for my treatment of Father. Never, never! If only I would have listened to him. I could have been spared this pain and he might be alive today. I must know, Ms. Helmes, what became of the money and who is this Mr. Drake?"

"Almost the entire amount you invested in your husband's company is sitting safely in Mr. Drake's account at the Boston Metro Bank. In answer to your second question, Mr. Joseph Drake is none other than Mr. John Demeter. It was the mark of true genius that your husband chose the alias of John Demeter so that his initials would correspond to his true name. Mr. Joseph Drake, whom we now know your husband to be, resides in the city of Boston. He lives there with his wife. Here is a photograph I was able to snap of him and his wife outside their home last week," Helmes said, handing the picture to our client.

"I think I would rather spare myself looking at that photograph, if you don't mind, Ms. Helmes!"

"I bring it to your attention for two reasons, Madame," Helmes explained. "The first of these is that you can plainly see your husband's attire to be that of denim jeans and a flannel shirt. We now know why his suitcase contained such apparel. When one leads a double life such a mishap is bound to happen. Finally, I have blown up a specific portion of the photograph. I need you to look at it as your identification of its contents is required."

Mrs. Fitzwilliam-Demeter examined the snapshot Helmes handed her and gasped, "It is my diamond, the Pink Diamond! I had completely forgotten about it. Oh Ms. Helmes, do not tell me he has given it to that, that woman!" she sobbed, breaking down entirely.

I rushed to her side; even with Helmes's help it took quite awhile before she was calm enough for Helmes to continue.

"I have taken steps, my dear lady, to begin to right the wrongs done to you. Let me outline them for you. I have contacted your solicitor. With his help, the funds in Mr. Drake's account have been frozen. So your money is safe until a court of law determines it should be returned to you. Mr. Drake and his wife have been taken into police custody. They are being held, even as we speak, to enable you to lodge a formal complaint against them. His wife was his accomplice throughout this and many other schemes. As for your heart shaped diamond ring, if you open the red box on the table to your left, you will see it is back with its rightful owner. Now, I think with your solicitor's help you can end this horrid chapter in your life quickly. Through it, I am sure you have become wiser for having endured it," Helmes said as she rose from her chair.

"There is just one more thing I need to know. Why did you ask me for a copy of Father's coroner report? John didn't . . . ?" our client began, but could not bring herself to finish her question.

"No, he didn't," Helmes answered. "I suspected that your husband may have gone to the extent of causing your father's death. My inquiries have proven that your father passed away as a result of completely natural causes. Further, I am assured by the top medical man in the country that your behavior towards him did not in any way bring on his deteriorating heart condition. So at least this is one burden I can spare you."

I do not know how to thank you Ms. Helmes," Mrs. Fitzwilliam-Demeter said while preparing to leave. "I am in your debt. You are the most amazing detective in modern history."

"My dear lady, it was through your logs that you were able to find a pattern in your husband's business trips. You also discovered where he had been going. Further, logging his checks enabled you to discern a pattern in his finances. Then, with the help of the bank president, you were able to locate where the money had been deposited. Additionally, it was your own discovery of the second set of clothes that first alerted you to a possible deception. Finally, it was your intuition that aroused your suspicions and caused you to bring this case to my attention. You had all the clues in your hands when you first entered my residence; I simply did some leg work for you. So, therefore, I would say that you are a mighty fine detective yourself," Helmes retorted as she escorted our client to the door.

After she had left, I turned to Helmes and said, "I have never known you to be in better form. You have worked through this maze as though it were child's play. I, too, am truly amazed!"

"Elementary, my dear Wastin, elementary!"

A log as it pertains to the realm of investigation is a written instrument in which one records daily occurrences. Although you can log any element of his behavior, there are six main logs with which you will probably come into contact. In any case, it is in a log that you will document the events or behavior of your spouse. Such documentation is vital to obtaining an overview of your spouse's activities. Further, a log enables you to note your observations and find his method of operation.

Although we will cover each log thoroughly, there are a few important points you should keep in mind. A log is a device restricted to the notation of facts. It is not a medium to allow you to vent your emotions. So as Sargent Joe Friday would say, "Just the facts, ma'am!" Further, a lackadaisically and sporadically kept log is not worth the paper it is written on. You must faithfully and daily add any significant data to it. It is because no one's memory is infallible that this type of record keeping must be implemented into your detective routine. Your dedication to your log is just as essential as the data you enter in it. Finally, it is imperative to keep your log or, as the case may be, logs carefully concealed.

If he should find them, your cover is all but blown. Unless, of course, you think he is dumb enough to buy the story that you were just holding them for a friend. My children honestly believe I would buy that type of explanation so if all else fails, try it. But if you do not wish to find yourself in that position, I suggest that you locate a hiding place for your logs that he will not discover. One client of mine went to the extreme of cutting a hole in her plaster board wall and then hanging a picture in front of it. This may sound all turned up collars and shadow slipping, but I assure you her husband did not run across her logs. This "addition" may or may not diminish your resale value. But the odds are with you that it won't, considering that statistics say that over forty to seventy percent of all married people will or have cheated. So your "For Sale" ad may read: "Three bedrooms, two bath Colonial with something for every member of the family, including special hideaway nook for Mom or Dad."

As we cover each type of log, I will address both its rationale and its objective. I have also included three sample logs for each type discussed. The first of these is the correct way to keep a log and contains the type of information one should be noting in this record. I have included this log to enhance your understanding of the date it should encompass. The second one is an incorrectly kept log. The third log I have left blank except for the outline and the headings. It has been designed so that you may enlarge it and run it off on a copy machine, saving yourself the trouble of creating your own. Further, each log's format has been developed in such a way as to reduce the time it will take to maintain it.

Hourly Movement Log

Rationale. This log is intended to keep you abreast of how your spouse spends his time. On it you should note date, the time and his activities. It will provide you with the ability to uncover his MO as it relates to hourly movement.

Objective. To discover those hours in which the affair is most likely to be taking place.

Pitfalls. Do not interfere with any activities he plans if it is out of character for you to do so. Neither should you encourage any activities that you would normally frown upon. Remember you are an observer. In that role, it is your job to take note of your subject's actions; any interference, negative or positive, will alter the normal course of events.

HOURLY MOVEMENT LOG

<u>Date</u> <u>Day</u>		<u>Time</u>	<u>Activity</u>
Oct. 2, 1989	Monday	7:00 a.m.	Jack left for work.
		6:17 p.m.	Jack arrived home.
		8:32 p.m.	Jack left to go bowling.
		11:49 p.m.	Jack arrived home.
(The right way)			

- -

Oct. 2, 1989	Monday	7:00 a.m.	Well, in the first place, "Mr. Wonderful" threatened the alarm clock for two full hours this morning.
(The wrong way)			

Personal Habits Log

Rationale. This log is intended to allow you to plot and determine his current personal habits. Personal habits include grooming, clothing and anything pertinent to one's appearance. In this log you will be noting only those occurrences that are of seemingly suspicious nature. This log will afford you the ability to flag those events. You should include the date and the day along with the event.

Objective. To discover a change in his personal habits that may signal when he is embarking on a rendezvous. Further, the logging of those incidents may allow you to determine when he is laying the preparatory groundwork prior to his actually engaging in an affair. (Remember that there is a "cleaning up your act" process. Therefore, it is conceivable that if you are able to detect the process, you may be able to nip the possibility of an affair in the bud.)

Pitfalls. Do not mistake a normal purchase of a much needed item, such as a work shirt, with a bona fide clue.

Special Note. The showering away from home is a definite episode to take note of and watch for.

Trick of the Trade. One former client marked one of her husband's socks with a dot of red nail polish. She then helped him on with his socks noting the dot to be on the right sock. When he returned home from working "overtime" and began to undress for bed, she casually helped him take off his shoes and socks. The red dot had mysteriously moved from the right foot to the left. One may take off his shoes during a course of a day, but his socks?

PERSONAL HABITS LOG

Date	Day	Time	Activity
Oct. 2, 1989	Monday	5:35 p.m.	Jack put on his new jeans and shirt to go bowling.
(The right way)			

Oct. 2, 1989	Monday	5:35 p.m.	Jack spent ten minutes laying on the bed trying to zipper himself into his new jeans.

(The wrong way)

Sex Life Log

Rationale. This log is intended to track your sex life. It should include sexual interludes, performances and who was the aggressor. You will need to make daily entries. This is also the place to note requests for new positions and the like. In addition, any genital discomforts or problems should be indicated in it.

Objective. To chart your sex life and determine the regularity and content of your lovemaking. Further, it is a catalyst to heighten your awareness of changes that might otherwise go unnoticed.

Pitfalls. Do not alter your sex life or push issues you normally would not. If you do so you will violate the validity of this log.

Special Note. In this era of AIDS and social disease, be constantly on the look out for signs of infection and physical changes in your body. The sudden onset of a yeast infection could tell a story in its own right. Physicians have found that when two people begin a sex life, they are exposing their genitals to a foreign environment. In doing so, they may experience infections or irritations. However, after a while the bodies accept one another and the problems dissipate. But if your spouse has sex with someone else, any irritations they encounter becoming adjusted to each other will probably be passed on to you. So, too, any infections, social or otherwise, will be passed on to you.

SEX LIFE LOG

Date	Day	Activity
Oct. 2, 1989	Monday	We made love. I was the aggressor. Nothing unusual occurred.
(The right way)		

— —

Sometime early October		Okay, here's the funny part. This guy who makes love like a rabbit thinks he is such a stud he wants to share the wealth. If he only knew I not only count the ceiling tiles, but I have given each of them names.
(The wrong way)		

Daily Personality Changes Log

Rationale. The purpose of this log is to keep you aware, on a daily basis, of his mood swings and/or changes in his normal personality.

Objective. To discover alterations in his normal personality. Further, your goal is to detect a pattern to these fluctuations.

Pitfalls. This is a very subjective log. In other words, you will be recording your opinion that he's behaving differently. So, be cautious not to project your theories in this log. Rather, report only what you observe in a factual manner.

Special Note. Be mindful that guilt is the motivating factor behind a personality change. So if his conscience is bothering him, he will probably act differently. His actions trigger his guilt and his guilt is the catalyst to variation in his normal disposition.

Trick of the Trade. In many cases a spouse will purposely start a fight out of the blue in order to get out of the house. Watch for this emotional trap.

DAILY PERSONALITY CHANGES LOG

<u>Date</u>	<u>Day</u>	<u>Incident</u>
Oct. 2, 1989	Monday	Jack was preoccupied and harsh before he left to go bowling. Then, when he returned, he was very distant. Note: Make an entry every day, even if the only thing to report is nothing happened

(The right way)

Oct. 2, 1989

(The wrong way)

Strange Telephone Call Log

Rationale. This log is intended to provide you with a continuous record of suspicious phone calls. You should indicate the nature of the call in this log. For example, was it a hang up or three rings, a hang up and one more ring? It is also important to note what reaction, if any, your spouse had to the call.

Objective. To detect a pattern in either your incoming or his outgoing telephone calls. Further, this log can be used in conjunction with past and present itemized telephone bills to confirm a pattern and discover to whom the calls were placed.

Pitfalls. When he is on the phone do not lift the receiver as the chance of detection is too great. If he catches you listening in on the call, he will become guarded. Remember, there is more than one way to skin a cat. We will discuss other methods later in the book.

Special Note. Sequential ringing is usually a signal with a definite meaning. Be on the look out for them.

STRANGE TELEPHONE CALL LOG

Date	Day	Time	Call
Oct. 2, 1989	Monday	7:45 p.m.	Hang up.
		11:52 p.m.	Jack picked up a call. He listened for a moment and then slammed the phone down.

(The right way)

- -

Date	Day	Time	Call
Oct. 2, 1989	Monday	8:37 a.m.	Mom called wih her recipe for upside down peanut butter and banana fruitcake. She also told me Uncle Frank is a transvestite. She recognized him on the *Oprah Winfrey Show* yesterday. She is thinking of resigning from the IYWANAUYWBHT Club. She is convinced that after the members of "If you were as normal as us, you'd be happy too" find out about Uncle Frank, they will boot her out anyway.

(The wrong way)

Mileage Log

Rationale. This log is intended to establish a record of the miles your spouse travels in a single day. Then, when you discover a discrepancy, you can not only zero in on the time it occurred, but will also have a radius of miles to investigate. For example, if his normal round trip mileage to and from the bowling alley was 18 but you discover 3 extra miles on the odometer during that time, you have a clue. It would then be safe to speculate that he did something other than just bowl, and he did so within a 3-mile radius.

Objective. To ascertain the normal amount of miles he travels in a single day in an effort to detect when he is driving to a clandestine destination.

Pitfalls. Be very careful not to let your spouse see you noting the mileage on the car. It would cause him to become suspicious. So if you have to get up in the middle of the night to check the odometer, do so. Better safe than sorry.

Special Note. It is imperative that you make yourself familiar with his normal route to his regular activities. To do so, invent an excuse to drive with him to each of the activities in which he is normally engaged. Note both the route and the mileage involved. This information will come in very handy both now and if, in the future, a vehicular surveillance is required.

MILEAGE LOG

Date	Activity	Odometer Reading	Miles Traveled
Oct. 2, 1989	Before work	40036	
	After work	40073	37
	After bowling	40091	18
(The right way)			

Oct. 2, 1989		I forgot today	

(The wrong way)

While the compiling of information in any one of the above logs is simple enough—and, in fact, the habit of doing so will become rote—the assimilation of the results could become muddled and confusing. The onslaught of various data could seem even more overwhelming if your particular investigation calls for you to maintain two or more logs simultaneously. So, in an effort to simplify your detection of his method of operation and discover his pattern of behavior, I have supplied you with overview charts. The first of these was designed to give you an overview of one log. The second chart can encompass the data from all the logs. You can utilize this chart whether you are keeping one log or as many as six.

The charts are set up on a weekly basis. Every week you will need to go through each log you are maintaining and flag those incidents of a suspicious nature. Then, by using the chart, you can place a check mark on the day the event took place. If you are keeping more than one log, you will need to use Chart Two wherein all flagged information can be recorded. In this manner, you will be able to ascertain a forming pattern at a glance.

For example, if you were maintaining an HOURLY LOG and three times in a week suspicious incidents occurred, your chart would look like this:

HOURLY MOVEMENT CHART

<u>Date</u>	<u>1</u>	<u>2</u>	<u>3</u>	<u>4</u>	<u>5</u>	<u>6</u>	<u>7</u>
Day	Sun.	Mon.	Tues.	Wed.	Thurs.	Fri.	Sat.
	✓		✓		✓		

You could also incorporate the suspicious time frame in the chart to save yourself the time of constantly going back over the logs. Your chart would then look like the following:

HOURLY MOVEMENT CHART

<u>Date</u>	<u>1</u>	<u>2</u>	<u>3</u>	<u>4</u>	<u>5</u>	<u>6</u>	<u>7</u>
Day	Sun.	Mon.	Tues.	Wed.	Thurs.	Fri.	Sat.

Time							
	8:32 p.m.		7:48 p.m.		8:13 p.m.		
	11:49 p.m.		10:58 p.m.		11:37 p.m.		

Therefore, all of your log information is contained in one chart. This same formula is adopted in every Log Chart. I have supplied you with individual Log Charts for each of the six logs. You can enlarge them and run them off on a copy machine to save yourself time.

HOURLY MOVEMENT CHART

<u>Date</u>	<u>1</u>	<u>2</u>	<u>3</u>	<u>4</u>	<u>5</u>	<u>6</u>	<u>7</u>
Day	Sun.	Mon.	Tues.	Wed.	Thurs.	Fri.	Sat.

Time

PERSONAL HABITS CHART

Date	1	2	3	4	5	6	7
Day	Sun.	Mon.	Tues.	Wed.	Thurs.	Fri.	Sat.

Event

- -

SEX LIFE CHART

Date	1	2	3	4	5	6	7
Day	Sun.	Mon.	Tues.	Wed.	Thurs.	Fri.	Sat.

Event

- -

DAILY PERSONALITY CHANGE CHART

Date	1	2	3	4	5	6	7
Day	Sun.	Mon.	Tues.	Wed.	Thurs.	Fri.	Sat

Event

- -

STRANGE TELEPHONE CALL CHART

Date	1	2	3	4	5	6	7
Day	Sun.	Mon.	Tues.	Wed.	Thurs.	Fri.	Sat.

Time

Call

MILEAGE LOG CHART

Date	1	2	3	4	5	6	7
Day	Sun.	Mon.	Tues.	Wed.	Thurs.	Fri.	Sat.

Odometer Reading

Miles Traveled

All suspicious events which are recorded in your logs should be flagged in the following chart.

OVERALL LOG CHART

LOGS	1	2	3	4	5	6	7
	Sun.	Mon.	Tues.	Wed.	Thurs.	Fri.	Sat.

HOURS

HABITS

SEX

PERSONALITY

PHONE CALLS

MILEAGE

You are now equipped to detect his pattern which is, of course, his method of operation. I have given you the tools. Your observation and log keeping are your ammunition. You are prepared to do battle with ignorance and, thereby, discover the truth.

A few words of advice: you must continue your record keeping throughout your investigation. One former client halted the maintenance of her logs after she uncovered a pattern in her husband's hourly moement. When she went to catch him in the act, he was nowhere to be found. As it turned out, the mistress had changed her work hours so, consequently, the client's husband changed the hours he saw her. My client had to start all over from square one. Don't let this happen to you. Be loyal and diligent to your logs. They will become your crystal ball in which you can read his future.

CHAPTER EIGHT

THE CLUES

The captain needs her ship and the artist needs her canvas and paint. Just as the writer needs her paper and pen and the soldier needs her gun, the detective needs her tools. Every occupation has its own equipment that is essential to that trade. The absence of the correct tools can be the determining factor in getting the job done.

Although the basic tools needed in the investigative field have been extensively covered in a previous chapter, there is one more set of tools that must now be officially added to your list: clues. A detective without a clue is like an artist without paint. A canvas and a brush are not enough to assist the artist in the creation of her masterpiece. She must have her paint, and the detective must have her clues. For without them, her binoculars gather dust and her camera's usefulness extends only to a somewhat bizarre necklace. If the detective does not have a clue to run down, the possession of long range walkie-talkies is fairly meaningless. Of course, you could always have them wired and turn them into matching lamps, becoming, thereby, the proud owner of unconventional and distinctive conversation pieces.

However, your goal is not to get on *That's Interesting*. Your goal, rather, is to amass and trace clues so that you can discover the truth behind your spouse's current behavior. There is a rationale behind a man's sudden obsession with the application of Grecian Formula to his chest hairs. Your mission is to discover the rationale behind your spouse's behavior. To do so, you need both the tangible equipment outlined in Chapter Three and the intangible tools which are clues.

The pursuit of pattern detection and the ascertainment of his modus operandi are imperative to your acquisition of clues. However, there are several other areas in which clues can be found. The focal points of this chapter are the detection and gathering of those clues within a 500-yard radius of the chair in which you are now seated. Those clues can be likened to the artist's paint laden brush. With them you can do your job. Instead of staring at a blank canvas, you can now go to work and begin to sketch a picture.

The concept of becoming a do-it-yourself detective is a sound one. Not only do you save an enormous amount of money on investigative fees, but most of the clues needed to catch him are probably so close to you, you could reach out and touch them. A woman wrote me recently. In her letter she told me she was amazed that her husband was stupid enough—her words not mine—to leave clues right out in the open. He did so because he never thought she would think to look for them. He was wrong. Further, he had no idea my first book had arrived at his home in a plain brown envelope to assist her in that search.

Another reason why conducting your own investigation makes so much sense is that you, as a spouse, are privy to all of your spouse's effects. A paid investigator would have to break several laws just to get a look at your spouse's wallet. You, on the other hand, can browse through it at your leisure, especially if he is asleep and left his wallet on the dresser. You can meticulously go through anything in your home and be free from prosecution. A marriage license affords you the freedom of access to everything. The law sees a married couple as one unit in many instances. In other words, regardless whose name appears on the ownership document such as a house deed, the property is jointly owned unless another document has been duly executed stating otherwise. You can, therefore, go through his clothes, his wallet and so forth and rest assured that there is not a Personal Effects Gestapo coming for you. Fortunately or unfortunately, both of your individual privacy rights become badly muddled under the umbrella of a marriage license. The aforementioned statement extends to all real and personal property held by either person in the marriage. If he owns it, you own it, period! So you can go through your home, your vehicles, any business either of you own and any personal effects found therein. I just love wherefores and thereins, it makes me sound like I am an attorney. I am not, but I have checked my facts with a reputable one. So you can safely begin your search for your trade's intangible tools which are, of course, clues.

I have divided the 500-yard radius of your search into three sections. Your exploration should be performed one section at a time. Further, you will need to conduct your examination in a methodical manner, taking great care to be attentive to the smallest of details. An actual criminal scrutinization of a possible piece of evidence could take hours. Further, it could be conducted so extensively that each fragment of that item would be throughly inspected before the search is considered complete.

As a matter of fact, there are those in the criminal investigative field who will section off a room into 2-foot by 2-foot squares. Then each section is examined minutely. Drawers are turned out and scrutinized on all sides, long needles are inserted into upholstery, furniture is overturned and examined at every angle and so forth. Your examination need not extend to that length and depth. However, you should carry out your search with the same seriousness a policeperson adopts at a murder scene. A detective who is meticulous in her efforts will reap the rewards of her hard work.

Remember, you are looking for clues. A clue is anything that appears to you, the investigator, as being suspicious. Moreover, you will be concentrating on obtaining physical clues. A physical clue is one that you can actually touch, such as a receipt.

As a general rule you should never take the original clue. Rather, you should make a copy of it. The rationale is that if he notices its absence, he will become guarded. So, therefore, unless it is impossible—for whatever reason—to copy a clue, do NOT confiscate it! The extraction of one clue that is only a small part of a much larger picture can be likened to a policeperson taking a syringe from a drug dealer's possessions. The syringe doesn't tell the investigator who the dealer's connection is or how the stuff is being transported; it simply lets her know she is possibly on the trail. However, the commandeering of the clue could cause the suspect to fly.

Now the physical clues you are searching for include telephone numbers, pictures, mementoes, matchbooks, strange keys and so forth.

Section One: Areas to Search, In and Around Your Home

Wallet
Purse
Briefcase
Personal telephone book
Diary or journal
Drawers
Closets
Desks
Clothing
Etc. . . .

Your attention to detail is imperative. One former client found that his regard to a small calculation was the decisive factor in his discovery of THE clue.

THE CASE OF DAVID J.

"David, are you sure you have everything you need?" Paula asked as she prepared to leave the house.

"Yes, babe, you go along. It's just a head cold. I'll be fine," David croaked from their bedroom.

But she came to check on him one last time anyway. He pulled the covers closer to his chin and shivered as she bent to kiss his forehead. He eyes caressed his wife's figure and face as he watched her go from his prone position. She appeared as youthful and beautiful to him as she did seventeen years ago when on bended knees he asked for her hand in marriage.

Thinking back over their marriage, he saw the years scroll by as if he were watching an old film or flipping through a dog-eared photograph album. Turning the pages through his memory, he saw the years of struggle, years of growth, years of strife and years of joy. Though he had been raised in a era in which men did not cry, he could not suppress the sob that rose from the depths of his aching heart. He felt that something was threatening to wash away his marriage just as surely as if a tidal wave was bearing down on them. Yet he felt powerless to stop or even stem the tide.

The sound of the latch catching in the front door arrested his thoughts. He listened until the last sounds of Paula's engine had died away far down the street before rising from their bed. Pulling on his faded jeans and tee-shirt, he walked swiftly into the front room. All of his pretended symptoms vanished as he focused in on the task before him. Gathering his briefcase, he sat down at his desk and examined its contents. Alighting on the paper he sought, he closed his briefcase and placed it on the floor. His eyes ran over his list of possible locations of clues to his wife's suspected affair.

He approached his suspicions of Paula's affair with the same organized precision he exercised in his position in corporate quality control. He was analytical in his planning and relentless in his execution. Running over his list, he checked off her purse and her briefcase. He had spent the last few nights going through these with minute care in the wee hours of the morning. Satisfying himself that he had scrutinized every compartment, therein he was sure that he had been thorough. Yet his search had yielded nothing concrete in his pursuit of clues. Nevertheless, though David hadn't unearthed one scrap of evidence, he sensed he was on the right track. He knew this on a level that defies the physical but rather depends solely on intuition.

Shaking off any periphrastic doubts, David recorded his findings, such as they were, on his list. He then turned his attention to the scaled paper before him. On this he made a rough sketch of the layout of the house. He diagrammed both the rooms and the large objects therein, such as dressers, tables and so forth. After accomplishing this, he set to work to search their three-bedroom ranch.

He began in their bedroom. He took out every drawer in their dresser, making sure to lay them out carefully so that they could be replaced correctly. Then he cautiously turned the contents out of each drawer. He examined every item for concealed letters, pictures and so forth. David then moved on, examining the dresser itself. He turned it over and looked at its bottom. He ran his hand over every section of it both inside and out. He similarly inspected every drawer before returning its contents and replacing it. Meticulously and slowly, he went through the entire house. He stripped beds, ran his hands under couch linings, checked behind every picture and every mirror. At the end of six hours of painstaking work, he sat dejected on the couch. Now he really was feeling sick. But this sickness couldn't be remedied with a pill or a spoonful of medicine. This sickness pulled at his heart and rankled his very soul. He leaned back on the cushions and closed his tired eyes. Although he had gone over or through every article and every object in their house, he had found nothing. Not one shred of evidence was he able to uncover. Yet he knew something had to be there. Somehow, he thought to himself, he had missed his mark.

But he felt at a loss to figure out how. Reclining there, a passage from Edgar Allan Poe's "The Purloined Letter" suddenly appeared before his mind's eye. In the passage, Monsieur G., the head of the Parisian Police, was questioned by Auguste Dupin concerning his search of Minister D.'s apartment. As the Monsieur recanted his detailed examination, he stated that he had measured every dresser, wardrobe and so forth. He further stated that he had then checked the outside dimension of each object with the outside measurements of its drawers. He did so in an effort to eliminate the possibility of a secret drawer or compartment.

"Well, if it's good enough for Poe, it's good enough for me," David said out loud, rising from the couch with renewed energy. He went to the kitchen and rifled through the junk drawer. Withdrawing a twenty-five-foot measuring tape, he retraced his steps to his bedroom. He then measured every object he had previously inspected, making his way once again to the dining room. He stood on a chair and hooked one end of the measuring tape onto the top of Paula's great-grandmother's china cabinet. Extending the tape, he took the height measurement. He continued to take the overall dimensions and then checked them against the drawers' outside measurements. They didn't match. There was a 6" by 60" difference. Suppressing his excitement, he again checked each figure but the results were the same. There was a definite discrepancy. Somewhere in the ancient china cabinet a secret compartment existed that was 6" deep by 60" wide. Pulling out each drawer once again, he began tapping the inside of the cabinet. He started with the top, then moved to the sides and finished at the inside bottom. It was there that his tap echoed back with a hollow sound. He had found the secret compartment. He felt the inside edges for a catch or a latch, but there was nothing. David then looked for a keyhole, but none presented itself.

Dumbfounded he sat back and thought. There must be some secret combination that opens it. But what! Looking over the entire cabinet again, he noticed a strange checkerboard pattern on the decorative piece of wood that skirted the bottom. Slowly he tried to manipulate the pieces of wood that made up the checkerboard and, to his amazement, they moved. After trying several combinations, he lined up all three rows to the left. He heard a click and the bottom sprang open.

Peering into the darkened recesses of this cavity, he spied several bundles of letters tied together with red ribbon, loose pictures and many other articles. He withdrew the contents with shaking hands and a trembling heart. Taking everything to the kitchen table, he began to shift through the letters. David forced himself to scan each of them. The impact of his comprehension was almost more than he could bear. He sat staring at the remnants of Paula's affair. It was an affair that spanned over eighteen years. The letters, the pressed corsages, the photographs of her smiling face turned up lovingly into another man's face were all dated. It had begun a year or so before they were married and the most recent letter was two weeks old. The other man was not some young hunk but a handsome, graying and middle-aged gentleman.

"Why had she married him, lived with him and had his babies; why, if she loved another man?" These thoughts tormented him as he sat there clutching the sides of the table.

David never heard Paula pull up or call out to him as she entered the house. She found him sitting at the table staring out into space as though in a trance, his knuckles turning white from the tension of his grasp on the table's edge. She immediately ran to his side and threw her arms around him.

"David, my God, what's wrong?" she began, but her words were no sooner out of her mouth when she saw her things spread out on the table. As though her life's blood had been abruptly spent, she collapsed in the chair beside him, suddenly exhausted.

Slowly David became aware of her presence. Turning to face her, he asked, "Why Paula, why?"

"Oh David, how can I explain something I scarcely understand myself? I met Chip two years before I knew you. We were in love and had planned to marry. But then something happened and we called it off at the last minute. Cold feet, I guess. But the love we felt remained with both of us, even though we knew we would never marry and weren't right for each other. Then I met you. I fell in love with you and you with me. I knew in my heart that you were the right man for me. So we married. But Chip was always there, buried in the back of my mind. I couldn't seem to completely let him go.

David, I gave you my life and my love, but one tiny space I held open for Chip. A few months after our wedding, Chip and I ran into each other. It wasn't planned, it just happened. We started to see each other again. Believe me, I broke it off with him a hundred times. Yet somehow, some way, it would begin anew. I guess I never let myself completely heal from our original break up before I became involved with you. So Chip and I never really ended. Can you understand any of this? Can you find it in your heart to forgive me? David, please speak to me!"

"You hid these things in your great grandmother's china cabinet behind an elaborate security system for all these years. You also hid a piece of yourself from me in your heart. I never knew, I never even suspected, that there was within you a secret schism I would never be allowed to see or fathom. You gave this man a place in your heart and in our home. In doing so, you have besmirched everything I held dear. Can you understand that?"

Paula didn't answer, she just nodded her head as the tears ran down her face.

David continued softly, "Did you actually go to the length of fixing up that secret compartment in the cabinet?"

"No. It was already there. I have known about it since I was a little girl. My great grandfather built it for Granny Ethel so she would have a place to hide her valuables from thieves," she sobbed.

"Well, you certainly chose the appropriate hiding place; you are the thief. You have robbed me of all my illusions of you and of us," he said, rising and turning his back on her.

"Oh David, please, please don't turn your back on me. Don't shut me out! I love you!" she cried as she watched him go.

David and Paula are still married. They never discuss Paula's relationship with Chip. David never questions her, and he is not certain whether or not their affair continues to this day. The only thing he is sure about is that he loves his wife more than he hates what she may be doing.

Section Two: The Car

Interior
Glove compartment
Trunk
Under the hood
Under the chassis . . .

This may or may not appear to you as a messy job, but the wealth of possible clues could be tremendous. It is also interesting and important to note that the car is the one place that you and your spouse's guilty partner will have both frequented. That is, of course, unless your spouse has been so incredibly low as to actually bring this person to your home. When I say low, I mean LOW—kind of like that stuff that forms between your garbage pail and the bag. So, when I say low, I'm talking really disgusting!

Further, it is a proven fact that the other man or woman may leave some item for you to find, accidentally of course. Keep in mind that, as a general rule, they know about you even if you do not know about them. The accident factor comes into play simply because he/she would not want to risk the wrath of your spouse which may subsequently risk their relationship. So if he/she has left something for you to find, by all means, be accommodating and find it.

You are looking for the same clues in this section as in Section One. However, I have added the following items to your list: unfamiliar cosmetics, jewelry, articles of clothing, notes, cigarette butts, flower petals and so forth. Further, check the car for secret compartments. If he has a key to the "other's" home, the car is the most likely place to stow it.

Let's look at the magnetically rivoting "Case of Detectives Detecting a Detective" to better understand how a car should and should not be searched.

THE CASE OF DETECTIVES DETECTING A DETECTIVE

Date: May 14, 1985. Day: Saturday. Time: 11:07 a.m. My name is Wednesday, Joe Wednesday. This is my partner Tuesday.

It was a bright and cloudless spring day. Tuesday remarked on the brightness and cloudlessness of the day as we drove south on West Street. However, my attention was not on the pleasant weather rather I was observing the suspicious actions of a man preparing to leave his residence in a blue four-door sedan. It was 11:07 a.m. as the car pulled on to the street. I followed him.

Arresting Tuesday's interest from the weather, I solicited his help keeping the subject's car under surveillance. We drove in silence except for Tuesday's noting that he had spied what appeared to be a cloud forming.

At 11:23 a.m, the subject pulled into a deserted parking area of a local forest preserve. He exited the vehicle. I parked inconspicuously next to him. Reaching to my sun visor, I pulled out a newspaper. I handed Tuesday the sports section. I had hoped the subject would not notice the headlines that told of Babe Ruth's Grand Slam. I had used this paper before. But the subject, taking no notice of us, went straight to work and began an extensive search of the vehicle.

He turned out the trunk's contents and spread everything out on the cement. It was 11:37 a.m. We casually watched as he came upon discarded nylons and a pair of high heels that had been stowed under the spare tire. I looked over at Tuesday and nodded. It was then that I saw that he had been hanging out the window. I think he has been living with his mother too long. I pulled him back into the car and shoved the sports section back in his face. Although our subject searched the trunk meticulously, he discovered nothing more that seemed unusual. He then returned the trunk's contents to their previous places. It was now 11:43 a.m.

We kept a sharp eye on our subject as he moved to the inside of the car. To our surprise, he began to search the interior. Tuesday reached for his gun, but I stopped him. I decided we would wait it out and see what happened. Tuesday was disappointed but I assured him I would let him shoot our subject if the need presented itself. Tuesday perked up. I glanced at my watch; it was 12:14 p.m.

The subject carefully went through the entire inside of the car. We watched as he came across two filter tipped cigarettes butts. These he deposited into his pocket. Then something flashed in the sunlight. Tuesday pulled out his gun and we tensed for an attack. It turned out to be a long gold necklace. The subject stared at it and then deposited it in the same pocket as the cigarette butts.

I had come across these perverts before—the kind that collect ladies nylons, jewelry and cigarette butts. But it still turned my stomach to see this weirdo at work.

It was 1:11 p.m. when our subject raised the hood and continued his examination. He ran his hands slowly throughout this area of the car. We heard him gasp as he discovered and withdrew several magnetic boxes in various sizes. They had been affixed to the chassis.

Sensing that our moment had come, Tuesday and I jumped from our vehicle. With guns drawn, we accosted our suspect.

How and Why Lovers Cheat

Tuesday threw him to the ground as I took possession of the boxes. I hesitated before opening them. I was sure they contained more sick, demented paraphernlia from this pathetic and twisted individual whose face Tuesday was grounding into the pavement. Sliding back the lids of the boxes, I withdrew the contents as our suspect groaned.

"Explain these!" I shouted, holding out two keys, a bank book and some snapshots.

"I will, if you get this animal off me!" he shouted back as best as one can shout while eating cement.

"Let him up, Tuesday," I ordered.

"But Joe, he is a sick, twisted flea on the body of a decent society," Tuesday whined.

"I know, I know. But even fleas have rights. Let him up," I answered.

Slowly and painfully rising to his feet our suspect growled, "You idiots! What the hell do you think you are doing?"

"Just the facts, Sir, just give us the facts!" I commanded.

Shaking, he moved to the car and from the glove compartment took out his ownership papers and his registration. Handing them over to me, he pulled out his wallet and retrieved his drivers' license. After placing all of these documents in my hands he said, "This is my wife's car. I was searching it for evidence of her affair."

"A likely story. Do you think we are stupid? We've heard that story before," Tuesday sneered, still pointing his 357 Magnum at the suspect. I noted the time; it was 1:34 p.m.

"Actually we never heard any story before, Tuesday. You always shoot our subjects before we get a chance to either question them or read them their rights. As a matter of fact, this is the first time I've gotten an opportunity to say my line, 'Just the facts, sir, just the facts,' in years."

"If you are going to jump on every little thing I do, maybe you should JUST find yourself another partner I hear Saturday is available!" Tuesday retorted snidely.

Handing back his papers to the suspect, I turned to Tuesday, "Listen old buddy, I didn't mean it. I promise you can shoot the next suspect on sight. JUST don't get mad. Anyway, we saved society from yet another psycho dirtbag with warped sexual tendencies," I ventured, walking arm and arm with him back to our car.

As we watched the suspect get into his car and drive away Tuesday asked, "Well, how come you get to narrate our cases and note the time out loud? How come I can't do that part.

All I ever get to do is kill people."

"I'm sorry," I answered. "By the way, what time is it getting to be?"

With a grateful tear in his eye Tuesday said, "It's exactly 1:50 p.m. No wait, I am fast; it's 1:47. No, I remember now, I reset my watch yesterday; it's 1:49. Anyway, it's between 1:40 and 1:50 p.m."

What's the moral of this story? Well, in the first place, check every inch of your car for clues and be mindful of magnetic boxes that might be affixed to it. In the second place, for heaven's sake, never search your car in plain view of an unmarked police car with the license plates "COPS" —especially if the occupants are wearing sunglasses at night. These men are truly armed and dangerous.

Section Three: Monetary Statements Found In and Around Your Home

Bank account statements
Charge account statements
Telephone bill statements
Bills
Receipts . . .

This section includes all of those clues which are documented on paper and have to do with evidence in the monetary realm. All of the above-mentioned clues can be found either in your vehicle or in your home. However, I have separated these clues because a certain amount of backtracking is necessary if you are to accurately determine the significance of the data you uncover. In other words, if you were to find a picture of your spouse in the arms of another person, it would not take a genius to figure out "AHA, IT IS A CLUE!" A telephone bill must be researched in order to determine whether or not a clue is contained therein. In illustration of this point, consider "The Case of Jacob D."

THE CASE OF JACOB D.

Jacob relaxed on his therapist's couch and waited. He looked about the now familiar chamber. The room was warm and soothing. It comforted him. He studied Dr. Birnes's ancient and well-worn chair. It seemed to dominate the small room with the same quiet strength the doctor himself possessed.

Dr. Birnes entered the dimly lit inner office softly. Gently, he bade Jacob a good morning and seated himself. He was a kind, elderly man deeply rooted in his religious beliefs. He spoke little during his sessions, trusting in his patients' own sense of timing and judgment. However, today he felt that he must push Jacob further on in his therapy. So he asked him to recount the events that lead up to his divorce.

Visibly surprised, Jacob stammered, "I don't think . . . I mean I don't know . . . if I'm ready to discuss Gina."

Interrupting, Dr. Birnes said firmly, "I believe that you have skirted this issue for weeks. It is time we delve into the matter straight on."

"All right, Doctor, I trust your wisdom. It all started the day we were married. After the reception, we went to our new home on Long Island. Our schedules did not permit us the time for a long honeymoon, so we opted to spend a long weekend alone at home. Happily, I carried my new wife over the threshold. I kicked the door shut behind us and, with her in my arms, began to ascend the stairs. Suddenly, she screamed. I was so frightened I nearly dropped her. Regaining my composure, I set her down gently and asked what was wrong. That is when the nightmare began.

"'Are you crazy! Just look at that mark you put on the door with your foot! I just had this whole house painted inside and out. Furthermore, if you think you are going to walk on $10,000 worth of brand new carpeting with your shoes on, you've got another thing coming. Now, take your shoes off and put them in the closet. Come into the kitchen when you're done, I've got something to show you,' she screeched.

"Dumbfounded, I obediently followed her instructions; hoping against hope that she was joking and a romantic surprise awaited me in the kitchen. Shyly, I entered the room looking for her laughing face or a huge present. Instead, I found my wife, grim faced, sitting at our glass kitchen table.

"Did you put away your shoes?" she asked. After I nodded, she waved me to a chair and handed me a copy of the paper she held in her hand. She then continued, 'All right, this is a list of Do's and Don'ts. If you expect me to be able to live with you, I have some very simple rules. Read along with me and try to keep up. Rule number one, don't ever wake me up when I am sleeping. Rule number two, NEVER let any water get on the floor of the bathroom. . . .'

"I will not bore you, Doctor, with the entire list, but it took almost a full thirty minutes to go through it. She then lead me into the bathroom and gave me a ten minute lecture on how to affix the shower curtain to the tile so that no water would spill on the floor. She wasn't satisified until I demonstrated that I had mastered this skill. I was asked to try it in her presence. Believe it or not, after delivering her speeches, she took my hand and lead me to the bedroom for what she called our 'Duty.'

"I can tell you that the mood was pretty well squelched at this point, but when she went through the nightly ritual of teeth brushing, clothes hanging, one hundred times hair brushing and pillow fluffing, I was fairly sure this was not the woman I wanted. Nervously, I reached for a cigarette, trying to figure out whether or not it was too early to ask for a divorce. I had no sooner put my lighter to the tip when she asked me—through clenched teeth—whether I had already forgotten Rule number sixteen. This, of course, pertained to NO smoking in the house.

"This rule really bothered me because she knew I was a two-pack-a-day man. Furthermore, I always had a burning cigarette in the ashtray when I was writing. Since I write at home, this was going to be a definite problem. But I was too tried to fight so I went outside to smoke. Standing in the ten-below-zero wind, thoughts of murder crossed my mind more than once, I can tell you.

"After smoking my cigarette, I went back inside, resolving to be patient and understanding. But as soon as she heard the latch catch in the door, she called downstairs 'Take your shoes off!' I yelled back that I had, and then she actually came downstairs to check. My fingers curled behind her neck unconsciously for a moment, but I said nothing and meekly followed her back to our room.

"Having completed all of her nightly tasks, she joined me in our bed. We made love for exactly ten minutes. She then said, 'I think that's enough for one night. Why don't you go clean up so that you do not soil the linen?' I went and had a cigarette.

"It continued this way for the next several days: the regimented compliance of the Do's and Don'ts list, the orders and the inspection of my every move. Did I mention that Gina picked lint off our garaged car and insisted I take a cab so as not to put unnecessary miles on her pride and joy? Or that she felt the bathroom floor every time I took a shower?

No? Well, did I tell you that I was not permitted to sit on the furniture because the fabric was so delicate that I might leave an indentation? No? Needless to say, I was not a happy man and I spent most of my time at the local donut shop. It was there that I could smoke, drink coffee and write in peace. I also got to know the regulars. It was also there that I met Roberta. Ah, Roberta. One evening she had given me a ride home to save me the trouble of calling a cab. She was blessedly normal. She drove her car right through a mud puddle. Can you believe it, Doctor, right through it? It was at that very moment that I knew that I could not go on with Gina, no matter what.

"I had entered the house full of this resolve, so with my muddy shoes on I stamped up the stairs and into our room. Gina wasn't there. I couldn't believe it. It was after ten o'clock at night. Gina always went to bed promptly at ten but our bed hadn't been slept in. I looked at the clock. It was a little after midnight. Defiantly, I sat down on our perfectly matched chase lounge and lit up a cigarette. Letting the ashes drop to the floor, I waited. It wasn't until four o'clock in the morning that Gina finally came home. I watched as she staggered and fell onto our bed, fully clothed. I don't know what shocked me more, the lateness of the hour, or the fact that she was passed out there with her clothes and shoes on.

"I unsuccessfully attempted to wake and question her, but she was out like a light. So I grabbed her purse and walked to the bathroom. Sitting there behind the locked door, I rifled through the contents. Among her matching checkbook and make-up case, I found a business card with a man's home number scribbled on the back and several suspicious receipts. One of these was from a Manhattan Hotel dated with that same day's date. Feeling reckless, I called the number on the card. A sleepy, male voice answered. Posing as the hotel's night manager, I told him that Mrs. Jacob D. had left her purse at the hotel in their room. He told me not to wory about it, that he would come and pick it up the next day.

"I suppose I should have felt hurt or despondent, instead all I could feel was pure, unadulterated—no pun intended—joy. I felt as though a one hundred and twenty-seven-pound weight had been lifted from around my neck.

"The next day I confronted Gina, filed for a divorce and asked Roberta for a date," Jacob said completing his story.

"So what exactly is your problem, Jacob? Why are you coming to see me week after week?" Dr. Birnes asked kindly.

"I found myself doing strange things, Doctor, after Gina and I broke up. For one thing, I can't bring myself to sit on my own couch and, for another, I check the bathroom floor after every shower. I think I caught whatever it was Gina had," he answered miserably.

"You poor, poor boy. Tell me about your childhood. Maybe you should come to see me twice a week," Dr. Birnes said sympathetically while Jacob picked lint off his jacket.

My grandmother use to say when I was looking for something, "It is probably so close to you that, if it were a snake, it would bite you!" This also is true for many clues. If you look carefully, you will find them. With them you can do your job—which is, of course, discovering and uncovering "the facts, Madame, just the facts!"

CHAPTER NINE

EASY
RESOURCES

This chapter is a reference chapter. In the course of building your case, you will probably find yourself frequently referring to the following information.

You can achieve three different objectives with this fingertip guide. First, it can be utilized to run down a clue presently in your possession. Second, it can be used to chain clues and leads together. Finally, it can be employed to uncover completely new clues. The following hypothetical situations will illustrate how you can effectively use this chapter.

Situation A

Fay presently possesses a clue which reveals that her husband's alleged mistress has recently moved, but she does not know where.

Consulting this guide, Fay can discern that the Post Office keeps change of address records and, also, that these records are OPEN to the public. Fay can, consequently, research the records and locate the desired new address.

Situation B

Let's suppose John has a clue which provides him with the "other" man's name. He then discovers a lead indicating that this man is a Vice President of a local corporation; John, however, does not know the name of the corporation. By using this guide, John can ascertain that the *Business Directory* lists most corporate executives by name. Further, this directory can be found at the local library and is, therefore, another OPEN record. After some research, John could locate the other man's place of employment and, in so doing, chain together two separate clues.

Situation C

Hannah wants to know whether or not her husband's mistress is married. Utilizing this guide, she can determine that all vital statistics records are OPEN records and that a marriage certificate is a vital statistic. So by researching those records, she can both answer her initial question and extract from this guide a completely new clue, such as her husband's name.

In each of these hypothetical situations, you may have noted my use of the word "OPEN" when referring to records. However, not all records are OPEN; some are SEMIOPEN; others are quite CLOSED. I will define each type of record for you; however, you must first understand that I have used the word "record" as an umbrella term. Within this guide, you will be familiarized with governmental files, business directories, credit companies and so forth. The word "record," therefore, applies to any data collected and preserved. With this bit of riveting information out of the way, let's look at the definitions of the three types of records with which you will be dealing.

Open Records

OPEN Records are those records that can be viewed by anyone. They are open to public scrutiny. Although not all OPEN records are govermental files, it may surprise you to discover how much information Uncle Sam has on all of us. In fact, governmental agencies gather and maintain vast amounts of diversified information on every citizen in the country. Further, just as surprising is the fact that this information is, almost without exception, accessible to anyone who wants to take the time to review it.

I am sure you have heard the saying "Big Brother is watching." Big Brother is, of course, the government, and he is indeed watching you. But in an effort to be completely fair—and also avoid a tax audit—let me say this in defense of our great and mighty government: with millions of people occupying this country, some tracking methods and record keeping are necessary. (Do you think they are buying this snow job?) So, therefore, "Big Brother" records our births, marriages, deaths, political affiliations and so forth.

Now as much right as "they" have to keep tabs on us, we, in turn, have some rights to keep tabs on them. After all, it is our tax dollars which pay "their" salaries and supports these governmental agencies. Consequentially, we as citizens do have the right to have access to information gathered by our government with very little exception. So, if you ever want to scare the pants off a governmental clerk, recite the Freedom of Information Act to her. It's fun, try it.

The Freedom of Information Act is a piece of legislation which states that the general populace has the right to scrutinize public records. This Act is a powerful tool and I recommend that you obtain a copy of it from your local library. If "they" shut a door you know should be OPEN, this will be just the key that turns the lock. Knowledge is power and, as my Mom says, "The squeaky wheel gets the grease." Okay, some of my Mom's sayings are dumb, but she is my Mom and if I don't put some of her sayings in this book, I can't come to Thanksgiving dinner. (This little tidbit should get me a turkey leg.)

Governmental agencies are not the only source from which one can obtain OPEN records, as you will note in the coming pages. You will also discover that your local library's reference section contains a veritable wealth of information and resources. In any event, as we go through each type of record, I will both explain the record's function and indicate where you can gain access to it.

Keep in mind that records are an important source of information which, if properly utilized, will assist you in your pursuit of clues. Therefore, take advantage of the fact that someone else has compiled the information you seek and avail yourself to data which may, in the end, save you many hours of legwork. Remember that all records are not equally accessible; the accessibility of a record determines whether it is OPEN, SEMIOPEN or CLOSED.

Semiopen Records

SEMIOPEN Records are those records that have limited access. The limitations could be in place for any one of several reasons. Those reasons include the assurance of personal privacy, a business policy, a legal dictate or a combination thereof.

Let me give you some examples to assist your understanding of these limitations: employment records have limited access to insure personal privacy; electric bill information is limited through a business policy, while a medical record is limited due to various state statutes.

While the general public's access to SEMIOPEN Records is limited, access is readily availble to the person whose private information is directly contained therein. At least, that is the way the system is suppossed to work. However, an individual may give another person or agency written permission which, in turn, would allow access to the SEMIOPEN record. For example, if you were involved in a workmen's compensation claim, you may need to give your attorney written permission to obtain a copy of your hospital medical file.

I do not intend to belabor this point. I will, however, reiterate that you can not secure SEMIOPEN records unless they are either YOUR records, or you have acquired written permission from the concerned party; this written permission is a document commonly known as a release form. A signed release form grants you the right to secure otherwise private information. I have included a general release form below so that you may become familiar with it. This basic format can be adapted to fit any record you wish to obtain.

This form authorizes_____, or their agents, to examine, inspect, or make copies of all_____.

To_____ Sustained by_____ on____
When_____Was involved in_____With_____
Signature_____Date_____
Witness_____Date_____

(NOTE: Spouses usually can obtain their spouse's SEMI-OPEN Records as easily as if they were their own. Remember the world and the law views a married couple somewhat as one person.)

Closed Records

CLOSED Records are those records which are closed to public scrutiny. These records include FBI reports, some military records and documents dealing with national security. As a general rule, these records can be examined neither with written permission nor by utilizing the Freedom of Information Act.

But rules are made to be broken, and every rule has an exception. The exception, in this instance, is a court ordered disclosure; we have most recently witnessed its effectiveness in the Contra scandal. Another exception is the declassification of documents. The motivating factors behind a declassification are numerous. A declassification could be due to a normal departmental policy change. There are also cases of public pressure being brought to bear; an example of which is the publication of the Watergate tapes. The media also applies pressure for disclosure. An illustration of media-inspired provocation can be seen in the declassification of the FBI surveillance reports concerning John Lennon. Actually, for all we know, the motivation behind any one of these examples could have been a combination of numerous factors. In any event, I believe in order to truly understand any rule, one must understand the inherent exceptions to that rule.

It is doubtful that you will ever need to obtain a CLOSED Record within the scope of your infidelity investigation. But, if the unlikely situation does occur, you should know that the application of pressure utilizing the Freedom of Information Act COULD cause the scales to be tipped in your favor. However, the wheels of justice and governmental agencies move slowly; not as slowly as civil servant clerks, but pretty darn near. The bottom line, therefore, is, there are some records that you will PROBABLY not be able to get your hands on.

This chapter has been entitled "Easy Resources," rather than "All About Records" because the resources contained in this guide are not all in the form of paper and microfiche. Some resources of which you can avail yourself have a quite different form altogether; that is, flesh and blood. Certain well-placed individuals can, in fact, be more valuable to your investigation than the net worth of Michael Jackson. Okay that might be pushing it, but you get the basic idea.

The suggestion of using another person as a resource may go against your sense of right and wrong, but it is a firmly established practice in the world of the professional investigator. Consider, if you would, that the policeperson has her snitch, the private investigator has her telephone company contact and so forth. It is all part of the job. Looking beyond the realm of the investigation field, one can find several other interdependent relationships within many other professions. For example, television producers use doctors to help them locate potential talkshow guests. Photographers use hospital personnel and records to help them locate new parents for baby pictures. The list goes on and on.

It is the word "use" that most likely vexes our sense of morality. In an effort to help dispel any apprehensions you may be experiencing, let me recount an analogy told to me by Marlene Chicco, a female private investigator who instructs other private investigators in their craft.

The Rhino and the Oxpecker

The rhinoceros suffers horribly from parasites. As many as twenty species of ticks have been found feeding on one rhinoceros. These parasites, at best, can cause severe infections; at worst, they can endanger the rhino's life if left unchecked. Happily, however, these ticks are the preferred food source for a small, gray-brown bird called an oxpecker. A single rhino may play host to up to three of these birds at any given time. The oxpeckers ride on the rhino's back, constantly feeding on its ticks and always on the alert for danger. When they see or sense peril, they fly up and sound an alarm in a piercing, screeching call. This adscititious alarm system is extremely valuable to the rhino as its eyesight is very poor.

Let's closely examine the interdependent relationship between this small bird and this immense animal. The rhino protects the oxpecker from predators and acts as a constant food source. The oxpecker, meanwhile, rids the rhino of health threatening parasites and acts an alarm system, warning its host of potentially dangerous situations. Therefore, each "uses" the other in many different ways.

The question is, is this USE negative? Could it be that each member equally contributes and extracts benefits from one another? Can anyone truly be used who does not want to be used? Maybe, maybe not; you need to make these determinations for yourself. Let me pose the following questions: Could the rhino not rid himself of this tiny bird if he chose to do so? Is the bird not free to fly away at any time? But then, how would it benefit the rhino to chase the oxpecker away? Who would protect and feed the oxpecker if it did not avail itself of the rhino's parasites?

Each interdependent relationship has ever-changing and varied advantages for its participants. The scales can tip back and forth constantly. For instance, the host rhino may experience periods in which its parasite population is minimal, thereby causing a food shortage for the oxpecker. During the same period of time, the screeching call from the oxpecker might have saved the rhino's life many times over. Just as possible, the rhino may feed and protect the oxpecker for years and then be fatally wounded by a poacher before the bird has a chance to sound its alarm.

The lesson to be learned from "The Rhino and the Oxpecker" is simply this: any interdependent relationship has built-in advantages and freely given choices of involvement for each party. Further, each member in the relationship gives the other unspoken permission for its "use." Therefore, manipulation and exploitation are not viable or applicable charges to be levied.

Successfully extracting information from a human resource is considerably different from obtaining information from a written one. Most of the differences are conspicuously apparent and flagrantly obvious. However, there are a few distinct aspects to be considered when dealing with that ever fluctuating paradox which is man.

A written resource provides one-dimensional information and is usually extremely restricted in scope. A person, however, can provide you with comprehensive and extensive details. A written record is either available to you or it is not. A person, on the other hand, could be persuaded to change their mind from closed to open, bend a policy or break a rule entirely. In other words, you can not bamboozle, con, charm or even bribe a piece of paper. But a person, well . . . human beings are as fickle as they are flexible. So, never say never.

Point of fact: While there are SEMIOPEN and CLOSED records, those records are in the OPEN hands of a very unpredictable entity. Consequently, when you are working with mortal resources, accessibility is a completely unknown variable, and your battery of investigative talents will be truly tested. A creative story, appropriately timed and told with confidence and realism, could unlock the front doors to Fort Knox. Since we will be discussing cover stories in Chapter Eleven, I will not go into them here; however, it is essential that you realize that eliciting data from an individual requires all of your investigative skills and a delicate and cultivated touch.

The touch to which I am referring is your approach. I have found that a person is more willing to verify information she "believes" you already possess, rather than to volunteer previously undisclosed facts. For example: if you were to call an airline and ask whether or not Mr. Smith booked a seat for "Mrs." Smith, they will be, at best, uncooperative. However, if you were to ask the same airline personnel to VERIFY "Mrs." Smith's reservation, they would both confirm her reservation and provide you with her compartment section and seat number.

The rationale governing the latter of these two approaches is simply this: no one wants to be a snitch. When we were kids, snitching was punishable—at least, on the playgrounds in my neighborhood—by a severe blow to the face. As adults, we usually are hesitant to divulge details or facts thought to be unknown as such disclosures conjure negative feelings. On the other hand, it gives us a warm, positive feeling to help someone recall or verify information.

> "What a piece of work is man! How noble in reason;
> how infinite in faculties . . ."
>
> —Shakespeare

Your easy resource guide has been divided into four categories. They are OPEN records, SEMIOPEN records, CLOSED records and PEOPLE. In each of the four categories, I have listed several resources that I feel you may most likely need to conduct your case. Happy hunting!

Open Records—A Listing

Vital Statistics

Definition:
Vital Statistics records include birth, death and marriage certificates.

Where they can be found:
They are filed in the county in which the event took place.
Data needed to obtain the record:
Birth Certificate—full name and birth date
Death Certificate—full name and date of death
Marriage Certificate—full name of both spouses and date of the marriage

Fees:
The fee varies, but $3.00 per record is the norm. This nominal fee usually covers both the record search and a copy of the certificate.

In the event that you can not furnish the clerk with exact names and/or dates, she will research their files for you. As a general rule, records are examined in three-year intervals. However, there is an additional fee charged for each of these searches. This could, therefore, become a costly undertaking if you are unable to provide the clerk with accurate and precise information. So it is extremely advantageous to arm yourself with as many facts as possible before requesting a vital statistic record. However, finding yourself in a position of lacking seemingly necessary data is not one that should cause discouragement. A first and last name, together with an approximate year are sufficient to commence your search. While the employment of a hit or miss method may not be the preferred means by which to obtain a record, it is a means to your end and, therefore, adequate.

Interesting note:
Vital Statistics records are neither kept as computerized data nor cross-indexed; they are retained on microfiche. As a result of this practice, researching documents can be both labor and time intensive. In short, this system of retention promotes both inefficiency and wastefulness. Do not be surprised, therefore, if you should find yourself encountering some bureaucratic snags while pursuing Vital Statistics records.

Court Files

Definition:

Court files include divorce, annulment, criminal and civil proceedings. In other words, these records include any legal procedure that occurred within the court system and has been legally adjudicated. However, cases that are a still in the process of being litigated are usually unavailable to the public until a finding has been handed down.

Where they can be found:

They are filed in the court system in which the litigation took place. There are several divisions within our court system. Those divisions include the U.S. District Court (also known as the Federal Court), the Federal Appellate Court, the Federal Supreme Court, the Circuit Criminal/Civil Appellate Court and the State Supreme Court. Then there are subdivisions within these individual courts. For example, divorce litigation is adjudicated in the County Circuit Civil Court, Divorce Division.

Working with these record is not as difficult as my preceding statements might have made it appear. One simple call to your local Circuit Court record/file department should provide you an answer to where the record you are seeking can be located. My previous statements were made in an effort to increase your understanding of the court system and its various divisions. However, if you can not get an answer from a clerk in the Records Department, there are a few other avenues you can take. For instance, you can call a very good attorney and pick his brain. This is exactly what I do with an attorney I know by the name of Herb Wishe. But do not call him, find your own lawyer. I think one freeloader is all Herb can take. One avenue you can utilize to get your questions answered is either the State Attorney's Office or the administrative offices of your local Circuit Court. Unlike a private attorney who would be doing you a favor by allowing you to pick his brain for free, clerks of the court and state attorneys are public servants. As such they are somewhat obligated to answer your questions. Remember you pay their salaries. However, you would do well to write out your questions prior to placing a call to them. Doing so will serve your ultimate ends well as preparing your questions is an efficient use of both your time and theirs. Public servants or not, the offices in which they work are usually understaffed. As a result thereof, frustrations tend to build quickly, particularly when questions are not properly framed. So, save yourself unnecessary frustration—or being on the receiving end of another's wrath—and prepare your questions well in advance.

Data needed to obtain the record:

You will need to locate the appropriate court in which the litigation took place. You will also need at least the name of one of the parties involved in the case and the approximate year in which the case was heard. Of course, if you were to have the case number (also called the docket number), your search would be expedited with greater ease and timeliness.

Fees:

The initial search for a court file is, as a general rule, free. However, there is usually a small fee of approximately $3.00 or $4.00 for every search conducted thereafter. Furthermore, you will be charged for every additional search you request.

Interesting note:

Court records, unlike Vital Statistics records, are computerized. So, therefore, the searches can be conducted with greater efficiency and speed.

So much information is contained in a court file that the file alone may provide you with several other leads. Further, although the court files are not cross-indexed between Criminal and Civil jurisdictions, the file itself may contain references to past lawsuits and/or settlements.

Last, your entire investigation of court files can be done over the telephone and through the mail. As long as you pay the appropriate fees in advance, you can request any and all searches you deem necessary and receive copies of all documents contained within those files.

Registered Voters Listing

Definition:

This is a list of the registered voters. The information gathered by the Registrar Of Voters includes names, addresses, places of birth, occupation and signatures. Each listing pertains to those voters within a specific local voting district.

Where it can be found:

This list is compiled by the County Board of Elections; your research should commence here. However, the Registered

Voters Listing may also be available to you at either the village or town municipal building or the local library. As Ma Bell says, "Phone First."

Data needed to obtain the record:

You do not need any data other than the nearest location of the list.

Fees:

The list is free to the public. However, there may be a nominal charge to cover copying costs.

Interesting note:

Remember, information gathered from one resource can often enable you to obtain leads to additional information and/or resources. For example, let us suppose that your goal is to secure a copy of his mistress' divorce file. However, your present information on her is sadly inadequate. Further, without her ex-husband's name, you realize you are possibly facing a costly search process at the Vital Statistics department. But if you were able to gather some other facts on her, you could conceivably attain your goal quickly and inexpensively. Therefore, by first checking the Registered Voters Listing, you would be able to get both her date and place of birth. This information then would allow you to easily obtain her birth and marriage certificates. Then, armed with the data on her marriage certificate which includes her ex-husband's name, her divorce file is practically in your itchy little hands. This is called chaining leads together and that, my friend, is what detection work is all about.

Corporation Listing

Definition:

This is a listing of names and addresses of the principle stockholders of incorporated businesses in the area.

Where it can be found:

The reference section of your public library.

Data needed to obtain the record:

There is no data needed to obtain this listing other than its location.

Fees:

This listing is free to the public.

Interesting note:

Most corporations incorporate in their home state; however, there are exceptions to every rule. The exception to this rule is that one can and might incorporate their business in another state. The most popular out of state incorporation is done in the state of Delaware. Why? The reason for this is that Delaware's incorporation fees are minimal and its corporate tax rates are the lowest in the nation. If the corporate file you seek is not in its own home state, check the files of that original colony, Delaware.

Listings of Civil Employees

Definition:
These are separate lists of all the civil employees who are employed by a governmental agency or body. There are town, village, city, county, state and federal civil employees. These employees are paid with our tax dollars. The list exists so that tax monies can be accounted for. Each list includes names, occupations and salaries.

Where they can be found:
The Clerk's office of any body of government houses such a list or has the data to put one together for you. The Clerk might attempt to dispute the existence of such data or a list. Your right to review such a list and make a copy may likewise be disputed. In either event, these assertions are false. While the Clerk may not have an actual list ready for anyone astute enough to ask for it, she is obligated to produce one for you if you request it. This may be easily achieved in the Clerk is reminded to contact the office of budget and financial accounting wherein such data is readily available. Further, if the Clerk disputes your right to such a listing, do as Teddy Roosevelt suggested, "Speak softly and carry a big stick!" Your version of his words we've already discussed: hit her on top of the head with your Freedom of Information Act. Civil servants hate it when you do that, but they always come around to see things your way.

Data needed to obtain the record:
There is no data needed to obtain this record other than the location of the Clerk's Office for the governmental body which you are researching.

Fees:
This list is free to the public; however, a small fee may be charged to cover duplication costs.

Armed Forces Registrar Records

Definition:

These records include information on all active and retired officers of the Armed Forces.

Where they can be found:

With your fingers search the Yellow Pages.

Data needed to obtain the records:

There is no data needed to obtain these records other than the location of the Registrar's office.

Fees:

Nominal.

Business Directories

Definition:

A Business Directory is an annually updated reference book, giving you information on thousands of companies. It names the companies' officers and management personnel. It also acquaints you with the type of product or service the company provides. In some instances, it discloses the company's gross worth.

Where they can be found:

Most large libraries stock Business Directories in their reference section. Although reference books can not be checked out, you can photocopy any information contained in the directories.

Although I do not purposefully intend to be repetitive, I feel compelled to stress once again the tremendous asset your local library can be to your investigation. Furthermore, the personnel—the reference personnel in particular—are usually quite knowledgeable and helpful. So, take advantage of their help and guidance; they can certainly direct you to the right resources in a manner that is both expeditious and efficient.

Data needed to obtain the record:

There is no data needed to obtain this reference book other than the address of your local library.

Fees:

There are not any fees involved in using the public library. You simply need to remember to bring plenty of dimes to feed the photocopy machine.

County Tax Files

Definition:

These are the records of real estate property tax. They include the owner's name and the address where the the bill is mailed.

Where they can be found:

These records are kept in the Tax Assessor's Office in the county in which the property is located.

Data needed to obtain the record:

You simply need to give the clerk the complete address of the property in question.

Fees:

As a general rule, no fee is required. However, as in the case of most gratis records, a duplication charge should be expected.

Interesting note:

Although these are open records, you may want to take a soft approach when requesting them. My mother says, you can get more with sugar than with vinegar. So a line something like this may be all the sugar you need. "Hi, I'm interested in buying the house at 1234 Nowhere Street, Anyway Town, Illinois. Will you look up the owner for me?"

Multiple Listing Catalogue

Definition:

This is a monthly updated catalogue of all real estate presently on the market within a geographical area. It is compiled for realtors as a tool to assist them in buying and selling homes for their clients. The information in this catalogue is quite extensive; it is a detective's dream—facts at your fingertips compiled by someone else—come true. The data given on each home includes interest rates, name, address and phone number of the owners, mortgage holder, the balance on the mortgage, and the selling price. Of course, it also provides you with insignificant information such as square footage and whether or not the home has central air conditioning. But don't you just love it, all this data just for saying seven little words: "I AM THINKING ABOUT BUYING A HOUSE."

Where it can be found:
Any real estate office you care to visit.

Data needed to obtain the record:
All you need is the address of your nearest realtor.

Fees:
This information is completely free. While you are not allowed, as a general rule, to take the catalogue home with you, your friendly neighborhood realtor will copy any entry from it free of charge.

Interesting note:
Many realtors have computerized the information found in the Multiple Listing Catalogue; printing a Listing Sheet on the property in question is a simple task. Further, the data entered in the computer is usually more extensive and detailed than that found in the catalogue. So, one way or another, you can obtain all the facts you require.

Secretary of State Records

Definition:
These records include files on all licensed drivers of the state and all registered vehicles of the state. The data gathered and maintained on licensed drivers includes the following: name, address, social security number, driver's license number, physical description and, in some states, blood type. The records concerning registered vehicles of the state include: vehicle description, and the registered owner's name, address and driver's license number.

Where these can be found:
The Secretary of State records and files are kept at the agency's main office which is located in the state capital. You can obtain the address from your local library, currency exchange or by giving them a call.

Data needed to obtain the records:
Data on a licensed driver—full name and date of birth
Data on license plate—license plate number
Data on a vehicle owner—license plate number

Fees:
The fees to obtain any one of these records varies. Further there are extra charges if you can not furnish the Secretary of State with exact information, requiring them to research their files for you.

Interesting note:

As data, clues and leads can be chained together, the savy detective knows that one record can assist in obtaining another. Let us suppose that the questions on the table are: "Who is that man, I saw in the car with my wife?" and "Does he own that black Porshe or is it a rental he is using to impress her?"

Employing the chaining theory, you would commense your research a license plate number search. Having received the name, address, the driver's license number of the vehicle's registered owner and a description of the vehicle, you would then request a search on the driver's license number extracted from your from the data obtained in you initial search. This second search would give you all the information found on a driver's license including a physical description of the driver.

An analysis of all the data gleaned thus far should yield the answer to both of your questions. Comparing the description of the man you saw with the physical description documented on the driver's license record, you could make a positive identification. Having established a positive ID, you would then compare the driver's license number of this man with the driver's license number of the registered owner. If the numbers match, I'd say you've got your man.

County Recorder's Records

Definition:

These records include house deeds, state and federal liens, real estate and personal judgements, to name just a few.

Where they can be found:

These records are housed in the offices of your local County Recorder, usually located in the your local county's administrative offices. The address can be found in your telephone directory.

Data needed to obtain the records:

The data needed to obtain any one of these records is dependent upon the record you request. However, the personnel in this department are usually both well informed and helpful. Further, as a general rule, the county building that houses the Recorder's office also houses other agencies. So, the information you may need in order to acquire a record from the Recorder's office may be found just down the hall.

Let's suppose you request the owner's name of a certain house, but the Recorder's office requires the legal description of that property in order to process your request. You could conceivably walk over to the County Tax Collectors office and obtain a legal description from the address. Then, by furnishing the Recording Clerk with that data, you can secure the property owner's name.

Fees:

The fees vary from record to record and range from $1.00 to $10.00.

Interesting note:

The Recorder's office also maintains birth records of those residents born outside of the country. Further, records of county residents discharged from the Armed Forces are gathered and maintained in these offices.

However, there are a few drawbacks to attempting to work within this county agency. Most of the Recorder's offices contacted by this author required that you conduct any and all searches through their records yourself. In the event that the records must be researched by their personnel, very specific information would be required in order to conduct the research. Further, several of the larger counties do not conduct searches for you by mail.

The above stipulations notwithstanding, this office, in my opinion, is one of the largest warehouses of open data you may encounter while conducting your investigation.

Post Office Records

Definition:

Your local Post Office maintains two records to which you may need access in conducting your investigation—the Change of Address files and the Post Office Box receipts. The Change of Address files reveal to you the new address of a relocated resident. The Post Office Box records available to the public are more restrictive; information—name and address—available for general perusal is confined to corporate entities and/or individuals engaged in doing business with the general public.

Where they can be found:

These records can be found at your local Post Office.

Data needed to obtain the records:

Change of Address—a completed Change of Address Inquiry form and the complete former address

Post Office Box owner—the Post Office Box number

Fees:

Each of the records can, at the time of this writing, be obtained for $1.00. However, if the increases in the price of stamps are indicative of the possible increases for other Post Office services, I say you may need to mortgage one of the kids.

Semiopen Records—A Listing

Note: OPEN RECORDS can, at any time, change to SEMI-OPEN. If this does occur, react accordingly.

Utility Company Records

Definition:

Utility companies would include your local electric, gas, and water companies. As a matter of fact, we can stretch the point and encompass into this heading, the telephone and cable companies. The records kept by these companies include: name, address, telephone number, some credit information and billing data on each of their customers.

Where they can be found:

All the utility companies maintain customer information on their central computer systems. A telephone call placed to any one of their locations will put you in touch with a company representative, thereby granting access to all YOUR information.

Data needed to obtain the records:

Data from the Electric Company—name and address

Data from the Gas Company—name and address

Data from the Water Company—name and address

Data from the Telephone Company—name and phone number

Data from the Cable Company—name and address

Fees:

There are no fees for these records other than the cost of the telephone call.

If for some reason you can not remember your telephone number or your address, the representative will usually answer your question anyway. Further, as long as you have her on the phone anyway, this may be a good time to request a verification of the data currently kept on your file. You wouldn't want the utility company to have, say, the wrong, unlisted telephone number or the incorrect, hard to find address. Actually, the best time to do a little verification is during a billing question or complaint call.

Credit History and Record

Definition:
Every person who has ever obtained credit has a file with one of the Credit Bureaus. This file includes the individual's name, present and past addresses, telephone number, date of birth, social security number, credit rating and credit history. This file is usually referred to as a "Credit Report."

Where it can be found:
This report can be obtained through your local Credit Bureau.

Data needed to obtain the record:
To obtain a copy of YOUR credit report, you need to furnish the Bureau with YOUR name, address and social security number.

Fees:
The fee to obtain a copy of your credit report usually ranges from $10.00 to $25.00.

Interesting note:
Businesses can secure credit reports very easily. They simply acquire a membership to any local Credit Bureau. Then, by paying a membership fee—approximately $25.00 to $50.00—they are able to request credit reports on their customers. However, they are charged a fee of approximately $10.00 for each request.

Miscellaneous Records

Definition:
Each of the following entities may have records on YOU. Those records contain a wealth of information. It can be

likened to a wheat field waiting to be harvested. What are you waiting for? Go get your tractor.

Where they can be found:

In order to locate any of these entities, I suggest you begin with your local telephone book.

Data needed to obtain the records:

After you locate the entity, call them and ask what data you need to give them in order to obtain a copy of their file on YOU. Then call back and verify, verify, and verify.

Fees:

The fees are usually nonexistent or nominal.

Interesting note:

The two best pieces of advice I can give you are: first, remember that the Freedom Of Information Act is your best friend and most powerful ally; and, in using this guide, your motto should be "ADAPT, IMPROVISE and OVERCOME."

The following is a list of entities that may have records on YOU:

U.S. and State Attorney's Office
Justice Department
IRS
Your local law enforcement agency
Army data bank
Selective Service
Veterans Administration
Civil Service Commission
Department of Health and Human Services
Hospitals
Your doctor
Your dentist
Public schools
Colleges
Welfare Agency
Aid to Dependant Children
H.U.D.
Your insurance agency
Unemployment agency
Your place of employment
Clubs
Boy Scouts
Park District

These are but a few of the entities that may have records on YOU. Boggles the mind, does it not?

Closed Records—A Listing

It is enough to state that there are some records that, try as you may, you will not be able to pry loose.

Those entities which contain closed records are as follows:

C.I.A.

F.B.I.

Some police files

Pentagon (unless your last name is North)

Some governmental records

We can pretty well sum it up with the following maxim: Any record considered CLASSIFIED has been Filed Out of Your Class.

People—A Listing

Real Estate Agents

Real estate agents not only have access to the Multiple Listing Catalogue but also know the background on their sellers. Did you ever walk through a house with a realtor who was bent on besieging you with more personal information on the sellers than you ever wanted to know? A realtor knows, and is usually willing to share with you, the seller's marital status, occupational background, number of children, the make and model of their car and the type of fertilizer they use.

They usually divulge this information in an effort to instigate a reaction from you, not as a matter of unsolicited gossip. Those sought after reactions include the following: your identification with the sellers, your sympathy with their situation, and, perhaps most importantly, your ability to feel AT HOME with the premises. This is but one of the many strategies used in selling houses.

So, if your spouse's "other" has a house for sale, by all means, tour the house and listen carefully to what the gabby agent may be saying to you. Make a talkative agent's technique work for you. Hey, it's worth a try.

Bellboy/Maid

Bellboys and maids are the real cogs that turn the wheels of any hotel or motel. Further, these employees are usually underpaid and overworked. The irony of their position is striking; although considered by some to be on the lowest rung of the ladder, their presence is essential to daily operations. In fact, without them, the organization would grind to a halt. Also, these are the employees who know what is taking place within the establishment. They have access to rooms, room keys, and hotel records.

It is primarily these employees that I recommend you seek out for any one of a number of helpful services. Although the hotel desk clerk, managers and so forth can also be helpful, these employees usually are the ones in authority and you should be careful not to step on company policy toes. When in doubt, don't. Be ever mindful to make your approach a dignified one, and always be extremely clear as to your needs or desires. Further, it is a common practice to reward any help you receive with an appropriate gratuity.

It is a good idea not to appear ridiculously overconfident and self-impressed when dealing with these employees; this, especially, if they appear to be seasoned veterans. Detectives have a tendency to over play this aspect of their job, most probably as a result of too much television. Keep in mind that these employees work in this hotel everyday and can easily tell stories that would curl both your hair and your toes. So, it might be wise to leave your Mickey Spillane routine in the parking lot.

Further, you can be sure that they have seen the likes of you before and, undoubtedly, will again. I'm sure they laugh themselves sick every time a detective-type person swaggers up to them with a $20 bill protruding from sweaty hand and a looking-for-some-juicy-information gleam in the eye. Don't attempt to play games, and use good judgment when choosing the best candidate to assist you. Having made your choice, tailor your approach to fit both the situation and the person with whom you will deal.

My caution on your appearance of overconfidence is actually twofold. Just as important as not looking like a blithering idiot is your ability to appear neither as an easy make nor pasty. Detectives, also, have some curl-your-toes stories. Two maxims to keep you humbly on your toes: Never pay for any service until it has been rendered; and, never appear to promise something you do not intend to deliver (or, if should make such a promise, keep your room number to yourself!).

Neighbors, Friends and Relatives

Your nearest and/or dearest know more about you than you probably ever dreamed. Your life, to them, is like an open book. Who do you think spills all the beans to the *National Enquirer*?

It is around those people—the ones with whom you plan block parties and holiday dinners—that you really should be watching your Ps & Qs. Now don't think for one minute that I am cynical; I am not. I know that these people are as fundamentally trustworthy and loyal as the day is long, but they are also human. They can be bamboozled, conned, charmed and, I dare say, bribed. You may well say to yourself, "Maybe in your circle of neighbors, friends and family, but not in mine." Perhaps; but I say, don't kid yourself. You know as well as I do, that there is ONE—even Jesus had his Judas—in every circle. Such divulging of your life's intimate aspects may have been totally accidental or unintentional; the culprit: a dimwitted or gullible friend; a neighbor—the same one, incidentally, who was not invited to the block party you organized—with no occupation other than that of staring out her window. And then, of course, there is the family member from Hades. God knows, we all have one of those. I'm sure you know the type. If you ask them what time it is, they will tell you where, when and how their watch was made. In my family, this culprit is called "she who runs off at the mouth," and SHE knows who she is. Love her as I may, I know that if I ever did commit a serious crime and she was on the witness stand, I'd fry as fast as an egg in the Arizona noon day sun. Just remember, spilt beans are spilt beans, no matter how you view the pot.

What is the moral of this story? Well, if I have ONE and if you can now admit to having ONE, then the person you are investigating probably has ONE too. Your mission, if you choose to accept it, is to find their right ONE. Once you do so, any number of "cover" stories may work to obtain the information you seek.

One of the best ploys is that of a "survey taker." In Chapter Ten, I will outline a complete survey call for you. This "survey" format can be adapted to any person you are interviewing and to any situation with which you may be confronted.

Mailperson

A mailperson, although on a schedule, will usually stop a moment or two to answer any question you may have. They are excellent sources to utilize as they often know both the neighborhood and the residents on their route.

The best means by which to extract information from a mailperson is the "I'm buying a house in the neighborhood" approach. With this introductory line, you can then proceed from very general, neighborhood questions to specific inquiries about your suspect.

If you anticipate a lengthy conversation with a mailperson, it would be a good idea to walk as you talk. Both of you can then continue to do your respective jobs.

Policeperson

Every detective should have a police connection. So if you intend on being effective, or if you believe that your investigation will be both deep and intense, start combing the doughnut shops. I am completely serious. It is a known fact that cops hang out in doughnut shops. So to befriend one, go where they are. You could offer to buy him or her a cup of coffee on some pretense and then strike up a conversation. However, you will want to build this relationship somewhat gradually. Do not attempt requesting an immediate favor. It would be a better idea to "run into" your policeperson again, a few days later.

After you have established an acquaintance with him, you might casually say, "I've seen a suspicious looking car in my neighborhood recently. Could you check on his license number so I could see if this is a resident or not?"

If time is of the essence, then you might try going into the station and using the old "I think someone was following me" scam. They just may run the license plate for you so that you can rule out the possibility of a friend attempting to get your attention.

Regardless of your approach, a connection in the Police Department is essential. They are privy to a substantial amount of information and their computers can access fingerprint records, driving records, criminal records, miscellaneous reports made on any resident in the municipality, license plate information and other data maintained in both the federal and state governments' databases. In this capacity, the police are, quite literally, worth their weight in gold.

Here is just a small sampling of the output they can obtain with merely a minimal input.

Type of Computer	Input Needed	Output Obtained
Soundex/General Info	Name and DOB*	Address, Social Security #, license plate #
Soundex/Criminal Info	Name and DOB	Complete criminal record, address, Social Security #, tattoos, convictions, charges, etc.
Accessed to the Sec. of State Records	Name and DOB	Transcript of driving record, name, address, registration info (state), driver's license, etc.

The knowledge this guide gives you, and your awareness of the Freedom of Information Act, will provide you with the ability to comprehensively pursue your clues.

You can obtain a copy of the Freedom of Information Act from your local library. You can also write to Commercial Clearinghouse Inc., Publishers of Topical Law Reports, 4025 W. Peterson, Chicago, IL, 60646, for a copy of their "Citizens' Guide to the Freedom of Information Act." You can also write to the Center for National Security Studies at 122 Maryland Ave. NE, Washington, DC 20002.

* Date of birth.

TELEPHONE GOLDMINE

I have, throughout this book, stated that the telephone is the detective's most formidable tool. Its benefits are virtually immeasurable, and its potential is limitless. As a result of these and many other virtues, I have devoted an entire chapter to the very special and unique ways in which you can most take advantage of the telephone while conducting your investigation. You will learn, in reading this chapter, that the telephone is a detective's best friend—a time and energy saving device that allows you to be anything or anyone you so desire.

There are two main characters in this life drama: yourself and your mate. Within the parameters of this investigation, you are playing the detective, clad in a turned-up-collar raincoat, and your mate is the suspect—an oblique shadowy figure. Your role and goal are one and the same: detection and tracking of the elusive suspect. With stage defined and parameters set, let us take a moment to understand your suspect in relation to the telephone.

The big question with which you are immediately confronted—would your spouse be stupid enough to call the significant "other" from your home phone?—has an equally big answer: YES! Stupid maybe, but oh how true. Why? To understand the why is to understand human nature and recognize that "convenience breeds carelessness." Simply put, your mate would rather make an intimate call from his warm and comfortable home than from a cold and leaky phone booth. Furthermore, you are now, with the help of this book, an informed individual, but your increase in smarts does not mean that he has become any smarter.

After all, he hasn't read this book. Therefore, your increased enlightenment has no bearing on his present intelligence; he remains secure in his belief that his clandestine actions will glide by undetected. There are only two changes that have occurred: your new understanding of his motivations and your awareness that his expectations of your actions are, at best, short sighted; at worst, completely idiotic.

He will or has picked up the telephone and made that intimate call from your home. This, my friend, is a distinct probability rather than a rarity. If the affair is a lengthy one, you can be sure that he will, in all likelihood, receive either a telephone signal or a call from the "other" at your home. I know this because I have worked and communicated with thousands of spouses and have, consequently, studied their cases; some of which I have shared with you in this book. But most or all, I know this because I know that history repeats itself and a pattern is a pattern.

Recognizing these facts, we know that your first plan of attack, with respect to your utilization of the telephone, is the placement of your "tool of the trade" (Chapter Three). Once this is accomplished, you can go forth and mine the gems that will, undoubtedly, ensue. Before doing so, however, let's go over the points I touched on in this chapter's opening paragraph.

I briefly noted that the telephone is a time and energy efficient instrument. Let me give you an illustration of this statement's accuracy. In the same amount of time required to drive to your first lead, you can track down three or four leads on the telephone. So, the adage of "Phone First" contains great wisdom; it is a extremely good advice. Another point to remember: until we have a telephone system which allows the caller to be seen, the telephone will continue to offer us unsurpassed anonymity. You can depict, impersonate, portray, characterize or represent yourself to be anyone you desire. Rather than going through my entire Thesaurus to convey this assertion, let me cut to the bottom line. When speaking on the phone, you can pretend to be anyone you choose, and the recipient of your call need be none the wiser.

I have a bizarre friend by the name of Michael. Michael —I call him "Leprechaun"—is an Irish elf incarnate, complete with hidden treasures and a rare gift of the blarney. I'm sure you've met the type—those wonderfully gifted individuals who can charm the birds from the trees and put a sparkle in an angel's eye. In addition to all these marvelous qualities, Michael has an absolute genius for imitating vocal accents. This, combined with his unprecedented talent for blarney, renders him an excellent candidate for a detectiv—should he ever decide to turn his hand to the trade.

Now it's quite true that we can not become Michael, but we can, with practice, achieve his combination of good, old fashioned blarney and an ability to vocally become the part being played. It is this combination you should be seeking, and the means by which to attain this goal is simply being believable. In fact, it is this believability which separates the star from a crowd of actors.

If an actor believes in his character, the character comes to life for both the actor and his audience. So if you decide to make a call representing yourself as, say, a piece of celery, by all means become a piece of celery. Chevy Chase portrayed a golfer in the movie "Caddyshack." One of his best lines in that movie takes place while he is instructing another golfer in the art of golfing. It goes something like this: "See the ball; feel the ball; know the ball; be, be the ball." You must adopt this same philosophy: "See the celery; feel the celery; know the celery; be, be the celery." In other words, if you believe the part you are playing, others will believe it also.

We have, up to this point, addressed the probability of your spouse conversing on your telephone, the incalculable time the telephone will save you as you track down clues, and the metamorphosizing latitude the use of your telephone provides. We can now proceed in our exploration of the unique ways in which to use both the telephone and its related byproducts.

Itemized Telephone Bill

The telephone company keeps a record of every outgoing call made from your home so that they can correctly over—I mean, correctly charge you for the units you use. On this record, the following information is itemized: the date and time of the call, the number dialed, the minutes that elapsed during the call and the total number of units used.

Since you are financially responsible for your telephone

bill, you are entitled to this itemized computer printout of your charges upon request. It is a good idea to request your bills for a six-month period. The rationale in doing so is two-fold: you do not know when the affair began and a six-month span will provide you with a good overview of his telephone activity. Once you have obtained these itemized statements, you should make a few copies of each; several different processes of elimination may, in the course of your investigation, be required. In researching these statements, you will endeavor to locate a suspicious telephone number and/or a pattern within your spouse's calls. This suspicious number, of course, belongs to your spouse's other, and the pattern is how often he places calls to her.

A suspicious telephone number can be uncovered after a process of elimination has been conducted. In order to begin this process, take a highlight marker and run it through all of those numbers with which you are familiar. Then, look through your family's personal telephone and address books to further exclude familiar numbers.

In all likelihood, you will be left with a dozen or so numbers that you are unable to identify. Given this situation, your next step is the utilization of one of the three following gems: the Name and Address Service, the Criss Cross and a Survey Call. After employing one of these methods, you should be able to match those unidentifiable numbers with names. Each of these methods are equally viable. To become better acquainted with how they work, read on.

As you match names to unfamiliar numbers, you may be able to eliminate those numbers from the scope of possibilities. One may be the dentist and one may be the local deli. However, there is still a distinct margin for error. Although those numbers may seem to be matched to an innocent third party, they must not be ruled out all together. For the sake of argument, however, check them off your statement so that you can clearly see what numbers remain. Hopefully, moving through the unfamiliar numbers in this manner will result in just one or two numbers that simply scream "suspicious." However, such may not be the case, and you may find that Murphy's Law rules your destiny as it so often does mine. If you are not acquainted with Murphy's Law, allow me to introduce you: "Anything that can go wrong, will go wrong." Bearing this in mind, you can now go through your entire six-month span of telephone bills and success-fully match every number with a name and every name could

How and Why Lovers Cheat

seem completely innocent. Should this occur, there are two possible explanations: your spouse is the exception and not the rule, and never makes intimate phone calls from home; or, the number of the other may have been excluded from the realm of possibilities because it is either a familiar number, or belongs to a seemingly innocent party. In other words, the other is either your best friend or dentist.

Why then, you may be asking yourself, did I bother to instruct you in eliminating numbers if the process is only successful when the other is a complete stranger? The answer is simply that there is no other way to determine fact unless you go through the process. Further, although the process may not have given you a stranger's name and number, it may give you your first clue—the identity of the other is someone within your circle of acquaintances. Tell me, is the glass half empty or half full?

In any event, your itemized telephone bill can be used to locate a pattern with or without an establishment of the other's number. Furthermore, it is through pattern discernment that the acquaintance's identity could be revealed to you. For example, while searching for a pattern you may discover that your spouse makes frequent calls to your sister when you are away from home. You will not only have established a pattern, but may, also, have located his mistress.

To locate a pattern with a suspicious telephone number, simply use another copy of your itemized statement and highlight that number throughout the six-month period. Then check the dates and times that calls were placed to this number. By doing this, you should be able to ascertain both the frequency with which your spouse places the calls and the time at which these calls take place.

Even if you do not have a suspicious number, the process of pattern discernment is essential. Keep in mind that it may take several hours to extract a pattern from your bills. However, this gem alone—with one clean or, maybe, not so clean, sweep—could expose both the name and the number of the person engaged in an affair with your spouse.

Name and Address Service

A Name and Address Service is not available everywhere; however, if you happen to live in or near one of the lucky metropolises which has the service, you will discover its immense value. To determine whether or not this service is available in your area, call your local directory assistance operator and request their number. If one does exist, simply place a call to them and give the number about which you need further information. You, in turn, will receive the name and address of the person to whom the number is listed. However, this service can only give information on those numbers listed in the telephone directory; information on unlisted or unpublished numbers is not available. In consequence, you will have no choice other than to employ another gem.

Criss Cross

Alfred Hitchcock used the term "Criss Cross" in the movie *Strangers on a Train*. The term signified the idea of "one person killing an acquaintance's enemy in exchange for that acquaintance killing that person's enemy." The concept was that the enemy would be killed without a motive, and at a time when his enemy was immersed in a perfect public alibi; this being true, of course, for both killers. From the perspective of the police, each killer had a perfect alibi, and as no motivation could be discerned, perception is stymied and the cops are stumped. Furthermore, each of the acquaintances had the same goods on one another. So, as long as neither was caught actually committing the crime, both were home free and rid of an enemy. CRISS CROSS. Although this Criss Cross is different, it can be just as deadly to the continuation of your spouse's affair.

The Criss Cross to which I now refer is a telephone book published to assist business and credit collection personnel. The information contained therein has been designed in a very unique manner. Unlike the normal telephone directory, the Criss Cross is divided into towns. Each town, in turn, is divided by its constituent streets. After each street heading, all addresses on that street are noted with the name and phone number of the resident. The telephone number will only appear if that person is listed, however.

The Criss Cross is published by the Reuben H. Donnelley Corportion on a national basis. While the books are very expensive to purchase, they can be found in your larger local libraries. I told you you would learn to love your library.

You may be wondering what good this little ole book is going to do for you if the suspicious number is unlisted. Well, I'll tell you. There are at least four possible avenues of exploration available to you when using the Criss Cross.

OLD EDITIONS

An old edition of a Criss Cross may contain the present number of the person who is the object of your inquiries. Although the occurrence of such a situation is rare, it is worth your time to check past editions. There have been several cases with which I am personally familiar wherein this has occurred. For example, a newly divorced woman instructed the telephone company to change the listed status on her number without changing the number. She did so in an effort to protect herself from random crank calls to women listed in the telephone directory. This woman's number, while not listed in the present Criss Cross, was easily found in a previous edition. Therefore, by using past editions of the Criss Cross, you may discover a number that does correspond to the name and address of your subject. A simple phone call will decide the matter. Should you discover that you've hit upon the correct number, your quarter will certainly have been well spent. By the way, if you find an old number and discover that it is no longer correct, keep it; it may come in handy at a later point in your investigation.

One more thing. Do not rule out luck; remember that it plays a viable role in the profession we call investigation. I can not tell you how many times I simply tripped over something. The real trick is to make others believe that a clue's discovery is the direct result of your hard work and skill, which are both necessary if a little luck is to go a long way.

RIPE NEIGHBORS

Keeping in mind that the Criss Cross lists by address, we can deduct that our subject's number may be unlisted but this need not be the case for his or her neighbors. So, a survey call placed to a helpful neighbor may reap a treasure chest of information. Of course, the call must be both believable and one concerning the immediate neighorhood. How about a poll on the impending hot lunch program proposed by the local school board? Okay, if you don't like that one, make up your own. But be assured; in every neighborhood there is —at the very least—one neighbor who knows everything that is going on in almost every house on the block. We have "one" on our block whose self-appointed civic duty is to know the comings and goings of his fellow residents. For the purpose of your investigation, this is exactly the type of neighbor you need to find. They not only have the dirt on everyone, chances are they're more than willing to fling it.

Just as there is one "special" neighbor on every block, there is one "special" person in every family. You remember, the one who, when asked what time it is, will tell you where and how her watch was made. It is your goal to locate and milk your subject's "special" family member, and the Criss Cross may help you do so. Once located, you could use any one of several approaches to open up a conversation and build a rapport. You can do so with a survey call. We will be discussing survey calls in detail very shortly. Whilean opinion poll type call may work, the old school chum ploy usually does the trick in half the time and reaps more details. To add a little credibility to your story, you may want to throw in that old telephone number you found—and saved—during this conversation. I told you it would come in handy.

"WITH FRIENDS LIKE YOU . . ." FRIENDS

While a family member is usually privy to just the information that leaks out around the Thanksgiving dinner table, a friend MAY know every disgusting detail of your life. You must hope to find your suspect's friend—one of those "special" type people we've previously discussed who live in our neighborhoods, are in our families, etc.—and hope, also, that this is not the kind of friend you have. I know all my friends to be loyal, trustworthy and tight lipped. Okay, so they are reading this; it never hurts to spread it on a little.

I feel compelled to pause here a moment and address the aversion you may possibly be experiencing. How do I know that you probably do not joyfully contemplate the purposeful duping of an unsuspecting person? Very simply, because I've felt those feelings also.

As a teacher, it is my responsibility to teach you everything and anything that will speed you on your way, completeing the education that commenced with Chapter One of this book. As the student, it is your responsibility to make selections from those teachings presented which are consistent with your own morals and code of ethics. I am, therefore, duty bound to share with you every avenue that will assist your assimilation of both investigative process and individual techniques.

No matter how badly you want to know the truth, there will be moments during your investigation in which you will ask yourself the big question: "Does the end justify the means?" Only you can answer this question. Only you can decide whether there is honor for a soldier who did not ask to be called to fight. I can not assist you in your personal questions of conscience; they forever remain your responsibility. Now, I'm ready to proceed, are you?

You will discover, if you have not already become so aware, that much of being an investigator is playacting. As a matter of fact, that is exactly why this field is so over used in television, movies and literature. The profession allows the investigator to be anyone she needs to be in order to get the job done. In other words, an investigator must be a bit of a chameleon.

A chameleon is a small lizard which changes color to adapt to its surroundings. By doing so, it can successfully hunt its prey or elude a potential predator. In investigative work, one must have this same adaptability. For example, a policeperson, in order to successfully conclude a drug investigation, may be obliged to pose as a junkie prostitute and thereby gain access to her suspects. An investigator of infidelty may be forced, during a telephone conversation, to pose as an old school chum in order to learn more about her suspect. As I've said previously, "An investigator ADAPTS, OVERCOMES and IMPROVISES."

In order to adapt, overcome and improvise, you must understand the psychology underlying a successful extraction of information from an unsuspecting third party. Your questions must be both properly phrased and presented in the appropriate manner. This can only be achieved if you comprehend the psychological process that propels both the questioner and the person being questioned forward.

In an effort to introduce you to this psychological process, let's take a look at the psychology used in the interrogations of communist countries. They are, I should think, the natural choice; they've elevated interrogation to an art form, having the dubious honor of putting TERROR in the process and thereby gaining significant success in extracting information. You may not concur with the methods we are about to discuss, but one can gain knowledge from all things. With this in mind, let's explore their interrogation methods.

The questioning of a prisoner takes many forms. The method chosen is usually tailored to the type of individual incarcerated and the surrounding circumstances. For example, if the prisoner is expendable, the method of interrogation may be, shall we say, decidedly physical and horrendously zealous. However, if the prisoner must appear alive at some later date, a more subtle form of interrogation will be used.

It is these more subtle methods and the psychology behind them upon which we will forcus our attention. One such method includes a form of deprivation coupled with the techniques used in "brainwashing"; the deprivations used can be numerous and extensive. A prisoner may be deprived of all light or noise; this method is called sensory deprivation. During sensory deprivation, one loses track of time and space; the ability to concentrate is dramatically reduced. One may also experience bizarre sensations and, in some cases, hallucinations. This sensory torture breaks down the human spirit and prepares the weakened and demoralized mind of the prisoner for questioning.

The commencement of the interrogation and "brainwashing" are simultaneous. There are three basic techniques used in "brainwashing." The first of these is the complete isolation of the prisoner. This isolation robs the prisoner of all emotional and physical support. The aloneness instills fear and ensures vulnerability.

The second technique utilized is that of conditioning. If the answers provided by the prisoner are considered believable and viable to the examiner, the prisoner is rewarded with the return of a "privilege" previously denied. If the interrogation is unsuccessful, however, the sensory deprivation is resumed and, in some instances, either intensified or increased with the addition of yet another deprivation. For example, the prisoner formerly deprived of light may also find himself deprived of any means of warmth.

This conditioning is a derivative of operant conditioning. Among those psychologists who have contributed the most to our understanding of operant conditioning is B.F. Skinner, the creator of the conditioning chamber known as the "Skinner Box." This small box was fitted with a metal lever and a food tray. Skinner then placed a rat inside the box. The rat soon discovered that when the metal lever was depressed, a food pellet would drop into his tray. The food pellet then became his reward for depressing the lever.

In this way, the rat became conditioned to voluntarily act and expect a reward for doing so. Skinner and many other psychological researchers were able to conclusively prove the existence and effectiveness of operant conditioning. They further found that man could also be conditioned to respond to an expected reward. Understanding and applying this psychological principle, the interrogator conditions the prisoner to answer questions that are rewarded with that which had been previously denied him. The conditioning also includes an awareness, by the prisoner, that the reward will not be forthcoming if he does not respond appropriately. It is this awareness that shapes both his conditioning and his actions.

The third technique necessary to ensure the success of this "brainwashing" process is the prisoner's complete dependence upon his captors for the satisfaction of all his needs. This dependence strengthens the interrogator's control over the prisoner's mind and emotions. Further, this dependence kindles a strange relationship between the prisoner and his persecutor. The persecutor is in the role of the benefactor. Their relationship, therefore, becomes a source of confusion for the prisoner. Some prisoners have reported that this paradoxical relationship induced them into the belief that the interrogator was but a reluctant pawn in their torture. Therefore, cooperating with his benefactor would spare him the painful task of punishment.

My objective in detailing these interrogation methods is not to stroll through the realms of sadism; rather, it is to acquaint you with the interrelationship between the utilization of psychology and its techniques and the thinking, behavior and reactions of the person upon whom such techniques are employed.

The psychology applied to your questioning must be similiarly well thought out. The thinking, behavior and reactions of the person being questioned must be evaluated and her objections anticipated. To accomplish this feat, you will need to initially approach your subject in a relaxed and nonchalant manner. This approach puts her at ease and placates her natural defenses. This understood, let's look at an exchange between an investigator posing as an opinion pollster and an alleged mistress. Throughout the course of this example, I will point out the following three elements:

the psychology employed by the investigator, the possible mental objections that might surface in the mistress, and the goal of the question. As you are aware, the goal of a survey call is to extract information from an unsuspecting third party. However, many of the questions you will be asking have a goal specific unto themselves. Those particular goals include the ascertainment of a name, an address, an occupation, marital status and so on.

Survey Call

SAMPLE OPINION POLL

Pollster: Hello, this is Shirley with the Television Marketing Corporation. We would like to ask you about a new television program that we will be airing soon, called "Women in Business." This program focuses on teaching women how to begin and improve their businesses. Is this a program you might be interested in watching?

Investigator's Psychology—Put the recipient of your call at ease. In addition, let the interviewee believe that her opinion is both needed and valued.

Interviewee's Objections—None. Further, she will probably be excited to give her opinion on a new television program.

Question's Goal—To start a dialogue with the interviewee.

Interviewee: Oh yes, it sounds great! What time of day will it be on?

Pollster: It is tentatively scheduled to be shown at 7:00 on Wednesday evenings. We are endeavoring to narrow down a good time for our female audience. Would you mind telling me if you feel this is a convenient time slot for you or do you work in the evening?

Investigator's Psychology—The investigator is continuing to promote the value of the interviewee's opinion, giving the impression that her opinion is of great importance with respect to the determination of a programming slot.

Interviewee's Objections—A yellow flag may possibly go up on the personal part of the question, but it is doubtful.

Question's Goal—To ascertain her working schedule and whether or not she is employed.

Interviewee: I work during the day so 7:00 in the evening should be a good time for me.

BINGO.

Pollster: What do you do? Are you thinking of opening your own business?

Investigator's Psychology—Begin with a personal question, but offset it with a question consistent with the topic of the call. This will soften the personal question and start a rapport between the two of you.

Interviewee's Objections—None, if she feels comfortable. But if she is becoming either suspicious or defensive, or if she is just a private person, she may be reluctant to answer.

Question's Goal—Occupation and, hopefully, the name of the company where she is employed.

(Note: If she volunteers her occupation easily, then you may want to simply ask where she works. If she sounds hesitant just giving you her occupation, do not push the issue; continue the questioning. So, if she answers the question with "I am a receptionist," you could respond by asking, "Oh really, where?")

Interviewee: I work for XYZ Company as a receptionist, but have thought many times about opening my own business.

DOUBLE BINGO.

Pollster: That's great! Do you think your husband would be interested in watching our program?

Investigator's Psychology—This is meant as a continuation of both the rapport and the questioning.

Interviewee's Objections—None, or very little. If she has gone along with you this far, her defenses are probably down and will stay down.

Question's Goal—Marital status.

Interviewee: I'm not married.

BINGO.

Pollster: Well, we really appreciate your time and your help. As a token of our gratitude we would like to send you a gift certificate. Could I have the correct spelling of your name and your current address with zip code?

Investigator's Psychology—Reward the help supposedly given in an effort to completely dispel any lingering doubts the interviewee may have.

Interviewee's Objections—None.

Question's Goal—Name and address.

Interviewee: My name is Jane Doe. My address is 123 Elm, Anytown, Illinois 60000.

BINGO BINGO BINGO.

(Note: It is a good idea to really send the gift, as her suspicions will be aroused if you do not. Also, as my grandmother used to say, "Never burn your bridges behind you. You never know when you might need to cross that stream again.")

As you can see, any "survey call" can be successful if it is well planned and the right psychology is used. To understand your subject's possible objections to your questions will prepare you to deal with them if they surface. Basically, the formula that works best when extracting information from any subject is the following:

1. Think through the questions and their goals.
2. Introduce yourself.
3. Put the subject at ease.
4. Establish a rapport.
5. Be prepared for his or her objections.
6. Back off any issue he or she is reluctant to discuss.
7. Agree with your subject when ever possible.
8. Reward his or her help either verbally or monetarily.

Two of the most common and most successful survey calls are as follows:

The Opinion Poll

This call is one in which the investigator poses as an opinion pollster. The subject of the polls can run the gamut from a new television program to a neighborhood issue or a controversial political issue.

The Old School Chum

This call is one in which the investigator poses as a former friend of the person about whom she is seeking information. The premise is, she has lost touch and she wants help finding her friend.

Some other survey calls may use one the following premises:

School reunion
Inheritance
Insurance adjuster looking for an accident witness
Bill inquiries

Cops

The policeperson CAN obtain unlisted telephone numbers and information such as the address of the person that corresponds to that number. Will your friendly neighborhood cop get an unlisted telephone number for you? Therein lies the dilemma and possibly the challenge.

As I have mentioned to you several times throughout this book, a cop is a needed friend to an investigator. Even if you have such a friend on the force, however, you should understand the restrictions and policies with which the policeperson must comply. As a general rule, a policeperson may obtain an unlisted telephone number by making a request to the telephone company's security department; however, there may be one of three security safeguard policies with which he must comply before the request is granted. The policies are the following:

He MAY have to wait for a return call from the security department at the station. They do this to insure that the request came from a legitimate policeperson.

He MAY have to give the security department an "incident report number." This is easy enough to overcome if he is willing to give them either a bogus number or invent a bogus report.

He MAY have to make the request through a superior officer such as a Sergeant. This can be overcome as well, if he is a superior on the force; is willing to give that officer a bogus story or the superior is his friend. .

Regardless of the safeguard policies, if he wants to get the number for you, he can. Any policeperson who may be reading this may have his back up sanctimoniously. Put it back down. I was married to a cop and I know cops. As a matter of fact, I personally know two policemen who got the unlisted numbers of women they wanted to ask out on a date. So, let's agree to agree; if a cop wants an unlisted number, he can get it. The question is, will he get it for you?

THE OPERATOR GAME

Operator Game: Before the game can begin, you should know both the object of the game and the rules. Additionally, you will need to have your playing pieces ready. So let's set the game up.

Object of the Game: To capture the rook by obtaining its unlisted telephone number through the process of elimination.

Rules:

1. Know the name of your suspect and the town in which she resides. If you do not know the town, the game can be played to help you find it; however, the game then becomes both more lengthy and difficult.

2. Request the number each time you call directory assistance.

3. Run through the same statements each time you speak to a different assistant, varying it only with new information you receive. For example, once you have the right exchange, then give the next assistant that exchange and play the game with the first number of the last four digits and so on.

4. Stress in each call how important the acquisition of the number is to you.

5. Always lead her to believe she is helping you REMEMBER a number rather than giving you an unlisted number.

6. Jot down the name of the directory assistant. If the same assistant answers your subsequent call, hang up and try again. Never speak to the same assistant twice.

7. Never ask an assistant to give you an actual number. Rather, phrase your requests in a manner that allows her to give you a yes or no answer. If she gives you an actual number, or even a digit of that number, she could be fired.

Playing Pieces:

1. The playing board is the telephone.

2. The king is the investigator. The king can move forward, backward and to either side.

3. The queen is the directory assistant. The queen must, or at least should, move the way the king wants her to move.

4. The rook is your suspect. She is pursued by the king.

To prepare to play the game, look up the exchanges for the town in which the rook resides. This can be accomplished by using your telephone directory. Jot down those exchanges on a piece of paper. Exchanges, in this context, mean the first three digits of a seven digit telephone number. Also, have a piece of paper and a pen nearby to jot down the name of the directory assistants as you speak to each one of them.

Let's play a practice game! Your move, call Directory Assistance.

Queen: This is Susie. May I help you?

King: Hi, I would like the number of Jane Doe. She lives in Anytown. (Give her full name and address if you have it. It allows you to appear as though you really know her.)

Queen: I'm sorry, that number is unlisted.

King: Oh my gosh, she is my cousin and I have to get in touch with her. Her mother is very ill. Listen, I know I have her number buried somewhere in my memory . . . let's see, I think it starts with 555. (Give one of the exchanges you had looked up that corresponds to the town she resides in.) Is that right? If she replies with a negative, hang up and try a different assistant and a different exchange. IF she affirms your guess, push your luck.) Okay, let's see . . . 555, the next digit is five, right? (Always begin with the number five when pursuing each digit.)

Queen: No. (If she stays on the line, keep playing the game.)

King: Is the number higher than five?

Queen: Yes.

King: (Quickly) 6? 7? 8?

Queen: Yes. (She will say yes on the right number. Go for the next number, if she will keep playing with you. But if she is uncooperative, hang up and call another assistant.)

King: Thank you, I just remembered the number.

Use as many queens as you need to snare the rook and win the game.

You can also play the game to get your rook's street address if you do not have it presently. This game is played in just a slightly different manner. It would go something like this:

Queen: This is Dawn. May I help you?

King: Hi, I would like the number of Jane Doe. She lives in Anytown.

Queen: I'm sorry that number is unlisted.

King: Oh gosh, I have to get in touch with her. Is the number 555-1234?

Queen: Yes it is.

King: Thank you. Is she still on Park Drive? (All telephone directories include maps and an alphabetical street listing of the names of the streets in that town. Use that listing and pick a street from that listing. Keep track of her negative responses on a sheet of paper.)

Queen: No, that is not the name of the street.
King: But it does start with a "P," right?
Queen: No.
King: (Quickly) B? F? S?
Queen: Yes.
King: Thank you, I just remembered her address.

Pick from the streets beginning with "S" and go on with the game for as long as she will play with you. Do not become discouraged. It may take several calls to realize your goals and win the game. However, if capturing the rook is worth it to you, the time you expend in achieving this end will not be wasted.

If all else fails, or if you do not like this game, you may want to go a different route with the "Queen." You may want to "accidentally" bump into a person whose job just happens to be that of a directory assistant. I hear they hang out in the telephone company's parking lot. They like it there because their cars are there. After you bump into a "Queen," befriend her and get your information.

The manner in which you play the Operator Game is similar to the method used by the cowboy when meeting the Karate Black Belt for a showdown. The opponents stood in the middle of the street, sizing one another up. The Black Belt then assumed the attack position, moving his arms and yelling like Bruce Lee. The cowboy assumed the same position as his opponent, making similar noises and gesticulations. And then, suddenly, the cowboy stood up straight, squared his shoulders, pulled out his six shooter and shot the guy. The moral of this story: Play by your own rules!

TRAP AND TRACE

In Chapter One I told you the story of Alexandria. You may recall that Alexandria was able to uncover her husband's affair by having a trace put on her telephone. What you may or may not realize is that the placement of a trap and trace is something you actually can have done.

In order to have a trap and trace put on your telephone, you will need to contact your local police department. The purpose of the trap and trace is to enable the police to help you locate a prank caller, an obscene, a harassing caller or a caller who is threatening you. If you are receiving any of the above-mentioned types of calls on a regular basis, I urge you to call the police.

The police will talk with you and make out a report on the incident. If they are assured by you that you will follow through with signing a complaint once the offender is exposed, then they will initiate the process necessary to set up the trace. That process entails contacting the telephone company's security department in compliance with departmental policies. Once the trace is in effect, you are asked to keep a diary of all the disturbing calls coming into your home. Then, at specified intervals—perhaps bimonthly—you will be asked to check your diary against the telephone company's computer printout of all the incoming calls you received. You will be looking for a match between your diary and that computer printout. Once a match or matches are located, the police will take over and investigate the persons to whom the numbers correspond. A subsequent arrest may be made after you have signed the complaint.

The Trap and Trace is not something you should undertake lightly; it is a legitimate legal matter. Furthermore, you should be aware that the trace itself has a range endurance. Incoming calls can only be traced within a very specific mileage range around your home. So, if a call comes into your home that fits the bill in terms of being abusive but is out of range, it will not appear on the telephone company's printout. *Note:* You could also buy the new devices on the market that display the number of the person calling you.

A SPEEDY CONFERENCE CALL

This little gold nugget is a long shot, but believe it or not, it has worked enough times to warrant its inclusion in this goldmine.

In order for this gem to work, you would have to have two custom features on your telephone package. Those features are speed calling and conference calling. If you do not have these features presently and do not wish to have them installed, you could use the phone of a friend who has these services. Once you avail yourself of these features, you will also need to know the number of the suspect you are investigating. This number must then be programmed into the speed calling feature. These elements in place, the following call is made:

Nadine, the wife, calls her husband Perry at work or at home. While his number is ringing, she switches over to her other line and speed calls the mistress, Charlotte. Nadine then patches Charlotte into the line on which she called Perry. Now the three of them are on a three-way conference call. The conversation may go something like this:

Perry: Hello?

Charlotte: Hello?

Perry: Oh, hi. I'm glad I got a chance to talk to you. (Of course, each thinks the other called.)

Charlotte: Why, is that you, Babe? Aren't we on for tonight?

Perry: Well yes, but I need to change the time from seven to eight.

Charlotte: Okay, I have to run. I'll see you tonight, Hon, at the Knight's Roundtable, eight o'clock sharp.

Nadine: (Thinking to herself, Nice restaurant! I'll be there too, Hon.)

Perry: Bye, Sweetheart.

Charlotte: Bye.

I am not positive, but I believe Nadine "crowned" Perry at the Knight's Roundtable around 8:30.

Well, there ya go, amigo. Your telephone is a goldmine ready and waiting to be prospected. Before you swing that pickax and go to work on that first vein, let me leave you with a story filled with deep, dark shafts and winding, twisted tunnels.

A Sonnet's Anguished Plea

Grace rocked slowly in her ancient upholstered rocking chair. She closed her eyes and let the cool breeze from her bedroom window wash over her. The curtain gently moved with the wind. The sound of it lulled her away and she drifted off to sleep. Suddenly, she heard a moan; not a moan, exactly—an anguished call, a cry. It both beckoned and beseeched her. Although she had never heard it before, it was strangely familiar. It touched a part of her heart that had been closed these many long, lonely years. Her bewilderment was followed quickly by fear and a feeling of panic. It was as though she understood the cry on a subconscious plane. She fought against the rising panic within her that robbed her of her breath. Her heart beat like so many tom-toms and her hands shook uncontrollably. Grace struggled to calm herself —to breathe. The feeling that engulfed and held her prisoner wandered recklessly into her very soul, searching for its place—its home. Then, surprisingly, she wasn't afraid any longer; the fear that had only moments before threatened to beat her heart out of her chest, ebbed away. Slowly her breathing became regular and her composure returned. Looking about her old familiar room searchingly, she felt sure something in it would have changed. She felt as if she had been away for a very long time. But everything was in its neat and orderly place; only she had changed. How? She did not understand. Changed, how? The call, the cry, was still with her, but it no longer frightened her. It seemed to belong to her, but she did not know why.

Grace sat in her chair for several minutes. Then she rose and crossed the room to the window. She stood looking out, not really seeing the scene before her. A loud and distinct thud arrested her attention. It came from the front porch. Tearing herself away from the window, she shuffled to the front door and opened it.

Peering around the porch through the open door, she half expected to see someone. But no one was there. The porch was empty. Looking down, she spied her morning paper. How that paperboy managed to throw the paper every day into her prized potted begonia, she would never know. Smiling to herself, she plucked the paper from its flowery resting place and checked her plant for damage. Satisfying herself of its continued good health, Grace turned and walked back into her house. She went back to her room and to her comfortable chair. Settling down once again, she felt the call pulling at her but did not know how to go to it.

Hoping to shake off her uncertainity, she opened the paper, determined to occupy her mind with the news of the day. She glanced through the paper, catching a word here or a phrase there. But try as she might, she could not concentrate enough to actually read. As she neared the back of the paper, a man's face seemed to leap out at her from the page. She looked into his eyes—those tortured, haunted eyes. As she looked at his face, the words of the screaming headline began to filter into her brain. Holding the paper very tightly, she got up and went to her bedroom closet. She fumbled through the things stored on the top shelf, groping for a box just out of her reach. Then her hand closed over it and she pulled it towards her. Sitting once again, she opened the box and examined its contents, one by one. She returned each item back to the box, save one picture. Setting the box gently upon the floor beside her, she picked the picture up from her lap. It was a photograph of the same man when he was young, strong and handsome. The black curls of his hair fell untameably on the nape of his neck as unashamedly as a girl's. His tanned face seemed almost too handsome to be real. Yet, it was those eyes, those beautiful green eyes, that were riveting. They epotimized pain. One would know instantly that they were a window behind which anguish dwelt in a dark and secret place.

Grace held the young man's photograph to her bosom and began to once again slowly rock. One single tear slid down her cheek. The call came stronger now, beckoning her to come. Reaching out, she let it take her back over years and memories to a place when she was young. As she reached out, her hand felt his—this man that had once been her husband, her true love. And she remembered. She remembered the parting so long buried inside her. She remembered the pain that led to their end. She turned to go away, away from the pain and away from the past, but he grasped her hand firmly. She looked into his eyes and knew that, this time, she could not go—she would not leave him.

So together they walked, hand in hand, back through the years, back through time, back to the place that parted them; as though to brave it now—together—meant they could heal, separately and together. Holding tightly to one another, they went back to their own beginning—back to when they were so young and so in love. They watched themselves, two young lovers happily married, building a new life. But there was sadness about the man; he seemed somehow shamed and in pain. No matter how his new bride tried to dispel the ghost that hung around him, it steadfastly lingered.

They watched as a very particular day in their lives unfolded. It began with a telephone call from the young man's mother. As he listened he became very upset, though his young wife did not know why. He slammed down the phone and paced nervously around the room. She saw in him something that she thought she would never see. She saw terror. Again the telephone rang; once again the young man spoke with his mother. Now the wife knew that something was wrong, but what?

Her husband reacted as though he were resisting an order

—no, a command—from his mother. Again, he slammed down the telephone. It was no sooner in the cradle when it rang again. This time she could not resist her curiosity. She snuck into the bedroom and lifted the extension's receiver. They heard her and the conversation drew to an abrupt halt. She quietly hung up the phone. Had she heard what she thought she heard before they became aware she was on the extension? She tried to push it from her mind. She watched as her husband ended his call. With downcast eyes he left their home, telling her he had to go and see his mother.

The young girl waited nervously for her husband to return. They had only been married for ten days and she was not accustomed to being in the house alone. As the hours ticked by, the words she had thought she heard kept coming back to haunt her. She attempted to busy herself with the unpacking they had still not completed. As she was doing so, she came across one of her husband's old trunks. Thinking it would be fun to look at souvenirs from his childhood, she rummaged through it. She looked at pictures and mementoes for quite a while. Then she spied a yellowing envelope tucked inside an old school book. She opened it and pulled out a sheet of paper. It had been written by her husband; she immediately recognized his hand. It was a poem.

> I was asleep and she came to me,
> This woman who had once bounced me on her knee.
> She flung me into an abyss from which there is no reprieve,
> This woman from which I was conceived.
> Now my life is an empty shell, a tainted facsimile.
> This woman to whose safety I should have been able to cleave.
> Can no one stop this? Can no one see?
> This woman's lies are all believed.
> The shame, the pain, the humiliation, alone I grieve.
> This woman! It is my manhood, you thieve.
> I was asleep and she came to me.
> Oh Mother, how can thee?
> Oh can't someone hear my anguished plea?

The young bride fled out of their house and out of his life. She refused to speak to him or to see him. She buried her love and she buried her life.

The young husband went away too. He lived a loveless life with only his memory of her to sustain him.

Grace stood with him now, her hand clasped tightly in his. They turned away from the pain, away from the past. The cry faded and died. Together they walked away into the light.

They found Grace dead the next day, still sitting in her ancient rocking chair. His picture was clutched to her breast, and the newspaper telling of his death across her knee.

You may discover your marital truth on the extension of one telephone call, or you may have to search every shaft for the truth. That, my friend, is the reality of prospecting.

CHAPTER ELEVEN

CLOAK AND DAGGER

What picture do those words conjure up in your mind's eye? For me, the scene is a dark, narrow byway somewhere deep in the heart of London. The moonlight filters eerily down through the thick fog onto the cobblestone pavement. The light catches just for a moment the flash of steel as it reflects off—a dagger? Then the movement of something. A heavily cloaked man draws an arm across his face so that only his piercing, murderous eyes can be distinguished. He slithers in and out of shadowed doorways, dragging his twisted and useless leg. The only sounds are the intermittent dragging and scraping of his leg, followed by the tapping of his cane. The man fades from our view. Silence. A horrible, piteous scream. It rises and fades. Then there is a silence once more.

Okay, so I have an extremely overactive imagination; so everyone has to have something. This is my cross to bear. Actually, my scenario fits our present topic very well. The man is cloaked, and he uses his coat to cover his face. The cloak, therefore, is his disguise. At the very least, it serves to disguise his face—or, is he ugly as sin? For our purposes here, let's stay with the disguise concept. Furthermore, for all we know, the leg he drags behind him is not really malformed. So the pretense of a game leg only adds to his overall disguise. If that is true, then the cane he carries is only a prop which further legitimates his appearance. But we are forgetting the flash of steel. Was it the reflection of the moon on a dagger? Could it have only been a lock-picking jimmy?

If the cloak and dragging leg were only parts of an elaborate disguise, if the cane only served as a prop to substantiate the disguise, if the dagger is not a dagger but a door opening tool, what then? What then, for instance, was the scream?

Maybe, just maybe, what we really saw was a man, a husband disguised slightly overdramatically, sneaking up on his wife's rendezvous abode. Once there, he picked the lock to the front door and caught her "in the act." The scream was, therefore, genuine. You would scream too if you were caught, shall we say, sooo RAWLY.

For an investigator, a Cloak is comprised of the parts of a disguise necessary to achieve his goal. If he dresses up like a woman while not on the job, it is his preference and not our problem. Further, in order to substantiate or create a total effect for his disguise, the investigator may need to use a prop. Finally, the dagger may just be the key that turns the lock. Without it, all the wigs, shawls and wheelchairs may only get the investigator as far as the front door—the locked door.

Let me clarify further by defining a Cloak, a Prop and a Dagger.

A Cloak is a physical disguise. Included in this definition are wigs, makeup and clothing. (Why cloak? Cloak also means to conceal.)

A Prop is anything one uses to further support and legitimize the totality of the disguise. Props include both living beings and inanimate objects. The living beings could either be a person or an animal. The inanimate objects include such things as a cane, a doctor's bag, a briefcase, or a limousine. (Why is Prop not in the title? Because it doesn't sound right. Cloak, Prop and Dagger. See? It loses something in the translation.)

A Dagger is the instrument that authenticates the disguise and the corresponding prop. Daggers are fake identification. The identification includes business cards, I.D. cards, name tags and so forth. (Why Dagger? Well, you would feel pretty stabbed if you poured out your guts to an investigator who was only pretending to be on staff for Venereal Disease Control.)

While the possible combinations of disguises and props are infinite, there are only two purposes that render their use essential to the investigator: integration and impersonation.

Integration, in this context, is meant as an all-inclusive term for blending into one's surroundings. One would appear, out of place, at best, sitting in a park in an evening gown or dressed as a clown in a church. Furthermore, appearing obviously conspicuous would be profoundly detrimental to your case. In many instances, the ramifications could be irrevocable. If you blow your cover, or your presence is detected, your effectiveness is obsolete. But once you outright expose yourself and your spouse knows you are investigating him, then you might as well blow taps over your binoculars.

An analogy that best epitomizes integration is animal photography. If the photographer went into the bush dressed in orange coveralls and a purple hat, guess what pictures he would end up shooting. Nothing! Right! Why? Because all the animals would be holed up in their hiding places, laughing themselves sick. But if the same photographer wore camouflage clothes and built a viewing shelter known as a blind, he could take the kinds of pictures that made *National Geographic* world renowned.

Disguises and props allow the investigator to fit in—blend in—with the environment in which he is operating. Disguised as, say, a jogger, an investigator could jog around a particular neighborhood for hours. But if he just stood around, he would be flagrantly noticeable and therefore draw unwanted attention to himself.

The second essential purpose for which an investigator uses disguises and props is impersonation. A Cloak and a Prop and a Dagger are the tools the investigator uses in order to carry off a "part."

In the movie *Tootsie*, Dustin Hoffman played a man pretending to be a woman. He had to speak and walk like a woman and adopt feminine mannerisms. But once the actor made the internal adaptations necessary for his character, he still needed to make the external changes. Those changes included shaving his legs, plucking his eyebrows, and wearing false eyelashes and dentures. He also had to wear padding on his chest and rear end. Then he added a wig, makeup and female clothing. Frankly, I don't think the man got paid enough, no matter how much he got paid. Furthermore, I hope they kicked in a little something for his wife. I understand Dustin started his metamorphosis into a woman weeks before production began on the movie. Regardless, his transformation was complete and his character depiction was sensational.

Now, I am not suggesting that the husband/investigator should shave his legs, nor the wife/investigator learn how to belch and scratch. Rather, my assertion is, in order to become the part you are playing, you will need to make both internal and external changes. Those external changes are Cloaks, Props and Daggers.

I do not recommend that you attempt difficult disguises or obtain unnecessary documentation. Therefore, your watchwords are K.I.S.S.—Keep it Simple, Sally. The more complicated the disguise, the more cumbersome it will be to work within.

Cloak

WIGS

Wigs, for our purposes, include any false hair. We can then add hairpieces, women's wigs, sideburns, eyebrows and mustaches.

The use of wigs for the investigator is to change one's present appearance into the character being portrayed. It can not, therefore, be viewed as something that will necessarily flatter. While it is true that a woman with long blonde hair may look cute in a curly blonde wig or a clean shaven man may look so Elvis in sideburns, this is not your intended goal. Cute and Elvis will not assist you in your investigation. Instead, you need to CHANGE your appearance so that it is suited to the character that you are playing. Furthermore, if your investigation precipitates your presence in close proximity to your spouse, your disguise must be both believable and convincing.

Achieving a direct correlation between character and disguise requires common sense and the ability to always be cognizant of your K.I.S.S. watch words. Achieving an inconspicuous obscurity when in close proximity of your spouse is slightly more complicated. In order to achieve an obscurity, let's look at why and how you might arrest the attention of your spouse. Once you understand the motivating factor needed to get attention, you can work towards avoiding it. The motivating factor is perceptible stimuli. Perception is the process of meaningfully organizing sensation. Stimuli is any physical energy that has some effect on an organism and evokes a response. So to get someone's attention, one would need to send out stimulating energy —whether consciously or unconsciously—that is perceived by another person. Further, some stimuli are more intense than others. Those stimuli are brighter, louder, larger or repetitive. Motives also play a major role in directing attention. For instance, if you are hungry, you will notice restaurants and billboards picturing food with much greater alacrity than if you had just completed a six course meal.

Therefore, to avoid perception, never appear brighter or larger than your surroundings. Dress down. Never sound louder—actually being more quiet than your surroundings is always your preferred mode as an investigator. Finally, understand the motive that will arrest your spouse's perception is the FEAR of seeing you. So do NOT look like you. In other words, if you have long blonde hair, your wig of choice should be short and dark. If you are clean shaven, opt for a beard. As undiscernible as you are is as undetectable as you will be.

One last word on the subject of wigs. Be sure to secure the false hair properly. There is nothing as perceptible as a hanging mustache or red hair hanging out of a gray wig. There is nothing quite so funny, either.

MAKEUP

The makeup you choose should fit three bills. The first of this is applicability. The makeup should match both the character you are playing and the disguise you are wearing. The second bill to fill is staying within the confines of K.I.S.S.. Your investigation may call for you to play the part of a person thirty years or more your senior. However, attempting a theatrical transformation complete with synthetic wrinkles and age spots is unnecessary. The third bill you need to fill is one ever mindful of not causing your detection. So if you normally wear no makeup at all, now you will do so. Basically, subtle changes from your norm is the goal you need to attain in order to keep out of your spouse's perspective feelers' reach.

CLOTHES

When choosing your clothing while on the job, you will need to follow the same edicts prescribed in "Wigs" and "Makeup." However, there are two more recommendations to guide your choice of appropriate clothing. They are comfort and mobility. Your disguise may call for you to wear an evening gown, but if you choose one so tight you can not breathe, you will neither be comfortable nor will you be able to jump a fence should you be so compelled. Keep in mind, at all times, that you are on a case. The disguise may, in fact, afford you an entrance into an exclusive club. Once there, however, you may be forced to hide in the men's bathroom with your feet up on the seat. After sitting thus for two hours, you may then have to race to your car parked six blocks away so that you can tail your spouse. A dress that looks like it has been painted on will not work. You may laugh at my example, but I'll bet my bottom dollar Jessica didn't laugh because that is exactly what she had to do to catch her husband. It seems he had this bathroom fetish. (One man's candy is another's porcelain.)

The proper attire serves yet another purpose for the detective. That is, it sometimes negates the need for credentials. Let me give you some examples. Envision a person dressed in the clothes I will describe, and then note to yourself the associations you make:

1. A woman dressed in white pants, white smock shirt and white shoes
2. A man dressed in gray pants and a gray shirt
3. A man dressed in royal blue uniform pants, a matching blue shirt and black shoes
4. A woman dressed in surgical greens
5. A man or woman dressed in a business suit

What associations did you make?
1. A nurse, doctor's receptionist or a hospital staff employee?
2. A mechanic, factory worker or a delivery man?
3. A policeman or security guard?
4. A doctor or surgical nurse?
5. A business person?

There is an old saying "Clothes make the man," and they make the woman too.

We associate a mode of dress with a profession, period. The association is so strong that if we were in a hospital and we needed to ask a question, we would approach anyone in white. Therefore, clothes in their own right can create the persona you want to portray. But a simple white pants suit will only get you near the door. It is the Prop and the Dagger

How and Why Lovers Cheat

that will both support and authenticate the fabric. These we will discuss shortly.

I am duty bound to give you a few words of caution as they relate to clothes and impersonation. It is illegal to impersonate a policeperson. But understand this, if you do not say that you are a policeperson, nor do you wear a false badge or municipality insignia patch, nor attempt a police action such as forcible entry, then you are not impersonating a police person. Your badge may say investigator, your identification may say investigator, your clothes may appear to be an official uniform. If you are mistaken after identifying yourself as an investigator for a policeperson, then it is your good fortune and your suspect's blunder.

In that same vein, exercise good common sense when dressed as what might be associated with medical personnel. You would not want to carry your characterization to the point of being shuffled into the operating room or making a stab at CPR.

As a general rule, you are completely on the right side of the legal line if you do not say EXACTLY something that you are not: investigator rather than policeperson; connected with, rather than an actual employee of. One can be connected, however loosely, with any company by having walked by the building, having called on the phone, or simply living in the same area.

Props

There are simply too many inanimate props that you may incorporate into any one of your disguises to make a listing feasible. Furthermore, compiling such a listing is intellectually insulting. So instead, I have put together the following list to give you some ideas and incite your imagination into action. Be ever mindful that a prop both supports and legitimizes your disguise.

INANIMATE PROPS

Sunglasses
Camera
Pizza box
Purse
Handcuffs
Tool belt
Guitar
Stethoscope

I previously made reference to props that were also living beings. However, I neglected to elaborate fully on the rationale which validates their inclusion herein. I will now correct that oversight.

A living prop includes both human beings and animals. The acquisition of such a prop can be more beneficial than all the stethoscopes in the world. Contained in the following listing are some potential living props:

Real estate agent
Friend
Your child
Cat
Dog
Snake

It goes without saying that an animal can neither be a willing nor unwilling accomplice, having neither the freedom nor faculties for decision making. So you can simply put a leash on a dog and walk him through your subject's neighborhood at your discretion.

Human beings, however, do have the latitude of choice. Therefore, as a general rule, you will need to obtain their consent to be used as a prop. Once assured of their cooperation, you can proceed. A friend may be utilized as a compatriot in any number of covert excursions ranging from a feigned dinner escort to co-driver in a vehicular stake-out. Every Sherlock needs his Watson. A Boswell is so many entities to the detective. He is his look out, co-conspirator, sounding board and sympathetic friend.

Now since the rules were made to be broken, let's break the one I proposed in the previous paragraph. You CAN, in fact, orchestrate and manipulate an unsuspecting human prop unknowingly into your service. As a matter of fact, they could be the forerunner in the entire escapade without ever having been aware that the adventure took place.

Let me give you an example. Suppose the "other" man's house was for sale. Enlisting the help of a zealous real estate agent could allow you to look through his house, obtain an overview of his finances, become familiar with his work schedule and so much more. Who was your willing though obvious accomplice? The realtor! So another rule bites the dust.

Dagger

BUSINESS CARDS

A business card is a two-inch by three-inch marvel. It can be likened to those combination jack knives of yesteryear. You know the kind, the one which combines a jack knife, a cork screw, a bottle opener, nail file, fork and fish scaler all into one casing. These cards open locked doors, clear away obstructions, make barred paths accessible, pry out information and authenticate impersonations. Yes, folks, this handy dandy sensation—this eighth wonder of the world and phenomenon extraordinaire—can be yours for the asking. Unbelievable, you say! If you think that's unbelievable, wait until you hear the price. Now I know that any one of you would pay $100.00 for a miracle device like this. But thanks to modern printing, you, friend, can get not one, not ten, but 500 of these little babies for the low low price of about $20.00. Now, here's the bonus friends: you can purchase as many different kinds of these astonishing wonders as you desire. Sure, you can put any names on them you want. Custom orders, folks, nothing but the best. You could have it say, Joe Shmoe, from the Livingston Girdle Company, Incorporated. We will even throw in a nice picture of a girdle at a nominal fee. And to top it all off, you can put a phone number on it. Say you don't have a phone. Well, I'll tell ya, I know this fella down Frisco way, put a phone number of a telephone booth on his card. What a cut-up Scooter is. He had guys calling the number, thinking they were calling his office and the phone would just ring and ring. That Scooter, what a card! Get it? Card!!

But listen folks, there is just one small hitch in this thing and I gotta tell you about it so you don't wind up in the clink. Don't ever put a cop insignia or anything like that on these cards. Those coppers don't take kindly to it. Yes, it's real serious. But if you wanna be official like, you can have something like "Investigator" put on it; just don't get real specific about the where and for whom. Get it? Now my time is just about up and I see a copper mozying on over here. So, I'll just leave my card with you so you can ponder the whole thing over on your own.

A sample business card could contain a catchy business motto, company name, your "cover" name, under that your "cover" occupational title, your company phone number.

Optional might be a company logo or an identification card.

An identification card affords you the same benefits as a business card. It also allows you to appear completely legitimate and authentic. There are certain professions that are expected by the public to be able to show an I.D. Card. Some of these professions are insurance adjustor, investigator, real estate agent and security guard.

This card should include the type of agency or profession you are "connected" to, your "cover" name, your description, your position in that company, a phone number and your picture. To achieve an official effect, you could put your thumb print on the back of the card and you should have the card laminated. A printer can print the card for your "business." The correct information can then be typed on the appropriate lines. One can usually find a discount store that houses a photo booth; a small picture of yourself should be relatively easy to obtain. A thumb print can be made using an ink pad or, for that matter, a black marker. Then the card can be laminated. Most printers and stationary stores have laminating machines.

I.D. cards are usually kept in a wallet of its own. They are the type that open to show two sides. One side has a plastic window for the I.D. Card and the other side could be plain or it could have an area for a badge. These wallets and, as a matter of fact, some badges can be found at leather good stores and gun shops.

A sample identification card might contain your picture (glue it in place), the name of your agency (do not include address), your "cover" name and your description, your position, the telephone number, a thumb print (on the reverse side).

Note: This card should be the size of a credit card.

OTHER FORMS OF IDENTIFICATION

There are several other forms of identification that you can obtain. However, do not waste your time, energy, or money doing so unless your investigation clearly requires you to do so. Each of these other forms of I.D. can be purchased through your suppliers or through ads found in army-type magazines and celebrity tabloids. They are specifically to be used for entertainment purposes, according to the law of the land. Some of those I.D.s are included in the following list:

Birth certificate
High school diploma
Private detective license
Marriage certificate
College degree
Other licenses

C.Y.A. AND COVER STORIES

To tie your Cloaks, Props and Daggers up with a bow, you need two more elements. Those elements are C.Y.A.—which means "cover your a . ."—and Cover Stories.

In order to C.Y.A., you will need to have a good excuse ready if you ever get caught in a compromising predicament. Early on in this narrative, we discussed a detective's need to always be prepared; preparation includes a good, viable cover story—a good excuse. It must be one that is well thought out and delivered with the appropriate emotion.

Cover stories include not only excuses to extract you from a bad situation, but are also the verbal premise of your impersonation. In an effort to better explain cover story excuses and cover stories, I have devised the following game. I call it Cover Stories. Catchy title!?!

Cover Stories

PART ONE: EXCUSES

I will give you a bad predicament and a few possible excuses from which to choose. You then choose the excuse you feel would best extradite you from the situation. Each answer is worth points. Once you have completed the game in Part One, add up your points and refer to the score evaluation to find out how you did.

Hi, tell us your name and a little about yourself.

Okay, are you ready to play Cover Stories? (applause . . . applause . . . applause . . .)

Predicament Number One

You are caught by the police rummaging through the alleged mistress' car. Do you . . .

A. Pour your heart out and tell him the whole sordid story?

B. Tell him you thought it was your car?

C. Tell him you are on drugs and you don't know what you are doing?

D. Tell him to bug off and mind his own business?

E. Tell him you were turning off the lights?

Predicament Number Two

You are caught by a hotel maid under a bed. Do you . . .

A. Tell her you are the Dust Bunny Vice Squad?

B. Say nothing?

C. Ask her to help you find your lost earring?

Predicament Number Three

Your wife spies you in her lover's neighborhood, but your case is not yet complete. Do you . . .

A. Confront her with evidence you have so far and hope for a confession?

B. Drive away at top speed?

C. Say nothing?

D. Run her over?

Predicament Number Four

Your wife's secretary catches you going through your wife's desk. Do you . . .

A. Confide in her and request her help?

B. Tap dance?

C. Tell her you were looking for something?

POINTS FOR PART ONE

Predicament Number One: Scores

A. 2 It might work but the chances are remote.

B. 2 It's original.

C. -5 You are nuts.

D. -5 You are going to jail.

E. 10 There are Good Samaritan laws that allow a person to enter another person's car to help out by turning out the lights.

Predicament Number Two: Scores

A. 2 Well, you are dumb but unique.

B. 5 Most people don't want to get involved, she may say nothing also and walk away.

C. 10 It is best in this situation to come up with a good reason to be there.

Predicament Number Three: Scores

A. 2 Probably wouldn't work; never confront your spouse until you are ready with conclusive evidence. If you can not prove it and they deny it, you're sunk.

B. -5 This is the best way to draw attention to yourself.

C. 10 This would be the best approach; don't say anything at all.

D. -10 You are going to jail and your car is going to be bloody.

Predicament Number Four: Scores

A. -5 This is not a good idea. Your wife signs this woman's paycheck.

B. 2 Original!?!

C. 10 This is the best approach. You can figure out what you were looking for later.

PART TWO: COVER STORIES

In Part Two of our game, I will give you a description of a disguise. Then I will give you a few possible cover stories. You choose the story that best fits the disguise and will accomplish the uncovering of the truth. Tally up your points for both Part One and Part Two. Then refer to the overall score evaluation to see what type of detective you really are.

Disguise Number One

A woman is dressed in a business suit carrying a briefcase. Her business card and I.D. card identifies her as an insurance adjustor. She knocks on the alleged mistress' door. Her premise is . . .

A. Hi, I'm Freda Horseinfeffer. I'm connected with ABC Mutual Life Insurance Company. I stopped by today to see if your cat is insured fully against dog collision. Do you mind if I step in to discuss it?

B. Hi, I'm Freda Horseinfeffer with ABC Mutual Life posing as an insurance adjustor so that I can find out if you are having an affair with my husband. Mind if I come in? I hope your insurance is paid up, Bimbo!

C. Hi, I'm Freda Horseinfeffer. I'm an insurance adjustor with ABC Mutual Life Insurance Company. We are investigating a hit and run accident. Mr. (her husband's name) has been identified as the driver of the car. He claims he was in your company at the time. I would like to discuss this matter with you and possibly get a statement from you. The matter is somewhat urgent as charges may be filed based on your testimony. Do you mind if I come in to discuss it?

Disguise Number Two

A man is dressed in surgical greens. He is wearing a hospital name badge. He enters the Doctors' Lounge. He walks up to the doctor who is allegedly having an affair with his wife, a gift shop employee. His premise is . . .

A. Hi, I'm Doctor Grant. How are you doing? Oh great, coffee! (Chit-chat.) Hey, who is that cute number in the gift shop? Oh, I'm sorry, you are Doctor Kirby. Someone said she goes out with you. Is that true?

B. Hi, I'm Doctor Grant. I've come here to consult on a special case. Seems a patient has contracted the dreaded Asdfghjwertyxcgitebism Syndrome. Yep, so they called me in. Best man in the country when it comes to stubborn cases of this syndrome. Say, who's the babe in the gift shop? Is she a friend of yours?

Disguise Number Three

A woman is dressed in a waitress uniform. She is recently employed at the same restaurant where the mistress is working. She begins a conversation with the mistress. Her premise is . . .

A. Hi, I'm Roxanne. I just started today. Gosh, I have a headache. Do you have some aspirins? Wouldn't you just know it, my first day on the job and I get my period, run out of gas while driving here and manage to have a huge fight with my boyfriend. (Uses same first name as your husband's and very similar last name. For example, instead of Jeff Berg, you may say Jeff Derg.)

B. Hi, I'm Roxanne. I just started today. What's your name? (Chit-chat on and off throughout the day.) Say listen, I'm new in the area and I've only met a few people. Tomorrow is my birthday and I thought I'd have a couple of people over for a party. Why don't you come and bring your boyfriend. What did you say his last name was?

POINTS FOR PART TWO

Disguise Number One: Scores

A. 2 Is that special! An unbelievable story is just that, UNBELIEVABLE! Although she had me until she mentioned dog collision. Everybody knows they only offer liability.

B. -10 Never reveal yourself or blow your cover.

C. 10 This story is true. The names have been changed to protect the innocent spouse. But "Freda" really did confront the mistress with this cover story. The mistress not only asked her in, wrote out and signed a statement swearing that Freda's husband had spent the night with her, but also invited Freda for lunch.

Disguise Number Two: Scores

A. 10 This story is also true. Once again the names were changed to protect the innocent spouse. The doctor not only spilled his macho guts about the cute little number he was seeing, but became graphic in his telling of the details. "Dr. Grant" lost his temper and, very shortly thereafter, it was "Dr. Kirby" who was in need of medical assistance. Men do that sort of thing. Women, on the other hand, usually just scream and pull hair. Femininity has its price.

B. -10 Never speak to a professional and try to buffalo them with contrived terms. They will spot you as a phony in a second. Furthermore, everyone knows that Asdfhjhrkyhfcybyrwqism is a tropical island in the South Pacific.

Disguise Number Three: Scores

A. 10 This story is true. A wife took a job at the same restaurant where the mistress was employed. After the aforementioned conversation took place, the wife dropped a name so similar to her husband's that her husband's mistress, her co-worker, requested that she repeat the name. The conversation ended with the women laughing over their respective boyfriends having such similar names. Roxanne's husband did not laugh, however, when she divorced him.

B. 10 This story is also true. Both of these premises are excellent. The twist in this particular case is that Roxanne number two was not satisfied with just confirming that the mistress was seeing her husband. She actually went so far as to invite them to a "party" using a girlfriend's address. When they arrived, the birthday party turned into a surprise party, complete with pictures. Boy, were they surprised!

SCORE EVALUATION

70 to 65—Sherlock. Either I'm a good teacher or you are a good student. This score puts you at the top of the class.

65 to 40—Dupin. This is a very good score. You may want to read this chapter again to further fine-tune your understanding.

40 to 20—Spillane. Okay, go back to Chapter One and read slowly.

20 to -25—Clouseau. Call me, we'll have lunch.

Note: Cloaks and Props need not be expensive. Do not go out and spend a lot of money; rummage, instead, through your own and friends' closets or your local resale shops.

CHAPTER TWELVE

SURVEILLANCE AND TAILING

It is a well-known fact that the dashboard has become, in our society, a prominent platform upon which to display one's affiliations and sense of humor. Examples of this can be seen on any street, country road or six-lane highway. Further, those objects propitious enough to be displayed are equally diverse: statues of the Virgin Mary, dogs whose heads bob up and down, the American flag and stick-on Garfield dolls are but a few examples. Though personal taste dictates the ultimate selection of the item chosen, I think we all can agree that the dashboard is an exalted and coveted place; the fortuitous opportunity of an auspicious placement thereupon is an unsurpassed honor—THE supreme compliment. Where am I going with all of this? What is my point? Well, I will tell you. You have been chosen—singled out as it were—to sit on this illustrious tier.

So, climb up, fold your legs and sit on my dashboard while we follow Elliot conducting a vehicular and foot surveillance and tail of his wife, Kelly.

Elliot has enlisted the help of his brother Duncan; Elliot will be in one car and his brother in another car. We will be following both of them. We will neither hamper nor assist them in any way; our role is that of an observer. As we have the good fortune to be riding in a futuristic car, we will be both driving on the street and flying in the air. I will interject my observations and criticisms as we proceed. Hopefully, these will assist your understanding of correct procedure.

I will use this time, while Elliot and Duncan are busy

preparing to embark on this phase of the investigation, to acquaint you with the facts of the case.

Elliot and Kelly have been married for eighteen years. Elliot is a concrete finisher for a large construction firm. Kelly operates a small cosmetics business in her spare time. She is also a full time homemaker and mother. They live in the suburbs with their four children, and have all the trappings of the typical suburban family: mortgage, mini-van, dog, weed whacker, PTA membership card, family doctor, bikes in the driveway and, of course, bills, lots and lots of bills.

For the first few years of their marriage, Kelly devoted herself exclusively to their home and children. As the children grew, so did their financial obligations. Kelly took on a part time job selling cosmetics to supplement their already strained budget and assumed responsibility for the monetary management of the family funds; these actions resulting in a substantial increase in the family's resources and Elliot's disassocition from the family's financial concerns.

As the children grew older and needed her less, Kelly spent more of her time expanding her business. She booked more parties, both in the daytime and evening. Although she was gone quite a bit, Elliot accepted her personal and business maturation, complacently. He felt their life to be good and happy.

Then one day all that changed. Elliot came across, quite accidentally, Kelly's business address book. As he glanced through it, he was amazed to find it filled with codes—at least, it appeared coded. Throughout the book, there was a series of figures followed by numbers. Although the code itself seemed innocent enough, something sounded inside Elliot; it was as though a shot rang out in the silent night. Since he could not shake his sense of foreboding, he decided to question Kelly about the address book. His suspicions rose dramatically when he confronted her with the book; she went completely white and grabbed it out of his hands. Later, she tried to glaze the whole incident over, explaining that she had been tired and had therefore overreacted. However, it was this overreaction that had aroused Elliot's suspicions, far more than the address book. So it was from that day on, with his inner voice spurring him forward, that Elliot embarked on the single most hell-raising task of his life: an investigation to discover what was behind that little black book. He vowed to stop if ever the trail he was following went cold. It didn't;

How and Why Lovers Cheat

every clue he chased down brought him yet another, and on he went.

He had begun by discovering where Kelly now kept the address book. After their initial confrontation, he never again saw it in her briefcase. It was several days before he was able to discover it's hiding place under the spare tire in her trunk. He then set out to break it's code. Since both he and Kelly were Sherlock Holmes buffs, his mind naturally turned to Sir Aruthur Conan Doyle's stories. Recalling that Sherlock had once been depicted by Doyle facing a similar decoding dilemma, he referred to that chronicle. Perusing "The Adventure of the Dancing Men," Elliot decided to attempt to use the same code breaking logic Sherlock had applied.

In the story, Sherlock endeavored to decipher a code which consisted of figures that appeared, at first glance, to be dancing men. Actually, the figures were stick men each made unique by the manner in which their arms and legs had been positioned. Additionally, some of the stick men held small flags in their hands. When these figures were placed in a line, they appeared to dance across the page; therefore, Holmes' client, Mr. Hilton Cubitt, referred to them as "dancing men."

HOW Sherlock broke the code was of extreme interest to Elliot. Once Sherlock had recognized · that each figure represented a letter, he was able to apply the rules that guide all forms of secret writings: the most frequently used figure is probably, the most frequently used letter. This letter is "E," so Sherlock subsituted an "E," the figure most frequently used. Now, roughly speaking, the order of frequency in which letters will occur in the English language is E, T, A, O, I, N, S, R, and D; T, A, O, and I are, however, nearly equal in frequency of use. Therefore, using all four letters and trial-and-error, Holmes was able to form words. Further, flagged figures were then determined to represent periods; the result was the formation of sentences and ultimately, deciphering the code. However, having deciphered the code and having understood the messages, Holmes was unable to forestall providence.

As Elliot reread "The Adventure of the Dancing Men" it occurred to him that if he were smart enough to use Sherlock's theory to break the code, Kelly may have been smart enough to use it to invent her code. Feeling sure he was correct, he set to work, staying within the confines of Sherlock's method for deciphering codes. His first order of business was to make an exact copy of all of the codes in

Kelly's little black book. He then replaced the figures with letters. Words began to form. After several hours, Elliot rose a triumphant but sadder man.

Using the broken code and the culmination of all of the clues he had uncovered, Elliot carefully prepared for the day upon which he would commence his surveillance. After recruiting the assistance of Duncan, he rented two four-door sedans, one blue and the other brown. These cars were chosen purposefully as both this car type and the colors selected are purported to be the least immediately identifiable and therefore most easy to obscure. Each car was equipped with a citizen band radio, a street guide map book, a thermos, a cooler, a tape recorder, binoculars, a 35mm camera with a telephoto lens, walkie-talkies, a flashlight and a video camera. Elliot packed two small duffle bags, placing in each a pair of sunglasses, two types of hats, a sweater, a jacket, a leash, a couple of different business cards and corresponding I.D. cards. In addition, he placed a self sticking mustache, a brunette toupee, a screwdriver and a special amplifier—with a range capability of approximately two hundred feet—in his own bag.

Prior to the designated surveillance day, and with all of these tools of the trade in place, Elliot scheduled a meeting with his brother. They went over the finer points of the case: their attack plan, goals, "cover" names, excuses and stories, disguises, and rendezvous point in case of separation. They selected safe CB channels to use, with the accompanying code to switch channels, should such become necessary. They then conducted a final equipment check with each item in its place and in good working order. Additionally, each battery powered tool was checked for new batteries, and both 35mm and video cameras were loaded with film and a reserve film supply established. Finally they reviewed any legal issues germane. Having concluded their joint preparations, they departed with a silent handshake, each holding his own personal thoughts firmly in check.

Driving home, Elliot felt his emotions welling up inside; his eyes became clouded and misty, objects slipped by as though floating through the sky. Realizing he was no longer in control, he pulled over and gave himself a good talking to. He mentally went over the decisions he had made, affirming to himself, once again, his desire and willingness to live with the end results of his investigation. He reviewed his short- and long-term goals in the light of the investigation's possibly unpleasant outcome, and resolved to forestall any further emotional involvement in the case. Success was dependent upon his ability to disassociate himself from fear, anger, sadness, rage and grief. As of tomorrow, he was no longer a husband; he would become a detective. Focused and steady in his mind, Elliot eased into traffic and headed home.

Elliot and Duncan are just about ready to leave, but before they do so, let me give you a few definitions to familiarize you with surveillance vernacular.

Surveillance: Close observation of one under suspicion.

Tailing: To follow.

Stationary Surveillance: Close observation while remaining in one location.

Mobile Surveillance: Close observation while on the move. This is subdivided into vehicular (car) and foot conveyance.

I believe Elliot and Duncan are ready, so if you would be so kind as to resume your dashboard position, we can begin.

Following Elliot and Duncan's good example I have, as you can see, similarly outfitted us with all of the tools of the trade. Further, I have filled our thermos with hot coffee and stocked our cooler with goodies.

Until the mobile surveillance actually begins we will hover over Elliot's neighborhood, just high enough to take in a few surrounding blocks of his house. Since Kelly's codes did not reveal the "when," Elliot has decided to start early and stay with the surveillance for the duration.

8:00 a.m.

Elliot leaves his house in his black Bronco. He heads west on Bedford Lane for one block and then turns north on Jones Avenue for three blocks. Pulling over, Elliot puts on his mustache, toupee, a Dodgers hat and a navy jacket.

Slipping back into traffic, he heads toward a nearby apartment complex. He parks near a brown sedan. Duncan is in the driver's seat, to his left is the blue sedan Elliot will be using.

Duncan motions Elliot over. "Man, oh man, I never would have recognized you. You look ten years younger. Hey, did you remember to punch a hole through her tail light last night?"

Nodding, Elliot walks up to Duncan's window. "Listen, let's do a radio check. Now, remember we will start on channel two and skip up or down two channels if there is too much interference to hear each other clearly. The code word for up two channels is Jump and the code word for down is Skip. Got it?" he asks, glancing at Duncan. Receiving an affirmative, he continues, "Okay, let's take up our positions." Starting to turn away, Elliot abruptly stops and, leaning once again on the window, he says seriously, "Thanks, Duncan, I can always count on you."

"You know it, Bro!" Duncan bellows, gesturing for a high five.

The brothers slap hands, Elliot begins to enter his sedan, then halts once again. "Duncan, you remembered to fill the tanks up, didn't you?"

"Are you kidding me! Gosh, I wish I could be calm like you," he muses as he passes by heading for the parking lot exit.

8:35 a.m.

Elliot takes up his position in the Baker Square Restaurant parking lot at the corner of Jones Road and Higgins Road. Duncan takes his position on Bedford in the driveway of a neighbor known to have already left for the day. He backs into the driveway so he can easily maneuver the car in either direction. The house is located several doors east of Elliot's home.

The brothers have made the calculated risk that Kelly will head toward Higgins Road; it is the closest main thoroughfare. If she acts accordingly Elliot will be able to ease into the chase; if she does not, it will be up to Duncan alone to keep Kelly under mobile surveillance until Elliot catches up to them.

The men must be sure to stay in constant communication and to speak calmly and clearly at all times.

Furthermore, since Duncan is both known to the subject and is out in the open, he must take special care not to be detected. This is the single most crucial phase of the tail. If Duncan can begin the tail totally unobserved and without arousing Kelly's suspicions in any way, he will have soared over the first and most vital hurtle. (Affixing a mirror on the interior of the car and pointing it in the direction of the subject's home provides the investigator with an excellent view while keeping out of sight.)

10:47 a.m.

Walking out of her home dressed both elegantly and demurely provocative, Kelly departs in her mini-van and heads west on Bedford. Duncan informs Elliot that the bird has flown the coop and details her progress over the CB. He allows her to get to almost the end of the block before he pulls out of the driveway in pursuit.

Never follow your subject closely on a side road; make sure you

How and Why Lovers Cheat

give a respectable distance between your car and that which you are tailing. If for any reason, you attract your subject's attention on a side road, and you are again spotted a couple of blocks later, your subject will, consciously or unconsciously, be on the alert.

Kelly drives north on Jones towards Higgins. Reaching the intersection of Jones and Higgins, she turns west; Duncan stays within a few cars lengths of her. After both she and Duncan pass, Elliot joins the chase. He, however, drives one block further north of Higgins to Salem. There he turns west, pacing himself with Duncan's radioed reports of Kelly's location.

Duncan—the lead car driver—must try to make every light Kelly does. Further, he must do so without drawing attention to himself. —in a manner that is neither noticeably erratic nor illegal.

Elliot is driving parallel to them; he may be in a position to head up the tail should Kelly suddenly turn in his direction.

11:01 a.m.

Noting to Elliot that Kelly has turned on her left turn signal, Duncan slides his car over accordingly. As Kelly actually makes the turn heading south on Roselle Road, the light changes to red. Duncan stops for the light and watches as Elliot, having turned pursuant to instructions and now traveling south on Roselle, shoots through the green light several cars behind Kelly. Easily spotting her van, Elliot jockeys to close the gap between them. He informs Duncan of his whereabouts and, one car length behind her, pulls over to the turning lane of the apartment complex she is entering.

Duncan was correct to have stopped for the red light as blowing a red light renders one most noticeable. In addition, Duncan knew, via the CB, that Elliot was in position to pick up the tail, and a detained, ticketed, arrested or dead comrade is of no use.

Kelly's car was easily identifiable because Elliot puched her tail light out; therefore it shined like a beacon each time she braked.

A spouse, even a well disguised one, should not unnecessarily get too close. Elliot should have gone a few driveways ahead and turned in. Do not take foolish chances!

Elliot parks some distance from Kelly and watches as she leaves her vehicle. In his peripheral vision, he sees Duncan also entering the complex. Speaking quietly into the CB, he instructs Duncan to follow her inside with a concealed video camera and a walkie-talkie. Kelly strolls inside confidently and pushes a buzzer. Her ring is answered immediatley and she walks through the inner doors.

Let's set our car/plane down and follow the foot tail.

Duncan is able to grab the essential equipment fast enough, but encounters some difficulty gaining entrance to the building. Finally, he leans on every buzzer until he gains admittance. He is able to reach the elevator as its overhead light shines, indicating a stop on the sixth floor. Waiting for the elevator to return, Duncan is delayed in reaching the sixth floor. When he finally does so, the hallway is deserted. Spying the stairway door, he noiselessly crosses to it.

Once behind the closed door of the stairway, Duncan cautiously informs Elliot of his location and progress via walkie-talkie. He is told to use the pinhole lens on the video camera. Sadly, Duncan informs his brother that the lens was left behind in his car; Elliot must bring it to him so as not to forfeit the stationary surveillance. Duncan lowers the walkie-talkie's volume control so that Elliot's oaths are barely audible.

Duncan's inability to ascertain Kelly's exact location is readily understandable; following an elevator on foot is impossible, and he acted wisely under the circumstances.

However, his absentmindedness is condemnable; simply put: "Do not forget your equipment!"

The pinhole lens makes more sense in this case; a standard lens would require a half open stairway door and, most revealingly, Duncan's exposure. A pinhole lens allows Duncan to remain concealed and the door to be only cracked open an inch or two. (We will be discussing video cameras and the pinhole lens in the next chapter, which is "Advanced Tools of the Trade.")

11:22 a.m.

Elliot has returned to his car and Duncan has the proper lens in place. The camera is on but the tape has not yet been activated.

12:55

Kelly appears, exiting an apartment. Duncan starts the tape. She is followed partially out of the door by a man. There they linger a moment, locked in a kiss. The man withdraws and shuts the door while Kelly heads for the elevator. Once the elevator doors close, Duncan informs Elliot of her recent activity and descent. Elliot asks for the man's description and makes a verbal note into his tape recorder: 12:57 p.m. BOOTS 100.

We will continue in the car at gound level for a change in scenery.

1:06 p.m.

Kelly leaves the complex heading north on Higgins, followed by Elliot and Duncan. Afraid of a possible detection,

Elliot asks Duncan to pass him and take the lead, the lights favoring him, Duncan is able to comply. They continue on Higgins with Elliot now lagging behind. Turning east on Golf Road, Kelly, unbeknowst to her, leads her entourage to an equally fashionable and expensive restaurant.

1:29 p.m.

She parks and enters. Elliot and Duncan wait impatiently a few moments and then dispense with the baseball hats. Donning sunglasses and sweaters, the cohorts also enter. Elliot heads for the men's room while Duncan asks to be seated and searches for Kelly. After spotting her, he requests a table several feet behind her. Elliot joins him with his duffle bag. He nonchalantly places the bag on the table. In this position, only Duncan can see the video camera's lens protruding from the bag. Duncan then focuses the camera on Kelly and her companion. Elliot and Duncan place their order, remaining silent with one another so as not to alert Kelly of their presence. Picking at their food, they await developments. Suddenly, Duncan looks at Elliot and, bewildered, whispers, "She is gone! Elliot, Kelly is gone! I saw her drop her napkin and bend over. I looked down, took a bite of my steak and when I looked back up, she was gone. What should I do? Oh wait! Oh my God, I see her! Don't look Elliot! Don't, what ever you do, turn around!"

Duncan looks down once again at his food and is silent. After a while he motions to Elliot to leave. Once he is gone, Duncan grabs the duffle bag, picks up the check, pays it and joins his brother outside. Over the walkie-talkie, speaking from their respective cars, Duncan describes the scene he has witnessed. Elliot makes another verbal note into his tape recorder:

2:37 p.m. EATERY 200.

2:54 p.m.

Kelly leaves the restaurant unescorted, gets into her van and heads north on Golf Road. Elliot takes the lead and Duncan is running parallel to them on the side street. By now the men have skipped and/or jumped all over the CB channels. While speaking on channel 10, a husky voice breaks in on their conversation: "Hey, what are you guys, cops or something? What game are you playing? I want to play too!" Desperately, Elliot tries to make Duncan understand that the gap between himself and Kelly is widening, but he can not shout over this idiot's insensate prattle. A car suddenly pulls out in front of him. He breaks; tires screech.

Surveillance and Tailing

The car in front of him swerves one way, he swerves the other. Just as he is about to let a sigh of relief escape, the scene in his rearview mirror causes him to hold his breath. The car behind him, desperately struggling for control, is bearing down on him. He feels as though he is watching a small-screen movie in which he is the next victim. He braces himself for the sickening crash. Closing his eyes, he waits; miraculously, it doesn't come. Peeping through slitted eyelids, he dares to look again in his mirror: The car had stopped inches from his back bumper.

Grateful to be in one piece, Elliot's mind returns to the matter at hand. Despondently, Elliot scans the sea of tail lights ahead of him but is unable to spot Kelly. He grabs his CB screaming, "Jump, Duncan, jump!"

It is to be expected, when working with an open citizen band radio frequency, that your conversation will be overheard. Furthermore, since any citizen can own a CB, you may just get a nut who has nothing better to do than hassle you. Although this can be frustrating, do not overreact; doing so will only make matters worse. To eliminate dealing with "good buddies" on an open channel, you may want to rent some two-way radios.

Additionally, losing someone due to a small mishap is part of the game. Learn to live with it. Keep two things in mind if you do lose your subject: it is better to let someone get away than be carried away, and as long as you did not blow your cover, you can start anew another day.

Switching to channel 12, Elliot hears his brother's voice, "Elliot can you hear me? What's going on? Can you hear me? Where are you? Are you okay? Answer me!"

"I'm okay!" Elliot shouts, "But some nut almost killed me, and that idiot wouldn't shut up; so, I didn't hear a word you said before. And Duncan, I lost her!"

"Listen, I'm at Pine Road and Woodfield Road. Where are you?"

Pausing to look around for a street sign, Elliot finally answers, "Golf and Center Road. That is about one mile south of you."

You must try to stay calm.

"Now I know she didn't cross my path, so we can pretty safely rule out her having turned east. She hasn't acted like she was suspicious at all today; chances are she didn't go south, but either turned off somewhere to the west or is still heading north. I place my bet on north; what do you think?" Duncan ventures.

"This isn't a damn poker game, Duncan; this is my life! You want me to play hunches?" Elliot shouts.

"Hey, calm down, Bro. I know this is your life but I also know we don't have any other choice except to play the hunches sometimes. Besides, who is it that always takes your money in poker?"

"Okay, we go north. Swing over to Golf and head north of Woodfield Road. Check out all the parking lots and driveways. I'll do the same between here and Woodfield and then double-check your path."

"Good plan!" Duncan teases.

Always play your hunches. Your inner voice more often makes more sense than your outer one.

3:39 p.m.

Each drives slowly, searching every lot and byway on both sides of the street for twenty minutes. They join up again near Woodfield Road and Golf in the Zayre parking lot. Each man gets out of his car. After standing together quietly for awhile, Elliot says in a rush, "I got a hunch; there is a forest preserve a couple blocks west of here off Meacham, and one of the codes might just fit it perfectly. Let's try it."

"We've got nothing to lose. I'll follow you," Duncan answers, trying to sound hopeful.

3:46 p.m.

Elliot drives slowly by the entrance. The entrance road curves this way and that, so he can not see into the park very well. Both men drive across the street and park their cars. They walk back to the narrow asphalt road. Staying as close to the tree line as possible, they proceed, each carrying their tools of the trade in a duffle bag.

Well, it looks like we have to take a walk.

Turning the last curve, they can see her van and a big black limousine. They both stumble into some nearby bushes. Duncan mans the video camera while Elliot mans the amplifier. Elliot has connected the amplifier, thus creating a feed directly into the video camera's audio track. While the picture of the long black car with dark windows remain unchanged, the sounds coming from the partially lowered window fluctuate dramatically. Coming in too clearly for Elliot's taste, he withdraws after only a few seconds and slowly walks back to his car, leaving his brother to complete this task.

Do not attempt to handle more than you can stomach; if possible try to be kind to yourself.

As the voices from within murmur farewells, Duncan moves backwards, pausing only to get a clear shot of Kelly as she emerges from the limo. This accomplished, he turns and runs back to his car.

Duncan shoots a questioning glance at Elliot. Although he appears composed, his brother's face is ashen. Hoarsely he mumbles, "I am in it till the end."

After a few moments, Elliot switches on his tape recorder and notes: 5:01 p.m. PARKER 350.

5:09 p.m.

Kelly emerges with eastbound traffic, followed by her shadows. She creeps along. Eventually, she turns north on Golf Road and heads toward Algonquin Road. Duncan, in the tail car, stays close; Elliot is nearly a block ahead of her. As Elliot can see Kelly's turn signal flashing, he continues north on Golf one block and then turns east on the next side street. He cuts back over to Algonquin and again spies her in his rearview mirror. Although unable to see him, Elliot knows, via the radio, that Duncan is about six cars behind Kelly. Nearly three miles down Algonquin Road, Kelly slows her pace and turns into a large hotel's parking lot. Elliot and Duncan do the same. They watch through their binoculars as she exits her van and walks into the hotel's lobby. They watch as she stops at the reception desk and asks a question. Nodding, she walks to the elevator.

Keeping a subject under mobile observation while in front of them is a common tactic used by law enforcement personnel. This tactic, used in conjuction with a tail behind the subject, creates a controlled sphere of surveillance. A guilty subject may check the cars behind them for a tail; few, however, are astute enough to check for a forward tail.

Once the elevator doors close, both men enter the hotel lobby. Duncan heads for the cigarette machine while Elliot walks briskly to the desk.

"Hi, my wife must have just come in. We are visiting some friends of hers who are staying here. My wife is blonde, pretty and is wearing a red satin dress. She must have gone to her friend's room without me. I can't remember their room number. What is it?"

"Yes, your wife just went up. Room 305," the clerk answers.

Elliot heads for the elevator, followed momentarily by Duncan. Stepping into the elevator, they ascend to the third floor.

"So what do we do?" Duncan asks.

"I was hoping you had another hunch or idea," Elliot wryly answers.

"Sorry, fresh out. So what do we do?"

"Gimme a minute, will you? I'll think of something," Elliot says, while standing very still with his eyes riveted to the carpet.

"This is stupid. The maid is standing over there staring at us like we are two perverts," Duncan whispers nervously.

"That's it!" Elliot excitedly gasps.

"What? We act like perverts?"

"No, the maid, the maid!"

"What, the maid is a pervert?"

"Shut up and follow me," Elliot orders.

Duncan follows behind Elliot, feigning subservience. They walk up to the maid. Duncan, hanging back, is only able to catch a word or two of the whispered conversation between Elliot and the maid. He sees money pass between the two. Reaching into his duffle bag, Elliot hands her the video camera after turning it on. She stuffs the camera into the laundry bag hanging from her cart. Stepping closer, Duncan hears Elliot promise her a hundred dollars more when the job is done. Walking swiftly to the stairway with Duncan at his heels, the brothers take their position behind the door.

Knocking on the door of Room 305, the maid is admitted. After pulling in her cart, she shuts the door. Several minutes pass; she once again emerges, shutting the door behind her. Giving them the thumbs-up sign, she goes on her way.

"Okay, let me in on it. What's the scoop?" Duncan asks.

"Well, it is fairly self-explanatory. Elliot talks to maid. Maid takes Elliot's life savings. Maid plants video camera wherever she can, first creating a disturbance to distract them. Maid will retrieve the camera, if they don't discover it first, after they leave. Elliot will give maid more money. Maid will give Elliot camera. Elliot will be unable to pay for his kids' college tuition. Got it?"

"No, I lost you after Elliot talks to maid."

Elliot glares at Duncan.

"So, shoot me. I was trying to lighten things up a bit," Duncan offers.

"You must be a barrel of laughs at funerals!" Elliot retorts.

Silence then permeates the air.

After almost half an hour, Elliot says quietly, "Sorry."

"Me, too," Duncan whispers.

Surveillance and Tailing

Kelly leaves the hotel room and heads toward the elevator. Duncan begins to descend the stairs in pursuit, but Elliot grabbing his sleeve, says, "Let her go, it is over. She told me this morning she would be working all day and she would be home by eight. One thing about Kelly, she is always home when she ways she will be. Let her go."

A few moments later, a middle-aged couple emerge from the room, smiling. They too head straight for the elevator. Ten minutes pass. The maid reappears, enters the room, retrieves the camera and brings it to Elliot. Once again, he fills her hand with bills.

Elliot took a big chance in paying the maid before she completed the service he requested. Furthermore, he took a even bigger chance when he paid her the other half of her reward; she could have simply left the camera in the wastepaper basket the whole time.

The brothers silently walk to their cars. They drive without speaking to each other to the car rental firm. Before exiting his car, Elliot makes one more verbal notation on his tape recorder: 7:18 p.m. DEUCE 400.

Riding together to retrieve Elliot's car, Duncan asks carefully, "What now? The kids are at our house; are you going to confront her tonight?"

"Yes."

"Should I stick around for moral support?"

"No."

They drive the rest of the way in silence. At last, pulling into the parking lot next to Elliot's car, Duncan stops and starts to speak to his brother; he decides against it, watching Elliot drag his weary body from the passenger seat. The day's events have finally hit Elliot. Duncan understands this. Although he wants to comfort and console his brother, he knows this is not the right time. Elliot has to be left alone. So without speaking, Duncan helps collect all of the tools of the trade from the car and stow them in Elliot's trunk. This accomplished, the brothers drive away in separate directions.

We will stay with Elliot.

Removing only the video tape and his tape rocorder from the car, Elliot enters his house.

"Kelly, would you please come into the family room? I want to show you something," he yells.

"What is it, dear?" she asks sweetly, entering the room.

"A movie. Please watch it with me. I want to know what you think and feel about it," he answers, popping the tape into the VCR. He rewinds it, presses play and then joins her on the couch.

The blank screen changes instantly to a hallway, occupied by two people: a man wearing a Stetson, a towel and cowboy boots, and a woman, Kelly. They are intertwined, locked in a deep, passionate kiss.

Kelly, watching the screen, puts her hand to her mouth. Shaking her head from side to side, she slowly rises. Elliot catches her by her arm firmly and pulls her back down on to the couch.

Without looking at her, he snarls, between clenched teeth, "You WILL watch this movie with me! You will NOT move until it is over!"

The couple on the screen disengage; the man disappearing into the doorway, Kelly walking down the hallway to the elevator.

Elliot stops the tape using the remote control. Picking up his tape recorder, he rewinds the tape back to the beginning. When the tape stops, he depresses the play button. His own voice is heard, "12:57 p.m. BOOTS 100." He stops the tape.

Kelly stares at him, unbelieving. He has just spoken this man's code name. She falls back against the cushions, thunderstruck.

Elliot restarts the video tape. The blank screen changes to a restaurant's interior. An older, well-dressed man is seen sitting with a woman in a red dress. Her back is to the camera but it is without a doubt Kelly. Elliot fast-forwards their luncheon conversation. He stops the tape at the point where Kelly has dropped her napkin on the floor. In a gesture to retrieve the napkin, Kelly is seen rising from her chair. Bending down, she collects the napkin, and, glancing around her, crawls under the table. The man's facial expression alters dramatically. Once again, Elliot fast-forwards the tape until the screen is again blank. Stopping the video tape, he starts the audio tape. His voice is heard again, "2:37 p.m. EATERY 200."

Elliot can feel Kelly's tension escalating, but she makes no further attempt to leave. He switches the video tape back on. The blank screen now changes to include a big black limousine in a forest setting. Voices are heard; both she and Elliot recognize her own seductive declaration: "Oh baby, you know I want you. Come here . . ." Elliot skips through the rest of the interlude until the screen is again blank.

Depressing the audio tape, he is heard to say, "5:01 p.m. PARKER 350."

Kelly is visibly shaken, her tension almost at the breaking point. Ignoring her, Elliot restarts the video tape. The blank screen changes to a hotel room's interior. A fuzzy yellow thing obstructs the top portion of the screen, but a bed can clearly be discerned. Three people, at last, gather on the bed, undressing and fondling one another: a middle-aged man and woman and Kelly. Several sex acts, almost simultaneously including all three partners, begin.

Kelly, as though emerging from a trance, grabs the remote control from her husband's hand and turns off the tape. Elliot complacently turns his attention to the audio tape; his voice is again heard, "7:18 p.m. DEUCE 400."

Clearing his throat several times, Elliot finally asks, "Tell me what you think and how you feel." He turns to look at her for the first time since he joined her on the couch. He can plainly see a dozen emotions flit across her face: guilt, bewilderment, humiliation, grief, rage, sadness and resentment. However, the one emotion that comes to rest on her face and in her eyes, he never expected to see: total resolved defiance.

"What I think, darling, is that you are a very smart man. You apparently broke my code with the same Sherlock Holmes story I used to create it. What I think, Sweety, is that I should have appreciated your intelligence before this; I could have taken steps to impede your detection. What I think is, if you would kindly remove your hand from my arm, I shall go and pack," she sneers, mocking him sarcastically.

Shocked, Elliot babbles, "Is that all you have to say after eighteen years of marriage and this incredible betrayal, this . . . this . . ."

"Whoring! Is that the word you are looking for?" she screams, ripping her arm from his grip. "Whore, yes, that's the right word. You want to know how I feel? I'll tell you, I feel just fine!" she yells, turning to leave the room.

"Kelly, I have some questions. I think you owe it to me to answer them!" Elliot shouts, grabbing her by the shoulders.

Twisting out of his grasp, she plops herself back down on the couch. "Questions! You have questions! You want all the juicy dirt, don't you? Okay, fire away, babe! I'll answer your questions!"

How and Why Lovers Cheat

For a long time Elliot stands glaring at her, trying to control and compose himself. He feels like slapping her senseless, but he wants answers more. So, leveling his voice, he shoots questions at her, "How long has this been going on? Are you a nympho or a prostitute? Are these figures your fees . . . ? I have more, do you want me to ask them, or can you just tell me the truth on your own!"

"Be glad to oblige! I am what is commonly referred to as a prostitute. A well-paid one, but a pro nonetheless. I started hooking back in college when I lost my job and couldn't pay the next year's tuition. I was turning tricks when I met you. When I fell in love and married you, I stopped. That is, until we hit hard times. Then I started again. They say 'Once a Pro always a Pro.' Understand so far?" she asks, pausing. When he does not reply she continues, "Those figures are my fees. I told you I am well paid. Do you want me to break down my services or can you spare yourself that?" she asks.

"Tell me everything," Elliot whispers.

Speaking quietly though none the less fiercely, "Well, let's see; I get one hundred for a straight lay, fifty dollars for a hand job, two hundred for head and four hundred for a threesome. No whips, but my customers are welcome to combine my services any way they care to." Rising regally from the couch, she asks, "Is this interrogation over, or do you want me to detail my actions today?"

"No. I don't want to hear that. But I want to know . . ." he begins—but his emotions cut his voice off. Collecting himself, he asks, "Will you stop?"

"I can't!" she confesses, walking out of the room.

Elliot collapses on the couch, dropping his head into his hands; his body shakes. He does not cry. He listens as she goes upstairs. Muffled sounds tell him she is packing. Then he hears her descend. Returning to the family room with a suitcase, she says, "I'm going. I'll send someone for the rest of my things. Please don't tell the kids. I like to think I have one clean place in my life." Then she leaves the house.

Suddenly seized with panic, Elliot runs out of the house and down the front steps after her. She roars out of the driveway, her broken tail light shining as though mocking him. A strong arm is suddenly around his shoulders, leading him into the house and to the sofa. Looking up, Elliot's eyes meet Duncan's and, putting his head on his brother's shoulder, the tears finally come—hot and bitter.

Let's leave them now.

A surveillance, as you have witnessed, is often the conclud-
ing chapter to an investigation. It can also be the most
painful; they say, "A picture is worth a thousand words."
More often than not, actually conducting a surveillance, and
tailing your spouse, is the only resort left open if you want
to discover the truth.

I will recap the Do's and the Don'ts for both surveillance
and tailing.

Do's

Enlist the assistance of a trusted comrade.
Think your plan of action through carefully.
Gather ALL of the tools of the trade you will likely need.
Go over your plan, goals, cover names, excuses and
stories, your cloaks and props, your rendezvous points and
the channels you will be using.
Check all of your equipment.
Be sure to include extra batteries and film.
Know the law and how it pertains to you and your
investigation.
Keep your emotions in check. While on the job you are not
a spouse, you are a DETECTIVE.
Be sure to pack food and beverage.
Break your subject's tail light.
Use a fueled-up, plain car in good working order.
Carefully choose your initial surveillance position ahead of
time.
Record, in some manner, your progress.
Stay close enough to catch every light your subject does.
Use the concept of parallel tailing.
Always stay in communication with your partner.
Keep track of names, addresses, license plate numbers and
other data.
Let your partner scout out areas ahead of you.
Use common sense.
Drive defensively.
Always play your hunches.
Use forward tailing.
Know when it is over.

Don'ts

Never draw attention to yourself.

Never follow too close on a side street.

Do not drive erratically.

Do not bend the law too much.

Do not blow red lights.

Never get too close to your spouse.

Do not take foolish chances.

Do not forget your equipment.

Never freak out. It will get you nowhere fast.

Never attempt to emotionally handle something you can not live with forever.

Epilogue: Elliot and Kelly are divorced. Kelly is still in "the life." Elliot is in counseling to help him deal with Kelly's betrayal. He never did tell the children the truth about their mother.

CHAPTER THIRTEEN

ADVANCED TOOLS OF THE TRADE

In Chapter Three, I covered the basic tools of the trade a detective may need to successfully conduct and conclude an investigation. I can not, however, consider your instruction in infidelity investigation to be comprehensive without addressing the advanced tools of the trade; I am sure there will be readers who will either need or desire this information.

A tool qualifies as "advanced", in my opinion, if it conforms to one of three categories: sophisticated or hi tech, particularly expensive and tools whose availability is restricted to law enforcement personnel. I might also add that a tool is "advanced" if it is an improvisation devised to overcome any obstacles posed by the three categories of tools mentioned above. As with all other areas we have discussed, ADAPT, OVERCOME, and IMPROVISE are the three watch words of which you must be frequently and consistently aware.

On the following pages, I will share with you nine tools which fall into one or more of the first three categories. I will also describe two improvised tools which were conceived in the brains of two extraordinary spouses determined to find a way in which to intelligently conduct their investigation: "Necessity is the mother of invention." In addition to describing their improvisations, I will relate their stories to you;

this so you may have the opportunity to fully appreciate their inventions.

Advanced tools which you may need and which correspond to the categories of hi-tech, expensive or restricted, are the following:

STAR TRON

The Star Tron Night Viewer is a telescope which allows one to "see" at night. This telescope utilizes the available light present at night, star and moon light, and amplifies it in a manner which allows the human eye to acquire night vision. As the telescope is adaptable to a camera, one can also photograph at night.

There are many infrared viewers on the market, of which the Star Tron is but one example. As those viewers are considered sophisticated tools, their price tags can be equally dear, ranging from between several hundred to a few thousand dollars. There is not, however, a restriction connected to their purchase or usage.

RIFLE MICROPHONE

The Rifle Microphone is a long microphone that allows one to hear conversations taking place hundreds of feet away. As its name implies, the microphone can be "aimed" at the subject in question. Only those noises which occur in the scope of the direction targeted are picked up and, with the use of a frequency equalizer, any other peripheral noises can be eliminated.

This type of microphone is considered hi-tech and, therefore, pricey; price tags vary but frequently range in the hundreds of dollars. There is however an inexpensive "amplifier"—Elliot in Chapter Twelve used one—priced under fifty dollars. Some of these microphones, depending on the specific type, carry limited restrictions on them.

SPECIAL LENSES

Numerous lenses can be purchased for your 35mm camera; variance is caused by the lens' length of range thus providing numberous options. Although these lenses are neither sophisticated nor restricted, they are exceptionally costly. Consequently, care should be taken in purchasing such lenses. One is best served if purchase is dependent upon an established, knowledgeable need. In short, choose a lens consistent with the scope of your investigation always in mind.

WIRELESS MICROPHONES

Wireless microphones transmit sound to a receiver without the utilization of wires.

These microphones come in myriad sizes and forms. The smallest, known generically as "bugs," are usually the most costly. The olive (microphone) on the end of the toothpick (antenna) is typical of this "Maxwell Smart" gadgetry.

Although considered hi-tech and expensive, there are some wireless microphones which are reasonably priced and as equally functional as the more expensive models. The use of some types of "bugs" by the general public is illegal; use of these is restricted to law enforcement personnel and, even then, a court order is often necessary.

LOCK PICK

A Lock Pick is not one tool; it is a set of tools comprised of instruments varying in size and shape which, either individually or in conjunction with one another, are used to "pick" the tumblers of a lock.

A lock is designed with a locking mechanism. This mechanism, inside a standard lock, is comprised of tumblers or pins. The tumblers must be depressed by the notches in an appropriate key to spring open the lock. In lieu of a correctly correponding key, picks can be utilized. Once inserted into the lock, the pick's purpose is to force each pin (tumbler) upward into the cord of the lock. Another tool, a tension bar, must be inserted to help keep each pin raised while the next pin is moved upward. When all of the pins have been raised, the tension bar can turn the lock.

Less complicated than a set of lock-picking tools is a device called the "Lock Aid Gun." this instrument, shaped like a staple gun, has a thin piece of metal jutting out of a muzzle. Upon inserting this thin piece of metal into a lock and depressing the gun's trigger, all of the pins are simultaneously stuck in an upward position. The small tension bar can then turn the lock. However, even with the help of this gun, your success may remain in question; this tool does not work on all locks, and one must be quite proficient in the art of lock picking for success to be as assured. I came to this realization one evening as I was crawling through my own window.

Lock Picks are neither sophisticated nor expensively priced. Their possession and use are, in most states, illegal, however.

You should be aware that is also illegal to gain entrance by using a diamond-tipped glass cutting tool with an accompanying suction cup to remove glass from windows or doors. Also, although glamorized by T.V. detectives, a credit card is not a lock-picking device and will rarely do the trick. As half a card will not be accepted for purchases, I suggest you leave this trick to T.V.'s detectives.

CAR BUG

Car Bug is my term for a magnetic transmitter and a receiver used during a vehicular surveillance. The battery powered transmitter can be attached under the car's hood or to its chassis. A powerful magnet holds the transmitter in place. Once properly placed, a signal is transmitted to the receiver located in the surveillance vehicle. The receiver translates the signal into audible pitches of sound; the closer the receiver is to the transmitter, the louder the sound becomes.

A Car Bug is a sophisticated and expensive hi-tech tool; its price ranging from one to several thousand dollars, depending on the strength of its transmission and reception capabilities.

Joe Q. Public can get his greedy little hands on this tool and, to date, there are no restrictions on its use.

VOICE ANALYZER

The Voice Analyzer analyzes the physiological stresses—often indications of lies—in an individual's speaking voice. Considered by some to be more accurate than the polygraph, this instrument can be applied to either a voice over the phone or a recorded voice on television or radio. As a matter of fact, many investigative reporters use this device to determine whether or not public personalities and politicians are speaking truthfully.

The Voice Analyzer is a highly technical and sophisticated instrument and bears an equally sophisticated price tag;

presently, its cost is in the vicinity of five thousand dollars. Although prohibitive in price, its purchase is without restrictions.

TELE-EAR

The Tele-Ear, and those devices similar to it, allows one to tune into a specific telephone and the area in which the telephone is located through the telephone line. The Tele-Ear is comprised of two parts: a monitor which is plugged into a standard wall jack and into which the telephone is then connected, and an activating device. Once the Tele-Ear jack (the monitor) is in place, one would dial the number to which it is connected from any outside telephone. As soon as the telephone rings, the activator is held to the mouthpiece and depressed. A signal is then sent to the monitoring component, which, in turn, activates the monitor and prevents the telephone from ringing. The caller can then monitor the room in which the telephone is located.

The Tele-Ear was designed to provide a means by which to monitor potential burglary or wrongdoing in either one's home or business while off the premises. When used within these confines, the Tele-Ear is completely legal. As a matter of fact, the use of most transmitters, receivers, and microphones is considered legal if confined to either personal/ recreational use or as a measure against possible criminal activity.

Although somewhat sophisticated, this tool is not, necessarily expensive; there are derivatives which are less costly and as equally effective as the five-hundred-dollar models.

VIDEO CAMERA AND THE PINHOLE LENS

A video camera is an incredible asset for an investigator, providing indisputable documentation of events.

Present legal thinking maintains that persons in full view of the public are not assumed to be inaccessible to public scrutiny. Therefore, one would not be infringing upon anyone's rights to film that which occurs in public. Additionally, as of this writing, a silent video tape is admissible in a court of law.

A video camera lens is usually powerful enough to bring into focus objects several feet away. Further, a pinhole lens can be fitted to the camera lens. This apparatus can be used in much the same way as that employed by Elliot. Also, a video camera can be rigged to a long-playing, voice-activated tape deck. Once these components are in place, the system can be left in a stationary position; a drop ceiling with a hole cut to accommodate the small lens may be one such example. The results could be, and often have been, illuminatingly conclusive.

In an effort to make your detective's palate drool, I have compiled the following list of other advanced tools of the trade you might consider useful:

Bionic Ear: a very sensitive electronic stethoscope which allows one to hear through any type of wall—including concrete—and can be used as a microphone when connected to a tape recorder.

Ten-Hour Recorder: a tape recorder, one and one quarter inches thick, which, with a built-in voice activator, will record sound for a maximum of ten continuous hours.

Cigarette Lighter Camera: an ultra-small, highly sensitive camera shaped like a lighter. When you flick your bic, you take a pic.

I thought these might get your blood pumping. Anyone care to run out and purchase a trench coat?

HOMEMADE DEVICES

These might include:
One briefcase or large purse
One small voice-activated tape recorder
A roll of duct tape

The Case of the "Time Bomb"

Bambi swept past her husband Jesse's secretary and barged into his office. Once inside, she slammed the door closed behind her. Rushing over to his desk, she screeched, "How dare you do this to me and the kids? You heartless pig! Don't think for one minute that I will let you go easily! You are not getting out of this so smoothly! Don't bother to deny it, I know everything!"

Jesse opened his mouth several times to speak, but nothing would come out. Instead, he sat there completely dumbfounded listening to her.

How and Why Lovers Cheat

As quickly as the tirade began, it was over. Then, without another word, Bambi turned on her heels and stormed out of the room.

The instant she left, Jesse picked up the phone and dialed his mistress. When she answered, he stammered, "Oh my God!" My wife was just in here! She said she knows everything and she's not going to let me get away with it! She was a crazy woman! What am I going to do? Listen, meet me at four-thirty and we can figure something out! Okay? Bye! I'll see you then."

Approximately fifteen minutes after Jesse had completed his call, Bambi once again barged into his office.

"I forgot my purse," was her only utterance, as she again whirled out the door.

Too eager and nervous to wait until she arrived at home, Bambi pulled into the first parking lot she came upon. Ripping open her purse, she began undoing the duct tape that held her voice-activated tape recorder in place. She had cut a hole in the seam, exposing the recorder's microphone. Having removed the tape from the microphone and the tape recorder from her purse, she rewound the tape and then depressed the play button.

Her own voice was heard to say, "How dare you do this . . . I know everything!"

Then Jesse's voice was heard to say, "Oh my God! . . . I'll see you then."

Bambi had played a game of chess that day. First, she made a "Time Bomb," placing her opponent in a position of possible check. He blindly fell into her trap when he called his mistress, thereby placing himself in check. Bambi now had not only a recording of her husband speaking with his mistress, but also knew about their arranged rendezvous that afternoon; the result: a checkmated mate! It would not be difficult to begin her vehicular surveillance armed with this information.

Bambi and Jesse are now divorced. With the help of the "Time Bomb," Bambi had been able to change roles from the prey to the hunter.

DEVICES NEEDED

The ingredients might include:
One tape recorder
One connecting wire
One pressure plunger

The Case of the Bedroom Ear

Penny lay stretched out on her chaise lounge in the back of her apartment building. She chatted with the other young mothers as they watched the children at play. Her bikini, or what there was of it, threatened further exposure each time she moved.

Although she was personally liked by her counterparts, each time she sun-bathed so scantily clad, a feeling of disapproval hung heavy in the air. Since she did so every afternoon of the summer, weather permitting, this disapproval was frequently present; so also was suspicion.

As the women sat together every day to trade gossip and quips directed at their husbands and household drudgery, they became like a family. No event could take place without it becoming common knowledge; this common knowledge particularly aware of the daily attention Penny received from the man who lived in the adjacent building, who worked nights.

It began innocently enough; he would walk by, greet Penny, and toss a ball to Kenny, her young son. As time went by, his attention shifted from the son to his mother. He began sitting with the women for extended periods of time, joining more and more into both the group and their conversation.

The women neither commented nor acknowledged that Penny and their newest member were simultaneously absent once or twice a week. As the absenteeism became more frequent however, comments started to slip out, mostly in sympathy for Penny's husband, Conrad. He was known to be a devoted father and an attentive husband. Furthermore, he often cared for the house while Penny worked at night. He even defrosted the refrigerator without being asked—a quality worthy of great respect and swooning.

So it went throughout the summer. One afternoon late in July, screaming could be heard throughout the group's building. The occupants, believing that someone was either being raped or murdered, rushed into the hallways. About twelve people, mostly women, rushed together toward the direction of the wailing. It lead them to Penny and Conrad's apartment. The door was wide open. Jan, the bravest of the bunch, tried to make herself heard over the noise and gain permission to enter. Finally, unable to withstand the din, the ladies rushed inside, down the hall and into the master bedroom. Dashing inside the bedroom the surge of bodies suddenly came to a halt. The horrifying scene they encountered was a pair of naked lovers—Penny and her boyfriend, Jason—with Conrad, seemingly delighting in watching the pair squirm, standing over them.

"Well ladies come in, come in. I figured her screams would bring you here. Since, for the entire summer, you all watched my wife cheating on me and remained silent—at least with me—I thought you might like to see the lovers in the flesh, so to speak. I want you all to know and bear witness that I never laid a hand on either of them. I admit that I was verbally forceful about their attempts to leave at that moment prior to your arrival. However, as you are here, let's step into the kitchen and have coffee. By the way, I want to thank the one—I won't say her name—who finally had enough guts to clue me in on Penny's "afternoon delight." Sometime when you ladies aren't busy, you will have to come over and listen to the tape I made of their lovemaking. It's a scream."

"Wait ladies. Surely you aren't going? Don't you want to see my little invention? You see, I attached a wire to a plunger and a tape recorder. I placed my "Bedroom Ear" under the bed. When weight from on top of the bed brought the mattress down, it depressed the plunger. Once the plunger was depressed, the wire activated the tape recorder. So the "Ear" heard all? What, no coffee?"

Shocked, guilt ridden and embarrassed were the three emotions that simultaneously ran through the group as they stood transfixed, listening to Conrad. His speech concluded, the women sheepishly walked from the room to their own apartments. One question, however, ran through each of the women's minds: Who told Conrad what was going on? Giving each other sideward glances, they searched for signs to reveal the responsible person's identity; nothing conclusive showed on anyone.

Penny and Conrad are now divorced. Kenny lives with his Dad in the same apartment. Penny and Jason moved to a different part of town. The women never did find out which one of them—if one ever did—told Conrad what was going on; doubt would ever after strain confidence between them, however.

I will prescribe the same advice I gave you in Chapter Three: try to borrow or rent any piece of equipment you need or desire. Once again, if you cannot locate any piece of equipment, write to me at the address given in Chapter Three.

| CHAPTER |
| FOURTEEN |

LEGALITIES

As you endeavor to navigate the maze of your investigation, you will encounter numerous situations wherein a legal judgment call may be required. Although I can not transform you into an attorney, I can attempt to provide you with an initial understanding of some of the legal issues with which you may be confronted. However, the manner in which you act is ultimately a matter of your own discretion. I encourage you to proceed, with any investigation you may undertake, in a manner that is cautious, knowledgeable and consistent with current, prevailing laws.

Let us commence our discussion with this working definition of a law: a law is a rule established by a local, state or federal authority. An example of local law is the village ordinance. A village ordinance may prohibit overnight, on-street parking. If this ordinance is violated, the vehicle in question may be either ticketed, towed, or both. The jurisdiction of local ordinances, however are restricted to the boundaries of the municipality. In other words, Poedunk may have a village law or ordinance which does not permit overnight parking; their police force may enforce this ordinance only in Poedunk, not in the neighboring town. Similarly, the state of Illinois dictates the legal drinking age to be that of twenty-one years of age. Noncompliance with this law can result in arrest, fine and imprisonment. However, this law is not applicable in Wisconsin, which formally mandated eighteen to be the legal drinking age. An underaged Illinois resident can, therefore, drink in Wisconsin—provided the individual is eighteen years of age—with complete immunity from the Illinois authorities. (As a matter of fact, this scenario occurred endlessly until Wisconsin changed its legal drinking age to twenty-one.) There are also federal laws which dictate and maintain jurisdiction on a country-wide basis. Although federal law may differ from one country to the next, rest assured that it is always present.

As an investigator, you must comprehend the three hues surrounding any given governmental edict. To assist that understanding, visualize a law as a straight line. Envision one side of the line black, one side white and the line itself gray. These three colors are the hues of any given law. Standing on the wrong side of the line places one in the black; on the right side of the line, in the white. If one stands on the line itself, betwixt and between, one is in the gray. Black is definitely illegal. White is definitely legal. Gray is a subtle combination of the two. To stand in the gray is to be in a position wherein your action is open to an interpretation of the law.

I will give you an example to better explain the law's hues. Let us suppose Gidget connected a telephone recording device to her telephone and a conversation was recorded between her husband J.J. and his mistress. The eavesdropping laws seem to forbid the intentional eavesdropping upon conversations with the use of any device. So is Gidget in the white, the black or the gray? If you answered gray, you answered correctly. Gidget's INTENTION in placing the TRD on her telephone could have been the monitoring of 900 calls made by her minor children; this with the further intent of stopping such behavior. As the recorded conversation between J.J. and Madam W was quite accidental, it would not be an actionable infraction of the law. The color is, therefore, gray. If, however, Gidget wished to use that same recording in her divorce proceeding, she could not. Audio recordings are not admissible in a court of law unless the tap was placed pursuant to either due process of law, or the prior permission of the recorded person to be recorded. Color this scenario black. Gidget could however, use the tape when confronting her husband with his affair, and as a basis for her decision to divorce him. Doing so would place the tape within the personal arena which, as previously discussed, is not illegal. Color this white. As you can see, the hues around a law can be as important as the law itself.

There are several laws with which an investigator will most likely come into conflict. Those laws pertain to eavesdropping, burglary, burglary tools, battery, assault, criminal damage to property, trespassing and theft. It sort of makes us sound more like criminals than crusaders. The reason we may brush against these laws is simply that our investigations may lead us into Hell's Kitchen. As any good cook knows, you can not bake a cake without breaking a few eggs. I do not advocate law breaking, but I do understand the difference between idealism and realism. The ideal situation is one wherein data is gathered without posing as a cleaning lady who, uninvited, enters an office late at night, rummages through desks and wastepaper baskets and, upon discovering something suspicious, may actually take it. In the very real world of investigation, this type of activity takes place. If you were a policeperson, such activity would be sanctioned as an undercover assignment. As a "private" investigator, you do not enjoy the same privileges, sanctions or justifications unique to a law enforcement official. Therefore, in our cleaning woman scenario, several laws would be broken: trespassing, breaking and entering, criminal damage to property, burglary and, if you are apprehended by a cop in a particularly bad mood, one or two more charges may be added to this lengthy list. As I said to you before, I am a realist. The scenario I have outlined for you is one which might, very possibly, take place. I do not encourage breaking the law. However, my honesty directs me to alert you to the real possiblity of finding yourself in a legally gray area. Therefore, you must familiarize yourself with the law and the hues with which certain actions may be colored. Here is a list of some actions with a complimentary color guide I have created for you.

ASSAULT

Assault is comitted when an individual is placed in fear of being the recipient of a battery. It is a threat.

White—One does nothing at all.
Black—One threatens to punch another's lights out.
Gray—Upon catching a spouse cheating, one states, "Have you ever seen the movie *The Burning Bed*? Notice, one is simply discussing a movie recently viewed on T.V.

Assault is a misdemeanor.

ASSAULT, AGGRAVATED

In addition to assault as previously defined, aggravated assault is constituted by either the use of a weapon or concealment of one's identity (i.e., use of a mask); or a combination of these two additional factors. Further, threatening a policeperson or an individual designated as high risk (i.e., teachers, and judges) also constitutes aggravated assault.

White—One does nothing at all.
Black—One makes a threat while holding a crowbar.
Gray—One changing a tire and, holding a crowbar in hand, speaks irritatedly (after all, they have been interrupted!); a terrible misunderstanding results.

Aggravated Assault is a misdemeanor.

BATTERY

A battery is committed when actual physical contact is made between two individuals without either legal justification or consent between the two. If one would so much as touch another person with the tip of their finger under these conditions, battery can be alleged.

White—One does nothing at all.
Black—One pulls out her hair.
Gray—One quite accidently spills a drink on her.

Battery is a misdemeanor.

BATTERY, AGGRAVATED

A battery is considered aggravated when the physical contact made either causes great bodily harm, or is perpetrated against an individual who is designated as a high-risk person.

White—One does nothing at all.
Black—One bends a crowbar over another's head.
Grey—One's foot is casually placed in the aisle down which a person in to the aisle is walking, causing said person to clumsily trip over his own feet and land on his face.

Aggravated Battery is a felony.

BURGLARY

Burglary is committed when without authority or prior consent, one knowingly enters or remains within a building, car, trailer, boat or aircraft with full intent to commit therein a felony or theft.

White—One does nothing at all.
Black—One enters an office and steals a picture of his wife in the arms of another man.
Gray—One, with the permission of a secretary, who did not refuse entrance, fetches the family checkbook upon which a picture just happens to be attached.

Burglary is a felony.

BURGLARY TOOL, POSSESSION OF

One is in possession of tools that can be used to gain entrance into the aforementioned places with intent to commit a felony or theft.

White—One does nothing at all.
Black—One has a diamond-tipped cutting tool and suction cup in their hand while standing outside a building.
Gray—One has a stubborn hangnail and the only thing that can sever it is a diamond-tipped cutter.

Possession of Burglary Tool is a felony.

CRIMINAL DAMAGE TO PROPERTY

This is when one damages another's property without the owner's consent.

White—One does nothing at all.
Black—One breaks down the "other" man's door.
Gray—One breaks down a door as cries of fire were thought to be heard coming from within.

Depending upon the damage sustained by the property, legal penalties for the change of Criminal Damage to Property can be either those of a misdemeanor or a felony.

DISORDERLY CONDUCT

This is a catchall statute for many different types of petty offenses which disrupt the peace.

White—One does nothing at all.
Black—One stands in front of the mistress' house, screaming for her husband to come out.
Gray—One yells for the occupants of a particular house to hurry out as an accident, involving their car, has just taken place.

Disorderly Conduct penalties range from those of a misdemeanor to those of a felony, depending upon the degree and duration of the disturbance.

EAVESDROPPING

Eavesdropping is constituted by the use of a device to hear or record oral conversation.

White—One does nothing at all.
Black—One puts a tap on the telephone of his wife's friend.
Gray—One puts a TRD on their own telephone.

Eavesdropping is a felony.

THEFT

Theft is committed when an individual exerts unauthorized control over property not his own.

White—One does nothing at all.
Black—One steals the mistress' keys.
Gray—One mistakenly grabs a purse believing it to be her own, discovering later it belongs to the mistress. An attempt to return the item to its rightful owner necessitates examining the purse's contents to discover the owner's identity.

If the value of the object taken is less than two hundred and fifty dollars, theft is a misdemeanor; any amount that it is upgraded over this sum, it is considered a felony offense.

TRESPASS ON PROPERTY

Trespassing is defined as the unauthorized entrance of an individual onto property other than one's own, or the refusal to leave said property when requested to do so.

White—One does nothing at all.
Black—One enters another's land and refuses to leave.
Gray—One enters another's property in search of a lost dog and, upon hearing the anguished cries of the puppy, refuses to leave until the dog is found.

Trespassing on Property is a misdemeanor.

TRESPASS IN A VEHICLE

Trespass in a Vehicle is committed when one knowingly, and without authority, enters any vehicle, watercraft or aircraft.

White—One does nothing at all.
Black—One enters the mistress' car to take a look around.
Gray—One enters the mistress' car to turn off her lights and happens to glance around.

Trespass in a Vehicle is a misdemeanor.

Misdemeanors, Felonies and Miscellaneous Legal Information

A misdemeanor is a crime punishable by a fine and/or imprisonment of up to one year in a local or state institution.

A felony is a crime punishable by imprisonment in the penitentiary for a period in excess of one year.

Knowing the law can afford one the ability to change his or her behavior or action from black to gray. Let's dissect an offense to assist this transformation. An offense can be broken down into two elements:

One commits a crime if: (1) he commits the act voluntarily; or (2) his mental state is (a) *intentional* (example: premeditated murder), (b) *knowledge* (example: he is a locksmith; therefore he has the knowledge to have opened the door),

(c) *recklessness* (drunken driver who hits a child), (d) *negligence* (he leaves his above-ground pool unfenced and unlocked and a child drowns).

Now, if an act were involuntary, it would then be an accident or it would have been committed under duress of great bodily harm. For example, most states have laws on their books that protect animals such as dogs from being purposely killed. But if you killed the dog accidentally, then the act would be deemed involuntary. It would also be an involuntary act if you killed Fido because a dog hater had a gun to your head and threatened to shoot you if you did not kill Fido. Furthermore, if your mental state while committing this furry murder was unintentional, without knowledge, not reckless or with neglect, then it would not be an actionable offense. So in order to have committed an actionable offense you must have a voluntary action plus a specific mental state. One plus one equals two. Eliminate one of the ones and you are then not an actionable doggy killer.

As mental states go, intent is the most difficult mental state to prove, and so much of a crime's definition hangs on it. For instance, look if you will at the crime definitions I previously gave you. Now remove the words "with authority," "knowingly" and "with intent." When you do so, you can see that without those words the crime falls like a deflated balloon. Furthermore, removing those words allows one to see clearly the gray emerging. So black turns into gray with the words ACCIDENT, SUPPOSED PERMISSION, UNKNOWINGLY and UNINTENTIONAL.

It will be up to your particular creativity skills to change your own hue.

I will list for you some other key factors you should know while on the "job," and walking the staight line of the law. I can not possible hope to address every question or situation which may arise in the course of your investigation. Further, as I am not an attorney, I cannot advise you to take specific legal action or recourse in any situation. I will, however, insist, prior to engaging in any activity which might be considered unlawful, that you consult an attorney regarding actions you are contemplating. Do not take the law in your own hands and do not rely upon your interpretation of the law. Get an expert, remember that he who has himself for a lawyer, has a fool for a lawyer.

I will again repeat that knowing the law is imperative if you are contemplating taking particular actions in the course of your investigations. However, even your knowledge of the law will not be sufficient to save you from arrest, should you choose to engage in unlawful activity. Therefore, please recognize that, regardless of the hues we have discussed, if you choose to engage in activity which is subject to prosecution, you may well be arrested and fined.

You can use your ear to hear, but with a device you are on thin ice.

Policepersons shoot criminals. Be careful out there.

No weapon in your control means no weapon to use if your emotions go out of control.

If it is legal in your state to carry mace, for protection, do so.

If you intend on going to court with your evidence, keep detailed notes and have a substantiating witness.

When in doubt, always consult an attorney or legal information service.

Note: Your author and your publisher recommend that you refer to your local statutes before purchasing and/or utilizing any equipment mentioned herein. In addition, we do not condone the illegal use of any such equipment or the engagement in activities which are unlawful in local, state or federal jurisdictions.

CHAPTER
FIFTEEN

CAUGHT, NOW WHAT?

"Now is the winter of our discontent. . . ."

King Richard the Third
Act One, Scene One
—Shakespeare

The Shakespearean quote above says so much, doesn't it? "Now is the winter of our discontent." When pain has no known depth and no known end. When it surrounds us and penetrates us and we become one with it. When we reach out vainly for consolation, for a comfort, for an end. When we reach out vainly for consolation, for a comfort, for an end. When it seems as though even our God cannot hear our anguished cries. When we shiver in the dark—alone. When we realize that it is alone that we must feel the searing agony of our own breaking heart. We must, we know, feel this way until we do not feel this way anymore. Nothing can ease it. Nothing can stop it, for its name is pain and it has come home to live in our heart. We feel it, it surrounds and penetrates us and we become one with it. For NOW is the winter of OUR discontent.

Discovering the truth brings with it responsibility; that responsibility is coping with that truth. Coping with its pain, with its grief, with its glaring light, and finally with making hard decisions. Decisions that will affect every area of our life.

Long ago, my friend, we addressed the question of your desire to know the truth. You made a decision then. But it is now that the true reality of that decision is borne. Bearing it can be one of the most painful tasks of your life. We both now understand this, so address your own pain. For you must alone feel it, until you do not feel it anymore. Neither I nor anyone can take this burden from your heart. But know this, believe this: "This too shall pass." Though it may not seem so now, the pain will lessen. The initial intensity will subside. It will end. But as the pain begins to ebb, grief will take its place.

Grief is essential to your adjustment to the truth. It is valid here. You have suffered so many losses. So many entities have died. Though each individual's life experience is unique, losses and deaths have befallen you. The loss of your love, your respect for your spouse, your dreams, your expectations and so much more.

So as the pain ebbs and grief comes to the forefront, you will go through a loss process in some manner. Elizabeth Kubler-Ross, a well-known author and physician, articulates the process better than I ever could, as she has spent years at the bedsides of terminally ill patients. She found that one goes through five stages toward accepting a loss. Those stages are denial, anger, bargaining, depression and then finally acceptance itself.

In the denial stage one attempts to avoid the truth, for avoidance stays off being plummeted into reality. We search desperately for another reality. Somehow, we want to believe that this is just all a terrible mistake. This did not really happen. And so we deny the truth to ourselves.

Then the anger comes. "Why did this happen to me? How could God LET this happen to me? I am a good person. I do not deserve this pain." Anger is born from the frustration of having everything that was ever valued stripped away. Anger comes from feelings of powerlessness and helplessness.

As anger abates, we begin to bargain with ourselves and with our God. "If this cannot be true, I will be a better person. If this can be untrue, I will change. Some way I will make my spouse love me more." These are but some of the verbalizations we utter.

When we recognize the futility of bartering over an event

that has already taken place, we fall into depression. The sadness of the realization that we cannot change the past hurls us into what appears to be a dark and bottomless pit. It is there we stay until acceptance comes upon us to rescue us and give us peace. This resolution grants for many a serenity neither happy nor sad, simply an acceptance for what cannot be changed. It is then and only then—when we have gone through our personal death-loss process—that we can come to a place from which decisions can be made.

Alcoholics Anonymous has a motto—no, a fervent prayer: "God grant me the serenity to accept the things I cannot change, the courage to change the things I can and the wisdom to know the difference." When you can pray that prayer, you will know you can go on to make the necessary decisions in your life.

But it is you and only you who can come to your own acceptance. You may or may not go through all five stages in the death-loss process. You may only go through one or two of the stages. You may not go through the stages in the order given. You may stay in one of the stages for what might appear to someone else as a long time. The reason is, you are a unique person with survival skills that are unique to yourself alone. No one can or should attempt to push you through the stages toward acceptance. This is not a formula on how to get on with your life. No matter how well-meaning the parent, sibling or friend, do not allow anyone to make YOUR acceptance. They may love you, comfort you, be a shoulder to cry on and a listening ear, yes. But no one can be you. Acceptance is your cross to bear—alone.

Before you can make decisions, you need to rebuild what the entire experience may have robbed you of. You have, though you may not as yet realize it, suffered personal losses as well. Those losses include self-esteem, self-confidence and self-worth. These losses occur because our SELF is usually so closely interwoven in our relationship with our spouse that not one can be disturbed without disturbing the other. It can be likened to the pulling on a dangling thread from a knitted sweater. Once one begins to pull more and more, the sweater unravels, until the whole thing falls apart.

Rebuilding and reconstructing oneself after these losses have transpired is, in my opinion, an easier task for you than accepting the relationship losses. You have, after all, power over yourself. You are no longer as helpless as a twig thrown about in a stormy sea. Though you cannot prevent, change or circumvent another's behavior, you do have dominion over yours. So you can rebuild yourself on a new and stronger foundation. While your old self may have been dependent and built upon another, your new self can be built upon yourself. The primary source, then, is transferred from the whims of an entity over which you had no power to you. You then become responsible, to define and nourish yourself. Like trees, all persons must gather their own water and sunlight to afford them personal growth. This is as it should be.

Then, after the acceptance and self-rebuilding, decisions must be made. Though you made decisions earlier on, you must reevaluate them now. Can your decisions and the truth coexist? Only you can decide. Involved as an equal partner in this life decision is your spouse. If you had decided and continue to steadfastly cling to staying with your spouse after the discovery of an affair, you must communicate with that spouse. His or her feelings and desires must now be weighed with yours. All of the hard questions must be asked and the real work must now begin. Do not be averse to seeking outside help with wrestling with these problems, both personal and marital. Yet no one—not family, friends, clergy or a therapist—can make or should make your decisions for you. Rather, their role is that of giving input. You must make your own decisions both personal and as a couple.

So "Caught, Now What?" is the onset of pain, the dawn of grief, reconciling losses, adjusting to acceptance, mediating decisions and striving for a resolve.

I, my friend, can only wish you well and Godspeed.

CHAPTER SIXTEEN

HEALING: ODE TO BITTERNESS AND VENGEANCE

We, my friend, have walked a long road together. You have walked through so many things with me, though you may not know it, and I have walked with you at least in spirit. Somehow author and reader become bound one to another on an inexplicable plane. Somewhere during this journey we joined. So before I can leave you to carry on—strong and alone—I feel compelled to address your pain and sorrow once more. For I want to know that you can heal yourself and become whole again.

We both understand that the two most predominant feelings that you will grapple with are bitterness and vengeance. The bitterness is a derivative of your pain and the vengeance is born out of your anger. These must be dealt with and resolved. Though examining the pain may seem masochistic, it really is not. We can assimilate and reconcile it only after dissecting it. *Understanding why we feel as we do* sets us on the road to recovery.

Most of us enter into a marriage or a love relationship with usually clear expectations: to be loved and to love, to be cherished and to cherish 'til death do us part. We give each other our pledge, our vow of fidelity. Therefore, fidelity is expected and deserved. If those vows are betrayed, then the pain can be devastating.

Why? Why would an act of infidelity ruin a marriage or wound the injured spouse so deeply? The fact is that even in our so-called permissive society there are still a majority who steadfastly believe in marriage, with all its limitations and responsibilities. One of the increasingly difficult boundaries of marriage is that of fidelity. It is the sacred thread that binds husband and wife. It therefore must be preserved. There need to be, have to be, some areas of our lives we do not share with strangers, some rules we follow, some commitments we honor, some boundaries we do not cross.

So . . . if sex, love, marriage and fidelity are all one and the same to you, the pain you will feel when betrayed is immeasurable. That betrayal is contrary to all your hopes, desires and ideals. To tread on these vows is to tread on everything that you are.

So bitterness takes root in our very soul. It is a constant state of pain that gnaws at the basic fiber of one's heart. It can threaten to consume us and swallow us whole. One can, like Miss Haversham in *Great Expectations*, stop all the clocks at the time of one's greatest pain—draw the drapes, let nothing be touched, leave everything to rot away and never live another second past that moment.

Do not do this. Ask yourself some hard questions. Where is the personal productivity in becoming embittered? Has not your former spouse moved on with his or her life? Does your life *only* have worth in conjunction with your spouse's?

Be hurt! You have a right to your pain. Wallow in it for as long as you really need to, if it helps. Scream, throw plates, punch the wall or whatever, if it helps. But for your sake, *heal* too. Get on with YOUR tomorrow. Even Miss Haversham realized how pointless her embittered life had been. Said she, "Had I only allowed in the sun's healing rays . . . "

Furthermore, do not, my friend, open the door and welcome vengeance into your heart. Vengeance is rooted in anger (though your anger is more than valid). Do not strike back. The best advice my mother ever gave me was about vengeance. I was wallowing in and being eaten alive by feelings of hatred and vengeance. I hated so bad I could literally taste it. Mama said, "In order to hate that much, to want to avenge yourself that much, you will have to trade in your heart and trade in your soul."

Are you willing to pay that price? I wasn't. Getting even is fruitless. The slate can never be wiped clean, for it was drawn on with indelible ink. I compare it to a murder. No matter how the murderer is executed, his demise will not bring back the victim. Nor if the father attacks his daughter's rapist with all his fury, will the rape be erased. What was done cannot be undone. So it is *how you live with it* that is truly important.

Get on with your tomorrow—because as unbelievable as it seems right now, there will be a tomorrow. It is up to you alone to make it as hopeful as it can be. When God shuts a door, he always opens a window. Find it!